"NEVER MAKE AN ATTEMPT TO GAIN OUR FREE-
DOM . . . UNTIL YOU CAN SEE YOUR WAY CLEAR . . .
IF YOU COMMENCE, MAKE SURE WORK, DO NOT
TRIFLE, FOR THEY WILL NOT TRIFLE WITH YOU.
THEY WANT US FOR THEIR SLAVES AND THINK
NOTHING OF MURDERING US . . . IF THERE IS
AN ATTEMPT MADE BY US, KILL OR BE KILLED."

*These words might well have been written by a Black
militant of today. Instead, they were written by a Black
militant, David Walker, in 1839.*

His *Appeal* is but one of the extraordinary documents in this book. Some are radical, some moderate,
some filled with love of humanity, some penned in
bitterness and rage. All combine to form a living link
between the American past and the American present, and to deliver a message that can be ignored only
at grave peril for our country and ourselves.

A NOTE ON THE EDITOR: Bradford Chambers, besides
his career as editor and author, has conducted various studies
and pilot projects in Harlem, as well as a noted World War II
survey of racial violence in American cities. He is currently
Acting Chairman of the Council on Interracial Books for
Children. He is a graduate of Amherst College and received
his M.A. from New York University.

Books of Related Interest

CHRONICLES
OF
BLACK PROTEST

*Compiled and Edited
with a commentary by
Bradford Chambers*

Original title: *Chronicles
of Negro Protest*

A Mentor Book
Published by The New American Library,
New York and Toronto

MENTOR TRADEMARK REG. U.S. PAT. OFF. AND FOREIGN COUNTRIES
REGISTERED TRADEMARK—MARCA REGISTRADA
HECHO EN CHICAGO, U.S.A.

MENTOR BOOKS are published *in the United States* by
The New American Library, Inc.,
1301 Avenue of the Americas, New York, New York 10019,
in Canada by The New American Library of Canada Limited,
295 King Street East, Toronto 2, Ontario

FIRST PRINTING, FEBRUARY, 1969

PRINTED IN THE UNITED STATES OF AMERICA

Let me give you a word of the philosophy of reforms. The whole history of the progress of human liberty shows that all concessions, yet made to her august claims, have been born of earnest struggle. The conflict has been exciting, agitating, all-absorbing, and for the time being putting all other tumults to silence. It must do this or it does nothing. If there is no struggle, there is no progress. Those who profess to favor freedom, and yet depreciate agitation, are men who want crops without plowing up the ground. They want rain without thunder and lightning. They want the ocean without the awful roar of its many waters. This struggle may be a moral one; or it may be a physical one; or it may be both moral and physical; but it must be a struggle. Power concedes nothing without a demand.

Frederick Douglass

To Leslie B. Tanner
and to Susan and Michael and Noel

PICTURE CREDITS

CONTENTS

Section III   LET NO MAN HOLD BACK

INTRODUCTION

We have not been honest with ourselves. What is infinitely more tragic, as parents and teachers, we have not been honest with our youth. We have sought to avoid the implications of our history by avoiding the facts of our history. For a time our obliviousness seemed to work, but we had contrived a world of unreality.

It is frequently insisted that the key to racial peace in America is "education." It is improbable that when all Americans are "properly educated" our racial problems will suddenly vanish; nevertheless there is perhaps more merit than we commonly recognize in helping our youth (*and* ourselves) to know more about the society we take for granted merely because it is ours. Ours is probably not the best of all possible worlds. Perhaps it could be made better if we knew more about our antecedent-selves—how our perceptions of ourselves and of others have evolved over the span of our brief history, and why.

In a democratic society where education is free and knowledge has social value, whatever is avoided or suppressed is inevitably brought to light. It is well that this is happening in America. A struggle is going on here. At the level of the obvious, it is a struggle about race. The central question is whether being "black" or being "white" has, or ought to have, significance in the structure of our social relations. Scarce values are involved: Jobs, education, prestige and status must be distributed. In the past, race has been a salient criterion of distribution. Suddenly there is a generalized concern that race is not a reliable index of human worth, not a proper basis for the determination of who gets what.

Because we have provided our youth with an interpretation of our history which has been highly stylized and selective, we have muddled their perceptions and compromised their preparation for coping with the hard problems of contemporary life. Neither black Americans nor white Americans have an adequate perception of themselves or of each other. Today's youth want—indeed they *demand*—more truth than we have been prepared to offer them. They want the information that will make their lives intelligible and equip them to make intelligent decisions about their relationships with each other.

This book is an important and timely response to "the need

11

to know." Bradford Chambers has opened a challenging new aperture through which we may focus on our society from a new perspective and in unusual dimensions. With artistry and skill he has put together a book that presents topical matters in a fashion accessible to all of us without sacrificing the value of the work for the more critical interests of scholarly research. In fact, his research into early American history of the black man has uncovered material hitherto overlooked by scholars of the period.

In trying to understand how racism became so pervasive in our culture, we have traditionally assented to an historical interpretation which allowed us to see our racial attitudes as developing gradually in response to pragmatic, economic interests. This book destroys that fiction and robs us of whatever comfort it made possible. The documents in *Chronicles of Black Protest* correct an historical error. They make it clear that the enslavement of the African was not incidental to his helplessness, but from the very first it involved a hatred of his blackness which was signified by an anxious willingness to believe in a mythical curse by a drunken old man that the black man was handed over by God for the white man's exploitation.

It is to the publisher's credit that they have had the courage to publish a book that departs from the standard technique of reducing socio-historical materials for laymen to easy "adaptations," which so often turn an exciting original work like this one into actual misrepresentation.

Mr. Chambers' book is a careful selection of historical documents, each preceded by an extended commentary that challenges our stereotyped concepts. Each document is presented in the political and sociological setting that projected it, with an insightful analysis of the circumstances from which it derived. Here is the substance of black protest—and the reasons for it—from the earliest times to the present.

Chronicles of Black Protest is peculiarly relevant for anyone who wants to understand the pre-occupation of the present-day black American to establish for himself a "negotiable identity." His struggle has been long. And hard. In this book the movement from radical protest, to moderation, to even more radical protest, is clearly discernible. The late Dr. Martin Luther King stands out as the last sentinel of nonviolent protest. One wonders what new chronicles might have been written had he been spared the assassin's bullet. He was a man standing against the flood. His wisdom and his nobility are captured here, but in his last days the rhetoric of militancy was loud and growing louder across the land.

Chronicles of Black Protest will help white people to fill in some of the perplexing gaps in their understanding of America. In "protecting" them from the errors we have made in the past, we have in effect implicated them in the errors we have projected for the future. This is not a pleasant contemplation. Unless drastic changes are made in our perception and behavior we shall soon move into the 21st century dragging behind us a 17th-century dilemma: race. Bradford Chambers has through a magnificent effort helped to diminish that possibility.

C. Eric Lincoln, Ph.D.
Union Theological Seminary

PREFACE

FORTY-TWO DOCUMENTS relating to black protest appear in this book. A list of libraries possessing major collections on black history—with designations for which ones possess the documents in this book—appear on pages 245–48. Some of the collections have a number of the documents; for example, copies of the same pamphlet or printed tract. Others are in only a few of the collections. These available sources are provided for the interested reader who may wish to verify the documents or search for additional ones.

The text of some of the documents is given in full; others have been shortened, but only to the extent that their meaning remains unaltered. Omitted text is indicated by ellipses (three points when words within a sentence only have been deleted, four points for a full sentence or more). Spelling and punctuation conform to the original documents.

A word about the slave statutes appearing on pages 35–41. Not until the early 1800's did state legislatures begin to commission official compilations of the original statutes of the colonies; they included all the colonial statutes, or as many as could be found, and were not confined to any particular topic. In the mid-1800's appeared compilations devoted exclusively to the laws regarding slavery, yet these were often published to promote sectional viewpoints. Reliance upon these collections may have resulted in some of the inconsistencies and misinterpretations on the role of black men in colonial America. These inconsistencies appear in modern historical studies, in encyclopedias and, most recently, in the Report of the National Advisory Commission on Civil Disorders. The slave statutes we have quoted are from the official collections of statutes originally commissioned by the various state legislatures.

For Section I, I wish to express gratitude to Bob Young for research assistance, especially his studies of the slave statutes. If we have come upon an historical oversight and tried to correct it, the credit is largely Mr. Young's.

The extremely complex issues involved in the Civil War and Reconstruction periods are presented in Section II, and for research and editorial help in throwing light on these issues, many thanks to Byron Williams.

Section III traces black protest in the 20th century, and if this book succeeds in helping the reader to a fuller understanding of the current struggle for human rights, thanks are due to Ken Linden for research and editorial help.

To Leslie B. Tanner for tireless assistance in the overall planning and execution of this book, very special thanks. I am warmly grateful to Alvin Tresselt and Tony De Luna for their encouragement and commitment to the book's objectives.

SECTION I

Who Would Be Free

"Who would be free, themselves must strike the blow"

Frederick Douglass

A FAMOUS CURSE

The origin of a myth

by the authors of the Old Testament

About The Document:

The ninth chapter of Genesis, the first book of the Old Testament, tells of a famous curse that for hundreds of years was made an excuse for buying and selling black men in slavery. From the 15th century when Portuguese traders raided Africa and brought the first Africans to Europe, to the 19th century when the slavery of black men was justified from the pulpits of white American churches—through all that time Noah's curse was held proof that slavery of Africans was not a crime against men but, rather, was the will of God Himself.

What was this curse? The Bible tells us that the waters of the Great Flood destroyed all the life that was on earth, except for the people and animals who were with Noah in the Ark. When the Flood receded and left the Ark high and dry on Mount Ararat, those who were in it emerged, resumed their lives, and began to multiply. Noah had three sons—Shem and Ham and Japheth—". . . and of them the whole earth overspread."

After the Flood, Noah planted a vineyard. The vines flourished; the grapes ripened, were picked and pressed into wine. And Noah "drank of the wine and was drunken; and he was uncovered within his tent." Ham entered his father's tent, found him lying naked, and went and told his brothers. The brothers—Shem and Japheth—took up a garment between them and, walking backwards into their father's tent, covered him without letting their eyes look upon him. When Noah awoke and learned what Ham had done, he uttered the fa-

19

mous curse: "Cursed be Canaan; a servant of servants shall he be unto his brethren."

That is the story as the Bible tells it, and for centuries Bible readers had no doubt about its meaning. Ham had been cursed, they said, and from him were descended the "dark races" of Africa. God had willed the inferior position of the black man. He was to be the eternal "hewer of wood and drawer of water" to his white brother.

Yet a closer look at the curse raises questions immediately. Since it was Ham who "uncovered his father's nakedness," why was it Canaan who was cursed by Noah? Canaan, the Bible says, was Ham's son, but we are not told why he was cursed for something that his father did. Simply because he was Ham's son, and Noah took that way of punishing Ham? But why Canaan and not his brothers? Yet, ignoring Canaan completely, Bible readers have for centuries referred to the "curse of Ham."

This old belief identified Ham so closely with the black race that blacks are often called "Hamitic." Yet modern study of Biblical literature has revealed no reference to the origins of the black African. The race certainly does not figure in the tables of the descendants of Ham. Besides Canaan, there were Mizraim, Phut, and Cush. From Mizraim were descended the Egyptians; from Phut, probably the Lydians of Asia Minor. Though Cush was once held to refer to Ethiopia, a country in the north of Africa, modern scholars have refuted that view. Most likely, the Cush of Genesis was father of a people who lived near Elam, more than a thousand miles from Africa. As for Canaan himself, he was the father of the Canaanites, a people who lived in Palestine. The Promised Land of the Israelites was Canaan; it was the land to which Moses led them from Egypt, the land that the children of Israel conquered after their long wandering in the desert. Its people held Palestine for a long time; they built cities and traded extensively along the Mediterranean; they are better known to us through history as the Phoenicians.

Nevertheless our forefathers, and their forefathers before them, firmly believed that Noah's curse showed that it was God's will that the black man be a slave. This is an important fact in understanding the historical background of black protest—a protest that began as a struggle against the most famous curse of all time, yet a curse that is now accepted by scholars of most faiths as a fraud. A notable exception is the Mormon Church, which to this day uses Noah's curse as the rationale for excluding black men from the priesthood and from positions of high office in the church hierarchy.

The Document:

Genesis 9:19–25
King James Version of the Bible

19 These are the three sons of Noah: and of them the whole earth overspread.

20 And Noah began to be an husbandman, and he planted a vineyard:

21 And he drank of the wine, and was drunken; and he was uncovered within his tent.

22 And Ham, the father of Canaan, saw the nakedness of his father, and told his two brethren without.

23 And Shem and Japheth took a garment, and laid it upon both their shoulders, and went backward, and covered the nakedness of their father; and their faces were backward, and they saw not their father's nakedness.

24 And Noah awoke from his wine, and knew what his younger son had done unto him.

25 And he said, Cursed be Canaan; a servant of servants shall he be unto his brethren.

THE "RICHES" OF THE NEW WORLD: 1494

Columbus envisions Hispaniola as a source of slave labor

by Christopher Columbus

About The Documents:

In 1494 Christopher Columbus began the slave trade in the New World. On his second voyage he brought seventeen ships, confident that he would send them back to Spain laden with gold and spices. What he found, as we all know, fell considerably short of his expectations. Columbus did send back a number of ships, but their holds were filled with 500 Indians, whom he ordered to be landed at Cadiz and sold as slaves at Seville. There is evidence to suggest that Columbus conceived of the new lands as a vast mart to compete with Africa in supplying slave labor to the European market.

The record also shows that on his second voyage Columbus sought to colonize Hispaniola with the aid of slave labor. He set a quota of gold dust that each Indian was required to mine every three months. Around his neck each Indian slave wore a brass tag, to be marked periodically as a quota was met. Frequent attempts at revolt were crushed ruthlessly.

The fact is that historians have regarded Columbus as in many ways just toward the Indians. Highly significant, therefore, are the documents below which show how strong were the prevailing attitudes of the time to permit a just man to show such unabashed enthusiasm for exporting slaves on a massive scale. But the dawn of a new morality was breaking upon Europe, and Queen Isabella felt that Columbus had not shown the Indians Christian mercy. She countermanded his orders to sell the Indians and decreed that they be sent back whence they had come.

A fierce and extraordinary debate now spread throughout Europe, especially in Spain, as to how world society should receive a human population whose existence had theretofore been unsuspected. Supporters of Columbus' enslavement policies cited passages in the Bible that sanctioned slavery, and learned theologians upheld them with the same logic they had employed but a short time before in their interminable arguments about the number of angels that could dance on the head of a pin.

Ultimately the humanitarian view won out, and the famous Laws of the Indies of 1542 established that the Indians were free persons and not to be taken as slaves.

The subsequent history of the Indian in the New World is a tragic one, but the laws that defined him as a free man were to have a vital significance. For a time Spanish colonists resorted to every devious ruse to circumvent these laws. One of them, a system called the *encomienda,* was supposed to "protect" the Indians. In theory the system was based on lofty ideals, but in practice its conditions of forced labor and starvation virtually exterminated the local Indian populations in places like Cuba and Santo Domingo.

Enter the black man from Africa.

As early as 1502 black slaves born in Seville and other parts of Spain were being shipped to Hispaniola, where Nicolás de Ovando had just succeeded to the governorship of Spanish possessions in America. (Those blacks born in Spain were the sons and daughters of the first blacks kidnapped from Africa by Portuguese navigators in the mid-15th century and sold to Spanish merchants.) At one point, Ovando asked the Queen to restrict the importation of black men to Hispaniola. Black slaves ran away, he said, and encouraged the Indians to rebel against the Spaniards. Within a few years, however, Ovando had decided that the need for black labor was greater than the danger of their mutiny.

In Hispaniola, Ovando was joined by Bartolomé de Las Casas, who came as a planter and remained to become a Dominican missionary called the "Apostle of the Indies." Las Casas was shocked at his countrymen's treatment of the Indians, and in 1517 he suggested to the new monarch, Charles I, that each Spanish resident in the New World be given license to import a dozen black slaves. Las Casas lived to regret his proposal; in his *History of the Indies* he confesses his error and attributes it to his zeal on behalf of the Indians. His idea was adopted, however, and Charles granted a patent to one of his Flemish court favorites, containing the exclusive right to supply the islands of Haiti, Cuba, Jamaica, and Puerto Rico with 4,000 black slaves annually.

Thus was launched the slave trade between Africa and the New World. There had been some selling of African slaves in

Europe, but the trade was limited and confined largely to Portugal and Spain. Columbus' miscalculation was of the direction of the slave trade; the big markets for slave labor lay, not in Europe, but in the West Indies. By 1540, more than 10,000 Africans a year were being brought to the New World.

The long-term significance of the Laws of the Indies is this: For the first hundred years of New World development, the vast majority of black men from Africa came to the Caribbean colonies owned by the Spanish and Portuguese. Spain's colonies in South America and Portugal's Brazil, however, also became important slave markets. Over the years, there developed in these countries precedents and laws and customs for treating people who were denied the advantages of the privileged classes. The Indian natives, though technically free (referred to as "slaves" only when taken as prisoners of war), fared not much better than slaves; but the brutalities against them lessened, and gradually written laws clearly defined the conditions under which they and the black slaves could live and work. By contrast with the system that grew up in the colonies to the north, slavery in South America was much more humane.

The Documents:

Letter published in Barcelona,
April 1493. Mailed from Lisbon after
Columbus' return from his first trip
to the New World. Extant copies sent
to divers high officials. Commonly
considered to be addressed originally
to Their Catholic Majesties, the King
and Queen of Castile and Aragon.

. . . FINALLY, and speaking only of what has happened on this voyage, which has been so hastily achieved, their highnesses can see that I shall give them all the gold they may need, if they will give me but a very little assistance; spices also, and cotton, as much as their highnesses shall demand . . . and slaves, as many slaves as their highnesses shall command to be shipped. . . .

Memorial brought by Antonio de Torres
from Christopher Columbus in Santo Domingo
to the King and Queen of Spain.
From *Libro de traslados de las
cédulas y provisiones de armadas para*

las Indias del tiempo
de los Reyes Católicos,
General Archives of the Indies, Seville.
Edited by Martín Fernández de Navarrete
in 1825, *Colección de los viajes,* Madrid.

YOU WILL say to their Highnesses that the benefit of the souls
of said cannibals [from Puerto Rico], and even those from
here [Santo Domingo], has brought the thought that the more
that are carried there [Spain] the better; and in that your
Highnesses could be served in this way: that seeing how necessary here are cattle and beasts of labor for the maintenance
of the people who will be here, and for the good of all these
islands, your Highnesses may give license and permission to a
sufficient number of caravels to come each year and bring
those cattle and other goods and things for settling the country and benefitting from the land, and this at prices reasonable to the costs of those who would bring them, which things
can be paid them in slaves from these cannibals, people so
rough and willing and well proportioned and of very good
understanding, which, taken from that inhumanity, we believe will be better than any other slaves. . . .

THE AFRICAN SLAVE TRADE: 1746

A pamphlet extolling the economic advantages of the slave trade to England

by Malachy Postlethwayt

About The Document:

Slavery in South America and Canada differed from the system that grew up in the English colonies of North America. Slavery existed in the Spanish and Portuguese colonies for a hundred years before it came to what is now the United States.

In the South American colonies a slave was not necessarily considered an inferior human being. To be a slave was regarded as a misfortune that might happen to anyone. Though the conditions of slavery were frequently brutal, these brutalities were against the law and punishable if discovered. Since the South American attitude did not hold that a black slave was incapable of being free, a freed slave had the same rights as any other citizen.

South American slaves could buy their freedom, usually at the price for which they had been purchased. In the cities they were legally entitled to work two hours a day for themselves, and in the country they were allowed to grow produce in their own gardens and to sell what they grew. Even as slaves they had the right to own property. Both town and country slaves could keep what they earned and save it toward purchasing their freedom. Under this system of slavery, the master owned the slave's labor, but not the man himself.

In the South American colonies slaves were considered subjects of the Crown; laws protected them against abuse, and each colony had an officer duty-bound to oversee their welfare. Priests were required to report slave mistreatment, and such reports were investigated.

The Catholic Church, very much concerned with the souls

of slaves and with the propagation of the faith, insisted that slaves be married in church, and owners could not separate married slaves from each other or from their children. Under this system, when a slave had earned his freedom he found a place for himself and his family within society. In the 18th century there were black bishops in Brazil.

This system of slavery developed as it did because of the Spanish tradition, dating to the Roman Empire, that a slave did not cease to be a man. He might be a very unfortunate one, but he was a man just the same, capable of the thoughts and feelings of any other man. The Greek and Roman master accepted the fact that slaves could think and feel and made it possible for them to change their status: they could buy or win their freedom.

Black slavery came to the French colony of Quebec not much later than it did to the English colonies. The first black man was sold in Quebec in 1628. Sixty years later, in 1689, Louis XIV approved the importation of Negroes to French Canada to fill the labor shortage. The French *Code Noir,* or the Black Code, set forth rules for the humane treatment of black men. They were allowed to marry, and families could not be broken up and sold to different masters. Yet when the English—who during the same period were evolving their own system of slavery—gained control of Quebec, the rights of the black slaves were abrogated. Black men were no longer allowed to marry, and their parental right to their children was rescinded, as was their right to own property.

To the south and north of the American colonies, then, social systems developed that accepted slaves as human beings and gave them inalienable rights. The slave system that evolved in the English colonies was unique in the New World—in fact, unique in all history. Although colonial laws governing slavery compared with ancient Roman law, popular attitudes made the difference. As in Rome, a slave in the colonies had no rights before the law, but Roman masters traditionally gave their slaves rights the colonists withheld. For example, Romans frequently granted to their slaves a *peculium,* or allowance, from which our word "peculiar" is derived. Freed slaves could fit into society and often rose to social prominence. Here in the colonies attitudes toward freed black men kept them in a position not far removed from outright slavery.

The differences in the attitudes of the Roman stemmed from his recognition that slavery could happen to any man and might happen to him, whereas the American colonist refused to identify himself with the black man.

In the colonies black slaves were not allowed to enter into

contracts; their word had no standing before the law, hence they could not marry. They were permitted and encouraged to live together to breed new slaves—and the children belonged to the woman's master. To avoid the problem of what to do with the children of slave mothers and white fathers, the courts decided that the father of a slave was "unknown to our law."

In the next section we shall examine the original slave statutes of the English colonists. The question we want to ask here is: *Why* did slavery in the English colonies develop so differently from the systems in South America and Canada?

Part of the answer lies in the double standard that characterized the mother country's attitude toward slavery. According to the Virginian colonist John Rolffe, a "Dutch man of Warre" sailed into Jamestown harbor in 1619 and exchanged "20 neggars" for "victualle." This was the first record of the black man's presence in the English colonies. Now, at that time in England, slavery was almost non-existent. The serfs of the Middle Ages were no longer; gone too were the serfs in most countries of Western Europe. The English people did recognize a system of work that combined semi-slavery with apprenticeship, known as "indentured servitude," about which we shall have more to say later. The English people, however, like most people throughout Europe, recognized the slavery of "infidels"; that is, they saw nothing wrong in making slaves out of Moslems and Turks captured in war. What the English and Europeans refused to accept was the slavery of fellow Christians. Thus, when a Turk or Moslem slave embraced Christianity and was baptized, the English automatically freed him. There were no written laws decreeing this. It was a matter of custom and tradition.

Moslems and Turks were slaves in the English colonies, just as blacks were slaves. But the New World colonies were two thousand miles distant from England. And the colonists were free to evolve a system peculiarly their own, or at least a system that did not go against the letter of the law of England.

The colonists did very little to convert their slaves to Christianity, for obvious reasons. They feared that once the slaves became Christians, England would demand that they be freed. As the years went on, and as the colonists developed a sense of independence from the motherland, they began writing laws that went counter, if not to the laws of England, at least to English tradition.

Virginia was the first colony in the New World to enact a statute that contradicted English tradition. The Virginia statute decreed that a black slave, even though he became converted and was baptized a Christian, could not thereby become free. Other colonies enacted similar statutes, and some of these the king of England vetoed, or countermanded. Why didn't the king order a halt to the enslavement of all Christians in the colonies?

As we have said, the English had a double standard. Probably they would have insisted on applying the same standards of morality to the colonists as they did to themselves, had it not been for one thing: money. England was becoming a sea power of importance, and her ships were bringing in fortunes from all over the world. Sir John Hawkins and Sir Francis Drake were the first English sea captains to pirate slaves from the ships of other countries, and after their time English involvement in the slave trade become more and more substantial.

This trade in slaves, the subject of the document that follows, was bringing truly enormous profits. More than half the African slave trade was carried in British ships, at first through an exclusive franchise granted to the Royal African Company and later, when profits grew so big, through free competition among shipowners. The English government even maintained at its own expense slave depots on the west coast of Africa, where black men were assembled before being shipped via the famous Middle Passage from Africa to the colonial markets. So huge were the profits from this trade that an English nobleman told his peers in the House of Lords that they owed their status to slaving; anyone who proposed to abolish the slave trade, he said, was an advocate of treason.

The document that follows is an argument by an 18th-century Englishman in defense of the trading company that had come under attack for its involvement in the slave trade. Reference is made in the document to the "Assiente Contract." This refers properly to the *Assiento*, a treaty with Spain permitting England to import slaves to the New World. In the Bull of Partition of May 4, 1493, Pope Alexander had given exclusive rights in the New World to Spain, and in Africa to Portugal. This was the famous "line of demarcation," dividing spheres of influence over lands recently discovered between the two great sea powers.

The Document:

From tract titled *The National and Private Advantages of the African Trade Considered,* London, printed for L. and P. Knapton, 1746

THE MOST APPROVED Judges of the commercial Interests of
these Kingdoms have ever been of Opinion, that our *West-In-
dia* and *African Trades* are the most nationally beneficial of
any we carry on. It is also allowed on all Hands, that the
Trade to *Africa* is the Branch which renders our *American
Colonies* and *Plantations* so advantagious to *Great Britain;*
that Traffic only affording our *Planters* a constant Supply of
Negroe-Servants for the Culture of their Lands in the Produce of *Sugars, Tobacco, Rice, Rum, Cotton, Fustick, Pi-
mento,* and all other our Plantation-Produce: So that the extensive Employment of our Shipping in, to, and from *America,* the great Brood of Seamen consequent thereupon, and
the daily Bread of the most considerable Part of our *British
Manufacturers,* are owing primarily to the Labour of
Negroes; who, as they were the first happy Instruments of
raising our Plantations; so their Labour only can support and
preserve them, and render them still more and more profit-
able to their Mother-Kingdom.

The *Negroe-Trade* therefore, and the natural Consequences
resulting from it, may be justly esteemed an inexhaustible
Fund of Wealth and Naval Power to this Nation. And by the
Overplus of *Negroes* above what have served our own Planta-
tions, we have drawn likewise no inconsiderable Quantities of
Treasure from the *Spaniards,* who are settled on the Conti-
nent of *America;* not only for *Negroes* furnished them from
Jamaica, but by the late *Assiente Contract* with the Crown of
Spain; which may probably again be revived, upon a Peace
being concluded with that Kingdom.

What renders the *Negroe-Trade* still more estimable and
important, is, that near Nine-tenths of those *Negroes* are paid
for in *Africa* with *British Produce* and *Manufactures* only;
and the Remainder with *East-India* Commodities. We send
no Specie or Bullion to pay for the Products of *Africa,* but,
'tis certain, we bring from thence very large Quantities of
Gold; and not only that but *Wax* and *Ivory;* the one serves
for a foreign Export without the least Detriment to our
own Product; the other is manufactured at Home, and afterwards carried to foreign Markets, to no little Advantage both
to the Nation and the Traders. From which *Facts,* the Trade
to *Africa* may very truly be said to be, as it were, all Profit to
the Nation; the direct Trade thither affords a considerable national Balance in our Favour, and is apparently attended with
such a Series of advantagious Consequences, that no other
Branch whatever of our foreign Traffic admits of.

And it may be worth Consideration, that while our Plantations depend only on Planting by *Negroe-Servants,* they will
neither depopulate our own Country, become independent of

her Dominion, or any way interfere with the Interests of the *British Manufacturer, Merchant,* or *Landed Gentleman:* Whereas were we under the Necessity of supplying our Colonies with *White-Men* instead of *Blacks,* they could not fail being in a Capacity to interfere with the Manufactures of this Nation, in Time to shake off their Dependency thereon, and prove as injurious to the *Landed,* and Trading-Interests as ever they have hitherto been beneficial.

Many are prepossessed against this Trade, thinking it a *barbarous, inhuman, and unlawful Traffic for a Christian Country to Trade in Blacks;* to which I would beg leave to observe; that though the odious Appellation of *Slaves* is annexed to this Trade, it being called by some the *Slave-Trade,* yet it does not appear from the best Enquiry I have been able to make, that the State of those People is changed for the worst, by being Servants to our *British Planters* in *America;* they are certainly treated with great Lenity and Humanity: And as the Improvement of the Planter's Estates depends upon due Care being taken of their Healths and Lives, I cannot but think their Condition is much bettered to what it was in their own Country.

Besides, the *Negroe-Princes* in *Africa,* 'tis well known, are in perpetual War with each other; and since before they had this Method of disposing of their Prisoners of War to Christian Merchants, they were wont not only to be applied to inhuman Sacrifices, but to extream Torture and Barbarity, their Transplantation must certainly be a Melioration of their Condition; provided living in a civilized Christian Country, is better than living among Savages: Nay, if Life be preferable to Torment and cruel Death, their State cannot with any Colour of Reason, be presumed to be worsted.

But I never heard it said that the Lives of *Negroes* in the Servitude of our planters were less tolerable than those of *Colliers* and *Miners* in all *Christian* Countries. However, while our Rivals in Trade receive great national Emolument by the Labour of these People, this Objection will be of little Weight with those who have the Interest of their Country at Heart; or indeed the Welfare of the *Negroes.*

COLONIAL SLAVE STATUTES: 1630-1740

Selections from early American laws governing slavery

Compiled from the original statutes of Virginia and other colonies

About The Documents:

White indentured servants comprised as much as two-thirds of the original labor force of the English colonies in the New World. By the system of indenture, a man made a contract with a shipping company for free passage, and in exchange he agreed to let the captain sell his services for a period of years to the highest bidder. Hundreds of thousands of white men from England, Ireland and Scotland (religious dissenters, paupers, prisoners, for the most part) came to the New World in this manner. They were called "bondsmen," "redemptioners" and "indented servants." After their time of service was up—two to seven years—the law required that bondsmen be given a new suit of clothes, a small parcel of land, and modest means to start their lives as "freemen."

A misconception of American black history—a misconception supported by a growing number of popular accounts —is that a more or less idyllic period existed between the time of the landing of the Jamestown blacks in 1619 and the enactment, some forty years later, of the first colonial statutes defining the black man as slave for life. During this interim period, we are told, the black man was treated on nearly a legal par with the white bondsman. An important corollary to this interpretation of history is that color distinctions, as a condition of slavery, became a fact of early American life *after* a series of colonial statutes decreed it so in the 1660's. According to this interpretation, the doctrine of the black man as an inferior being developed as a result of legal disenfranchisement. The inference is that the American forebears practiced racial equality and that a period of indeterminacy existed, following which—had the colonists been allowed to pursue their better instincts—black men might have been assimilated into the mainstream of American life.

The historical justification for this interpretation has tremendous bearing on our times. Suppose it were true that American denial of the black man's humanity originated in statutes and laws designed to promote the interests of the colonial planters and other privileged classes; in that event there would be massive logic for the aims of the protest movement of the first half of the 20th century, which directed its efforts toward breaking down legal barriers to racial equality. Since then, there has been a drastic revision in the goals of the black protest movement, and the conclusion becomes more and more accepted that there is something inherent in the makeup of white America that denies the black man his humanity, no matter how extensive the legal changes. Whatever that inherent something is, it became manifest at an exceptionally early period in American history.

The records of the early acts of the colonial assemblies and, in the case of Virginia, of the House of Burgesses—are not easy to follow, and they raise almost as many questions as they answer. Yet they do tell an astonishing story.

The first recorded statute that refers to the black man is a Virginia resolution of 1630, adopted eleven years after the landing of the Jamestown slaves in 1619. The time lapse hardly need surprise us, because the number of slaves in the colony was limited to a few cargoes, sold or traded at irregular intervals by Dutch ships. At the time there were not more than two hundred black men in the whole colony, out of a population of roughly 7,500. It wasn't until the colony was in a position to sell all the tobacco it grew and slaves were coming in increasing numbers that the House of Burgesses responded with legislative enactments affecting the legal status of black men. What should concern us is the fact that the Virginia colonists saw fit to adopt a discriminatory resolution against the black men when there were still so few of them in the colony. And we must presume that the resolution in question, and the acts adopted subsequently, were an expression of the attitudes and beliefs of the freemen of Virginia, since this was after all a democracy—the first experiment in democracy, as a matter of fact, in all of North America.

Consider the implications of the first three or four statutes that appear below, as they express the attitudes of the Virginia freemen. In the resolution, a white man is accused of dishonoring himself and defiling his body because he had intercourse with a black woman. Then a statute prohibits black men—no one else—from carrying guns. Next, in the statute of 1646, the wording of the text lists the black man in the same category as an object, not as a human being. These very early statutes reveal a decidedly discriminatory attitude already prevalent long before the acts of the 1660's gave it legal sanction. They hardly suggest a period of legal indeterminacy out of which black men might have emerged as the equal of other men. The Rhode Island reference of 1652 is to the "common practice" of the time, and the implication is clear that black men had been relegated to lifetime slavery from the outset.

The later statutes, beginning about 1660, reveal an almost hysterical fear of slave uprisings. These astonishing statutes are evidence that black men, even from the start of the slave trade, refused to submit meekly to the white man's domination, and that they did in fact rebel against their condition. Here again an important distinction is to be made between slavery in South America and slavery in the English colonies.

The Spanish had to contend with numerous slave insurrections, and they were often ruthless in the punishments they meted out; yet, fully conscious of their own morally untenable position, they seemed to accept the consequences and to face up to the rebellions as they occurred. The North American colonists were from the beginning seized by a collective fear of the black man; a fear so pervasive that they alone of the New World settlers sanctioned the most extreme repressive measures, hoping perhaps to avoid thereby the consequences of their own terrifying guilt.

It is important to know that the colonists possessed three categories of slaves. The first consisted of Indians taken as prisoners of war. The English colonists, like their Spanish and Portuguese predecessors, had come to accept what by then was almost a tenet of international law: that the Indians were free men. They were exploitable, but they were not to be treated as outright slaves, except Indians taken in combat, or Indians convicted of some kind of crime. Moors and Turks belonged to a second category of colonial slaves. It will be noted in one of the statutes that an English treaty exempted some Turks from bondage, but the statute establishes that the early colonists did enslave a number of the infidels. Colonial enslavement of Moors, Turks and some Jews (Jews were outlawed in England at this time) was sanctioned by unwritten law, on the ground that they were non-Christians.

Blacks were part of that second category, since they too were non-Christian, but they formed a third category of their own, because in addition to being "heathens," they were consid-

ered to be savages, set apart from human society, destined by
Noah's curse to perpetual servitude.

Selections from statutes referring to slavery appear below
in chronological sequence. Most of them are from the Virginia records, since that colony initiated slavery and other
colonies followed suit, but also included are the statutes of a
number of other colonies. (All text not set in italic type con-
sists of the original wording of the statutes. The spelling of
words, which boasts little in the way of consistency, has been
unaltered.)

The Documents:

The Statutes at Large being a
collection of all the Laws of Virginia,
published pursuant to an act of the
General Assembly of Virginia, passed
on the fifth day of February 1808.
Compiled by William Waller Hening.
Printed by R. & W. G. Barton, New York,
1823, and containing a letter of
commendation from Thomas Jefferson
to the compiler. Vols. I-III.

The Statutes at Large of South Carolina,
compiled by Thomas Cooper, Columbia,
S. C.: A. S. Johnson, 1836. Vols. I-V.

Records of the Colony of Rhode Island
and Providence Plantations, in New
England; compiled by John Russell Bartlett,
Secretary of State, Providence:
A. C. Green & Brothers, state printer,
1856–65.

Archives of Maryland,
Proceedings and Acts of the
General Assembly of Maryland.
Compiled by William Hand Browne.
Baltimore, 1889. Vol. VII.

1630 *Virginia* [Resolution] Hugh Davis to be soundly
        whipped before an assembly of negroes and others, for
        abusing himself to the dishonor of God and the shame
        of Christians, by defiling his body in lying with a
        negro, which fault he is to acknowledge next Sabbath
        day.

1639 *Virginia* All persons except negroes to be provided with arms and ammunition.

1646 *Virginia Treaty with the Indians, requiring that Necotowance* (*chief*) bring in the English prisoners, And all such negroes and guns which are yet remaining either in the possession of himselfe or any Indians.

1652 *Rhode Island* Whereas, there is a common course practised amongst Englishmen to buy negers, to the end that they may have them for service or slaves forever; for the preventinge of such practices among us, let it be ordered, that no blacke mankind or white being forced by covenant bond or otherwise, to serve any man or his assignes longer than ten yeares, or untill they come to bee twentie-four yeares of age, if they be taken in under fourteen, from the time of their cominge within the liberties of this collonie. And at the end or terme of ten years to set them free as the manner is with English servants. And that man that will not let them goe free, or shall sell them away elsewhere, to the end that they may bee enslaved to others for a long time, hee or they shall forfeit to the collonie forty pounds. *This was enacted by the Commissioners of the towns of Providence and Warwick, though it lacked the force of a general law.*

1660 *Virginia* In case any English servant shall run away in company with any negroes who are incapable of making satisfaction by addition of time, *be it enacted, &c.:* shall serve for the time of the said negroes absence.

1662 *Virginia* Whereas some doubts have arisen whether children got by any Englishman upon a negro woman should be slave or free, *be it enacted, &c.:* that all children borne in this country shalbe held bond or free only according to the condition of the mother.

1663 *Maryland* All negroes or other slaves within the province, and all negroes and other slaves to be hereafter imported into the province, shall serve *durante vita;* and all children born of any negro or other slave, shall be slaves as their fathers were for the term of their lives. Sec. 2. And forasmuch as divers freeborn English women, forgetful of their free condition, and to the disgrace of our nation, do intermarry with negro slaves, by which also divers suits may arise, touching the issue of such women, and a great damage doth befall the master of such negroes, for preservation whereof for deterring such free-born women from such shameful matches, *be it enacted, &c.:* That whatsoever free-born woman shall intermarry with any slave, from and after the last day of the present assembly, shall serve the master of such slave during the life of her husband; and that all the issue of such free-born women, so married, shall be slaves as their fathers were. *This statute was subsequently changed, for the following reason: It resulted in unscrupulous plantation owners forcing indentured female servants to marry slaves, to obtain the extended servitude of the women and the slave labor of the children of such marriages. In 1681 Maryland enacted a new statute defining the children as slave or free according to the status of the mother. The other colonies enacted similar statutes.*

1667 *Virginia* That the conferring of baptisme doth not alter the condition of the person as to his bondage or ffreedom. *This act for the first time negated British common law, which required that slaves who became Christian be freed.*

1668 *Virginia* Negro women, though permitted to enjoy their freedom yet ought not in all respects to be admitted to a full fruition of the exemptions and impunities of the English. *This statute denied equality before the law to the freed Negro.*

1669 *Virginia* Whereas the only law in force for the punishment of refractory servants resisting their master, mistress, or overseer, cannot be inflicted upon negroes, nor the obstinacy of many of them by other than violent means be suppressed. *Be it enacted &c.,* if any slave resist his master (or other by his master's order correcting him) and by the extremity of coercion should chance to die, that his death shall not be accounted felony, but the master (or that other person, &c.) be acquitted from molestation, since it cannot be presumed that prepensed malice (which alone makes murder felony) should induce any man to destroy his own estate.

1669 *North Carolina* Every freeman of Carolina shall have absolute power and authority over his negro slaves, of what opinion or religion soever. *The code of South Carolina granted even more authority to the slave-owner than did other colonies. The author of the code was none other than the famous libertarian John Locke, whose writings on political and religious freedom directly influenced the philosophy of the fathers of the Constitution of the United States.*

1670 *Virginia* Whereas it has been questioned whether Indians or negroes, manumitted or otherwise ffree, could be capable of purchasing Christian servants, it is enacted that noe negroe or Indian though baptised and enjoyed their owne ffreedom shall be capable of any such purchase of christians, but yet not debarred from buying any of their owne nation.

Virginia Whereas some disputes have arisen whether Indians taken in war by any other nation, and by that nation that taketh them sold to the English, are servants for life or term of years, it is resolved and enacted that all servants not being christians imported into this colony by shipping shalbe slaves for their lives; but what shall come by land shall serve; if boyes or girles, untill thirty years of age, if man or woman twelve years and no longer. *This act shows a relaxation of the prohibition against holding Indians as slaves. About this period Indian slaves in increasing numbers were being imported into Virginia and New England from the West Indies and the Spanish main. "By shipping" is also meant Negroes.*

1680 *Virginia* Whereas the frequent meeting of considerable numbers of negroe slaves under pretence of feasts and burialls is judged of dangerous consequence. . . . *This act, titled An act for preventing Negroes Insurrections, prohibits Negroes from carrying clubs, staffs or arms of any type. Lifting up a hand in opposition to any Christian is punishable by thirty lashes. A Negro runaway refusing apprehension is punishable by death. Negro slaves must have a pass to leave the grounds of their owner.*

1682 *Virginia* All servants imported or brought into this country, either by sea or land, whether Negroes, Moors, Mollattoes or Indians, who and whose parentage and native country are not christian at the time of their first purchase of such servants by some christian,

except Turks and Moors in amity with her majesty
. . . shall be adjudged, deemed and taken to be slaves.

Virginia Whereas a certaine act of assembly, held at
James City the 8th day of June, in the yeare of our
Lord 1680, instituted an act preventing negroes insurrections hath not had its intended effect . . . *This refers to the 1680 statute above and makes the punishments for insurrections even stronger than the first act.
It also sets a fine for a master or overseer who allows
Negroes not belonging to him to remain on his plantation for longer than four consecutive hours.*

1691 *Virginia* And for prevention of that abominable mix-
ture and spurious issue which hereafter may encrease
in this dominion, as well by negroes, mulattoes, and Indians intermarrying with English, or other white
women, as by their unlawful accompanying with one
another . . . and whatsoever English or other white
man or woman being free shall intermarry with a
negroe, mulatto, or Indian man or woman bond or free
shall within three months after such marriage be ban-
ished and removed from this dominion, forever.

Virginia That no negro or mulattoe be after the end of
this present session of assembly set free by any person
or persons whatsoever, unless such person or persons
. . . *heirs, etc.* . . . pay for the transportation of such
negro or negroes out of the country within six months
after such setting them free.

1692 *Maryland* Where any negro or slave, being in servitude
or bondage, is or shall become Christian, and receive
the sacrament of baptism, the same shall not nor ought
to be deemed, adjudged or construed to be a manumis-
sion or freeing of any such negro or slave, or his or her
issue, from their servitude or bondage, but that notwithstanding they shall at all times hereafter be and remain in servitude and bondage as they were before
baptism, any opinion, matter or thing to the contrary
notwithstanding. *Between the years 1706 and 1712,
other colonies including New York enacted similar
statutes. These statutes were contrary to English law.*

1705 *Virginia* That no person whatsoever already convicted,
or which shall hereafter be convicted, &c., of treason,
murther, felony, &c., &c., nor any negro, mulatto, or

Indian, shall from and after the publication of this act bear any office ecclesiasticall, civill, or military, or be in any place of public trust or power, within this her majesty's colony and dominion of Virginia. *The act defines mulatto in these words:* That the child of an Indian, and the child, grandchild, or great grandchild of a negro shall be deemed, accounted, held and taken to be mulatto.

Virginia That popish recusants, convicts, negroes, mulattoes and Indian servants, and others, not being christians, shall be deemed and taken to be persons incapable in law, to be witnesses in any cases whatsoever. *Later amended to allow Negroes to testify in court only against other Negroes.*

1723 *Virginia* Laws for the better governing of Negroes, Mulattos and Indians. Inasmuch as the present laws are found insufficient to restrain their tumultous and unlawful meetings, or to punish the secret plots and conspiracies carried on amongst them, and known only to such, as by the laws now established, are not accounted legal evidence. And it being found necessary, that some further provisions be made, for detecting and punishing all such dangerous combinations in the future, *be it enacted &c. . . . . Conspiracy of five slaves or more is deemed a felony punishable by death. The punishment for minor crimes not deemed a felony is stated as follows:* to have one ear nailed to the pillory, and there to stand for the space of one hour, and then the said ear to be cut off: and thereafter, the other ear nailed in like manner, and cut off. *All meetings by Negroes or slaves banned on any pretense whatsoever. No slaves to be set free except for some meritorious service, to be adjudged and allowed by the governor and council. Manslaughter of a slave (i.e., death resulting from corrective punishment) not deemed to be a punishable offense. Free Negroes are not permitted to vote.*

1740 *South Carolina* Whereas, in his majesty's plantations in America, slavery has been introduced and allowed, and the people commonly called negroes, Indians, mulattoes, and mestizoes have been deemed absolute slaves, and the subjects of property in the hands of particular persons, the extent of whose power over such slaves ought to be settled and limited by positive laws, so that the slaves may be kept in due subjection and obedience, and the owners and other persons having the care and government of slaves may be restrained from exercising too great rigor and cruelty over them, and that the public peace and order of this province may be preserved, it is therefore enacted that all negroes, Indians, mulattoes, and mestizoes (free Indians in amity with this government, and negroes, mulattoes, and mestizoes who are now free, excepted,) who now are or shall hereafter be in this province, and all their issue and offspring born and to be born, shall be, and they are hereby declared to be and remain forever hereafter, absolute slaves, and shall follow the condition of the mother, and shall be claimed, held, taken, reputed, and adjudged in law to be chattels personal.

"AN HEIGHT OF OUTRAGE AGAINST HUMANITY": 1775

Thomas Paine's first published article in America

by Thomas Paine

About The Document:

Thomas Paine was born in England in 1737, of poor Quaker parents. His father apprenticed him to a corsetmaker, but the trade was not to his liking, and he ran away. In the slums of London, he tried working as a grocer, as an excise man, then as a schoolteacher. He was unsuccessful; twice he was dismissed from his excise post for leading agitation for higher salaries. At thirty-seven, he was bankrupt, angry, and alone. Then he met Benjamin Franklin, who was impressed enough with him to give him letters of introduction to people in Philadelphia.

In 1774 Paine arrived in America, and within months he was denouncing the slave trade. He obtained a job on the *Pennsylvania Journal and the Weekly Advertiser,* and in the March 8 issue he wrote an article titled "African Slavery in America," which appears below. In April 1775 Paine helped a group of Quakers to launch the world's first abolition organization—The Pennsylvania Anti-Slavery Society. As early as 1696 the Quakers of Pennsylvania had urged their members not to countenance slavery, and they remained the only religious sect in the colonies to reject slavery. All other churches condoned the system; "Servants, obey your masters" was a frequent topic for sermons in colonial pulpits.

Paine's article denouncing slavery preceded by a year his famous pamphlet *Common Sense,* the argument for independence that so stirred the American colonists. Throughout the Revolution Paine marched with the troops, yet still found time to write a series of sixteen pamphlets called *The Crisis.*

Often he wrote by campfire light, after a long day's march, using a drum-head as a desk.

The Revolution did not make Paine forget his concern with slavery. In 1780 he was coauthor of legislation that led to the gradual abolishment of slavery in the state of Pennsylvania. Once, when Franklin said, "Where liberty is, there is my country," Paine answered, "Where liberty is *not*, there is mine."

After the Revolutionary War was won, Paine returned to England. There he wrote *The Rights of Man,* a call for the overthrow of the monarchy, which so upset England's ruling class that he was forced to flee to France. He took part in the French Revolution and was jailed by the Jacobins. Released in 1794, he remained in Paris, where he wrote *The Age of Reason,* a philosophical work attacking conventional religious beliefs. In 1802 he returned to America.

It had been Thomas Paine's writings that had made him so important to the American Revolution. Ironically, it was his last book—*The Age of Reason*—that turned Americans against him. Practically ostracized, Thomas Paine died in poverty seven years after his return to the land for whose liberty he had done so much.

The Document:

Magazine article titled "African Slavery
in America" appearing in the *Pennsylvania
Journal and the Weekly Advertiser,* March 8, 1775

To AMERICANS: That some desperate wretches should be willing to steal and enslave men by violence and murder for gain, is rather lamentable than strange. But that many civilized, nay Christianized people should approve, and be concerned in the savage practice, is surprising; and still persist, though it has been so often proved contrary to the light of nature, to every principle of justice and humanity, and even good policy, by a succession of eminent men,* and several late publications.

Our traders in MEN (*an unnatural commodity!*) must know the wickedness of that SLAVE-TRADE, if they attend to reasoning, or the dictates of their own hearts; and such as shun and stifle all these, wilfully sacrifice conscience, and the character of integrity to that golden idol.

* Dr. Ames, Baxter, Durham, Locke, Carmichael, Hutcheson, Montesquieu, and Blackstone, Wallace, etc., etc., Bishop of Gloucester. [Paine's own footnote.]

The managers of that trade themselves, and others, testify, that many of these African nations inhabit fertile countries, are industrious farmers, enjoy plenty, and lived quietly, averse to war, before the Europeans debauched them with liquors, and bribing them against one another; and that these inoffensive people are brought into slavery, by stealing them, tempting kings to sell subjects, which they can have no right to do, and hiring one tribe to war against another, in order to catch prisoners. By such wicked and inhuman ways the English are said to enslave towards one hundred thousand yearly; of which thirty thousand are supposed to die by barbarous treatment in the first year; besides all that are slain in the unnatural wars excited to take them. So much innocent blood have the managers and supporters of this inhuman trade to answer for to the common Lord of all!

Many of these were not prisoners of war, and redeemed from savage conquerors, as some plead; and they who were such prisoners, the English, who promote the war for that very end, are the guilty authors of their being so; and if they were redeemed, as is alleged, they would owe nothing to the redeemer but what he paid for them.

They show as little reason as conscience who put the matter by with saying—"Men, in some cases, are lawfully made slaves, and why may not these?" So men, in some cases, are lawfully put to death, deprived of their goods, without their consent; may any man, therefore, be treated so, without any conviction of desert? Nor is this plea mended by adding—"They are set forth to us as slaves, and we buy them without farther inquiry, let the sellers see to it." Such men may as well join with a known band of robbers, buy their ill-got goods, and help on the trade; ignorance is no more pleadable in one case than the other; the sellers plainly own how they obtain them. But none can lawfully buy without evidence that they are not concurring with men-stealers; and as the true owner has a right to reclaim his goods that were stolen, and sold; so the slave, who is proper owner of his freedom, has a right to reclaim it, however often sold.

Most shocking of all is alleging the sacred scriptures to favor this wicked practice. One would have thought none but infidel cavillers would endeavor to make them appear contrary to the plain dictates of natural light, and conscience, in a matter of common justice and humanity; which they cannot be. Such worthy men, as referred to before, judged otherways; Mr. Baxter declared, *the slave traders should be called devils, rather than Christians; and that it is a heinous crime to buy them.* But some say, "the practice was permitted to the Jews." To which may be replied:

1. The example of the Jews, in many things, may not be imitated by us; they had not only orders to cut off several nations altogether, but if they were obliged to war with others, and conquered them, to cut off every male; they were suffered to use polygamy and divorces, and other things utterly unlawful to us under clearer light.

2. The plea is, in a great measure, false; they had no permission to catch and enslave people who never injured them.

3. Such arguments ill become us, *since the time of reformation came,* under gospel light. All distinctions of nations, and privileges of one above others, are ceased; Christians are taught to *account all men their neighbors; and love their neighbors as themselves; and do to all men as they would be done by; to do good to all men; and man-stealing is ranked with enormous crimes.* Is the barbarous enslaving of our inoffensive neighbors, and treating them like wild beasts subdued by force, reconcilable with all these *divine precepts?* Is this doing to them as we would desire they should do to us? If they could carry off and enslave some thousands of us, would we think it just?—One would almost wish they could for once; it might convince more than reason, or the Bible. . . .

THE DELETED CLAUSE: 1776

*Action of the Continental Congress
July 2-4, 1776*

by Thomas Jefferson

About The Document:

Below is the controversial omitted clause as it originally appeared in Thomas Jefferson's draft of the Declaration of Independence. Jefferson was the representative of Virginia on the committee of five appointed to draw up the Declaration. The others were John Adams, representing Massachusetts; Benjamin Franklin, representing Pennsylvania; Robert R. Livingston, representing New York; and Roger Sherman, representing Connecticut. Except for an altered word and a phrase, and one or two altered sentences, the text of the Declaration was Jefferson's.

Jefferson wrote the Declaration in the upstairs parlor of a German bricklayer, in whose home he lodged during the Continental Congress then in session in Philadelphia. Seated at a portable desk of his own design, which he had brought with him, he wrote and rewrote the Declaration. He showed his final draft to Adams and Franklin, who approved it but made minor changes. (These alterations appear in the margins of the original draft and are marked "in the handwriting of John Adams" and "in the handwriting of Benjamin Franklin.")

On June 28, Jefferson and the committee submitted the Declaration to the Continental Congress. Beginning on the second day of July and continuing through to the fourth, the delegates acted as a board of editors. Like Adams and Franklin, they added a word here and omitted a word there—in all, they made thirty-eight alterations. The delegates omitted, however, one entire paragraph. It was the only substantive change in the Declaration.

The omitted clause, or paragraph, was a denunciation of the slave traffic, written as one of the several complaints against King George III.

It is sometimes noted that Jefferson himself was a plantation owner and a slave holder, and that in his book *Notes on Virginia* he questioned the black man's inherent capacities. He later repudiated this position, however, and admitted that his estimation of black men had been based on scanty evidence. Indeed, Jefferson was one of the first to recognize the accomplishments of the black scientist and mathematician Benjamin Banneker. It was Jefferson who recommended Banneker for the appointment by President Washington to the commission that surveyed what is now the District of Columbia.

Jefferson had known of the ex-slave Crispus Attucks who was the first to give his life in the Revolutionary War, as he tried to rally the Americans during the Boston Massacre of 1770. (Although George Washington tried to exclude black men from military service, in the end he relented, and at least 5,000 black men served in the Continental Army.)

Even while he held the typical Southern ideas of black inferiority, Jefferson made a clear distinction between capacities and rights. He wrote that in capacities there might be distinctions, but in rights all men are equal. Jefferson was one of the first to point out the crippling psychological effects of slavery on the white masters. As a young member of the Virginia House of Burgesses, he introduced a resolution calling for gradual emancipation and for colonization of blacks in Africa, where the United States would help black men to become a "free and independent people." This plan came to be called the "Jeffersonian solution," and Jefferson was frequently cited as an authority during the debates on colonization schemes that were to recur in post-Revolutionary times.

In another little-known statement from his *Notes on Virginia,* Jefferson perceptively explained the evolution of racist doctrines. He was showing how parents transmit "odious peculiarities" to their children and how, without conscious awareness, these peculiarities become so stamped upon the mind that their origins become completely forgotten generations later.

There must doubtless be an unhappy influence on the manners of our people produced by the existence of slavery among us. The whole commerce between master and slave is a perpetual exercise of the most boisterous passions, the most unremitting despotism on the one part, and degrading submissions on the other. Our children see this, and learn to imitate it; for man is an imitative animal. This quality is the

germ of all education in him. From his cradle to his grave
he is learning to do what he sees others do. . . . The parent
storms, the child looks on, catches the lineaments of wrath,
puts on the same airs in the circle of smaller slaves, gives a
loose to the worst of passions, and thus nursed, educated, and
daily exercised in tyranny, cannot but be stamped by it with
odious peculiarities.

Speaking of the contradictions between the American
dream of freedom and equality for all and the reality of
slavery, Jefferson declared:

I tremble for my country when I reflect that God is just;
that his justice cannot sleep forever.

Jefferson's plan to colonize blacks on the coast of Africa
included sending ships to other parts of the world to encourage an equal number of whites to come to the United States.
Jefferson foresaw race war and "the extermination of the one
or the other race" if the slave dilemma was not resolved in
his lifetime. He made that assertion in a rhetorical question
and answer involving his colonization plan:

It will probably be asked, Why not retain and incorporate
the blacks into the State, and thus save the expense of supplying by importation of white settlers, the vacancies they
will leave? Deep rooted prejudices entertained by the whites;
ten thousand recollections, by the blacks, of the injuries they
have sustained; new provocations; the real distinctions which
nature has made; and many other circumstances, will divide
us into parties, and produce convulsions, which will probably never end but in the extermination of the one or the
other race.

The Document:

From the Unexpurgated Draft
of the Declaration of Independence

HE [the king of Great Britain] has waged cruel war against
human nature itself. Violating its most sacred rights of life
and liberty in the persons of a distant people, who never
offended him, captivating and carrying them into slavery in
another hemisphere, or to incur miserable death in their
transportation thither, this piratical warfare, the opprobrium
of *infidel* powers, is the warfare of the *Christian* King of
Great Britain. Determined to keep open a market where
MEN should be bought and sold, he has prostituted his nega-

tive for suppressing every legislative attempt to prohibit or restrain this execrable commerce.

Postscript To The Document:

Who was responsible for the omission? Why was the clause deleted? In his *Autobiography*, Jefferson answers these questions with beautiful forthrightness:

> The Clause . . . reprobating the enslaving of the inhabitants of Africa was struck out in complaisance to South Carolina and Georgia, who have never attempted to restrain the importation of slaves, and who on the contrary still wished to continue it.
>
> Our Northern brethren also I believe felt a little tender under these censures; for tho their people have very few slaves themselves yet they had been pretty considerable carriers of them to others.

COLONIZATION SCHEMES: 1817

Resolutions opposing
resettlement of Africans

By the "Free People of Color" of Philadelphia

About The Document:

The first experiment in colonization—transporting free blacks and settling them somewhere in Africa—was made by a black man, a successful entrepreneur and shipowner, Paul Cuffee of Boston. In 1815 he took thirty-six ex-slaves aboard his brig, the *Traveller,* to Sierra Leone, at his own expense. (Sierra Leone was a colony on the west coast of Africa that had been established by the British for the slaves they had freed during the American Revolution.)

A year later the American Colonization Society made the first attempt by white men to set up a U.S. colony in Africa, and it won the financial support of the federal government. The Society was not an outgrowth of black protest, yet it had a profound influence on the protest movement.

The Society was formed at a meeting of prominent white citizens in Washington, D.C., in December 1816. The meeting followed the publication earlier that year of a book, *Thoughts on American Colonization,* by the headmaster of a boys' school in New Jersey. Among the leaders of the Society were Henry Clay and John C. Calhoun. Members included Quakers who honestly saw colonization as the black's best hope; it also included practical-minded Northerners who saw the scheme as an alternative to supporting freed slaves as paupers. A few members of the Society were free black men who viewed emigration as a last resort to escape white domination. But the largest segment consisted of Southern slaveholders. (Clay and Calhoun were themselves the owners of slaves.)

The Society's agents landed eighty-six blacks on the coast of West Africa in 1820. The expedition was poorly planned, and the colonizers were all but wiped out by malaria. The survivors found sanctuary in Sierra Leone, but the British let it be known that they didn't want any more settlers. In 1822 a second shipload of blacks was settled in an area that eventually became the Republic of Liberia. They faced indescribable hardships, not the least being the attempts by native black chiefs to capture and sell them as slaves again.

No more than a hundred blacks a year responded to the Colonization Society's efforts. After 1832—the year of the Nat Turner revolt—the Society increased its efforts enormously, but the project gradually collapsed as opposition to the Society—particularly among blacks—mounted. Yet the idea was to be revived later on by Abraham Lincoln. In all, the Society transported fewer than 15,000 blacks to Liberia.

From the beginning, the American Colonization Society had been essentially anti-black. Well-meaning liberals had been taken in by its missionary slogans, which it devised for the North's benefit. In the South the Society campaigned openly as the plantation owners' best hope of maintaining slavery. Southerners had always seen freed slaves as an everpresent threat, fearing that they would lead the slaves in revolts. The Colonization Society claimed it had the ideal way to rid the South of this agitating influence. In urging the governor of North Carolina to support the Society, for example, agent Calvin Jones on December 28, 1830, frankly stated that it would "rid us more expeditiously of our greatest pest and danger—the free people of colour."

For their part, most free blacks saw through the Colonization Society. A black convention in Hartford passed the following resolution:

This is our home and this is our country. . . . Here let us live, and here let us die.

One month after the founding of the Society, in January 1817, three thousand free blacks of Philadelphia met to protest the colonization scheme. The chairman was James Forten, one of the greatest of the pioneer black abolitionists. He had fought in the American Revolution and later, as a sail manufacturer, amassed a fortune of $100,000. It was this same James Forten who was to rescue William Lloyd Garrison's abolitionist newspaper *The Liberator* in a number of financial crises.

One effect of the anticolonization activities was to cement

the ties of the free blacks of the North with the slaves of the South, as is apparent from the petition that the Philadelphia free blacks adopted, which appears below. Another effect was to give free blacks a common front. The decade that followed the founding of the Colonization Society saw the birth of the black convention movement, the first black newspaper, *Freedom's Journal,* and the publication of the first truly militant black protest literature.

The Document:

Resolutions contained in pamphlet published
by William Lloyd Garrison titled *Thoughts
on African Colonization or An Impartial
Exhibition of the Doctrines, Principles &
Purposes of the American Colonization Society.
Together with the Resolutions, Addresses &
Remonstrances of the Free People of Color.*
Boston, Garrison and Knapp, 1832, Part II, pp. 62-63.

PHILADELPHIA, JANUARY, 1817

AT A NUMEROUS meeting of the people of color, convened at Bethel church, to take into consideration the propriety of remonstrating against the contemplated measure, that is to exile us from the land of our nativity; James Forten was called to the chair, and Russell Parrott appointed secretary. The intent of the meeting having been stated by the chairman, the following resolutions were adopted, without one dissenting voice.

Whereas our ancestors (not of choice) were the first successful cultivators of the wilds of America, we their descendants feel ourselves entitled to participate in the blessings of her luxuriant soil, which their blood and sweat manured; and that any measure or system of measures, having a tendency to banish us from her bosom, would not only be cruel, but in direct violation of those principles, which have been the boast of this republic.

Resolved, That we view with deep abhorrence the unmerited stigma attempted to be cast upon the reputation of the free people of color, by the promoters of this measure, 'that they are a dangerous and useless part of the community,' when in the state of disfranchisement in which they live, in the hour of danger they ceased to remember their wrongs, and rallied around the standard of their country.

Resolved, That we never will separate ourselves voluntarily from the slave population in this country; they are our breth-

ren by the ties of consanguinity, of suffering, and of wrong;
and we feel that there is more virtue in suffering privations
with them, than fancied advantages for a season.

Resolved, That without arts, without science, without a
proper knowledge of government, to cast into the savage
wilds of Africa the free people of color, seems to us the cir-
cuitous route through which they must return to perpetual
bondage. . . .

DAVID WALKER'S APPEAL: 1828

Pamphlet by a pre-Emancipation black militant

by David Walker

About The Document:

One of the great abolitionist pamphlets was *Walker's Appeal*, published in 1828. The abolitionist Benjamin Lundy wrote of it: "A more bold, daring, inflammatory publication, perhaps, never issued from the press, in any country." The *Appeal* ran through three editions in 1829, the year following publication, each containing language more militant than the preceding one.

David Walker was born in Wilmington, North Carolina, in 1785. His father was a slave; his mother was free; legally, therefore, Walker was born free, since by North Carolina law black children inherited the status of their mothers.

Walker left the South when he was about thirty years old, writing:

> If I remain in this bloody land, I will not live long. As true as God reigns, I will be avenged for the sorrows which my people have suffered. This is not the place for me—no, no. I must leave this part of the country. . . . Go I must.

He settled in Boston in 1826 and operated a secondhand clothing shop on Brattle Street. He became a leader in the Colored Association of Boston and served as the city's agent for the abolitionist newspaper, *Freedom's Journal*.

On September 28, 1828, appeared the first of the four articles which were combined as a pamphlet the next year and came to be known collectively as "Walker's Appeal." The *Appeal* is by far the most articulately militant work of its time. It implores, threatens, curses. One moment it is afire with burning vengeance, demanding the white man's blood, and the next it softens with the hope that the white man will change.

A bundle of fifty copies of *Walker's Appeal* arrived at the home of a black preacher in Savannah, Georgia, late in 1829, delivered by a ship's steward. Afraid, the preacher informed the police of his unsolicited receipt of seditious literature. The police forwarded the pamphlets to the governor, who issued an order placing in quarantine for forty days the ship that had carried the pamphlets. He then called the state legislature into secret session, to consider a bill making a capital offense the circulation of literature that might incite slaves to revolt. The legislature passed the bill and also offered a reward for Walker's capture: $10,000 alive; $1,000 dead.

In other Southern states the *Appeal* provoked similar consternation. Its discovery in several communities in Louisiana led to that state's enacting a bill that ordered the expulsion of all free slaves who had settled there after 1825.

Despite the *Appeal*'s fame, the author died in relative obscurity in 1831, some say under mysterious circumstances. But within months, David Walker's name was to become a byword throughout the nation. For on August 21, 1832, Nat Turner revolted, and the fearful predictions of white Southerners who had found such a threat in the *Appeal* seemed borne out.

The Document:

From pamphlet titled *Appeal in Four Articles, Together with an Appeal to the Coloured Citizens of the World, But in Particular, and Very Expressly, to Those of the United States of America*, Boston, 1828

I AM FULLY aware, in making this appeal to my much afflicted and suffering brethren, that I shall not only be assailed by those whose greatest earthly desires are, to keep us in abject ignorance and wretchedness, and who are of the firm conviction that Heaven has designed us and our children to be slaves and *beasts of burden* to them and their children. I say, I do not only expect to be held up to the public as an ignorant, impudent and restless disturber of the public peace, by such avaricious creatures, as well as a mover of insubordination—and perhaps put in prison or to death, for giving a superficial exposition of our miseries, and exposing tyrants. But I am persuaded, that many of my brethren, particularly those who are ignorantly in league with slave-holders or tyrants, who acquire their daily bread by the blood and sweat of their more ignorant brethren—and not a few of those too, who are too ignorant to see an inch beyond their noses, will rise up and call me cursed—Yea, the jealous ones among us will perhaps use more abject subtlety, by affirming that this work is not worth perusing, that we are well situated, and there is no use in trying to better our condition, for we cannot. I will ask one question here.—Can our condition be any worse? . . .

My beloved brethren: The Indians of North and of South America—the Greeks—the Irish, subjected under the king of Great Britain—the Jews, that ancient people of the Lord—the inhabitants of the islands of the sea—in fine, all the inhabitants of the earth, (except however, the sons of Africa) are called *men,* and of course are, and ought to be free. But we (colored people) and our children are *brutes!!* and of course are, and *ought to be* SLAVES to the American people and their children forever!! to dig their mines and work their farms; and thus go on enriching them, from one generation to another with our *blood* and our *tears!!!!. . . .* They keep us miserable now, and call us their property, but some of them will have enough of us by and by—their stomachs shall run over with us; they want us for their slaves, and shall have us to their fill. We are all in the world together!!—I said above, because we cannot help ourselves, (viz. we cannot help the whites murdering our mothers and our wives) but this statement is incorrect—for we can help ourselves; for, if we lay aside abject servility, and be determined to act like men, and not brutes—the murderers among the whites would be afraid to show their cruel heads. But O, my God!—in sorrow I must say it, that my color, all over the world, have a mean, servile spirit. They yield in a moment to the whites, let them be right or wrong—the reason they are able to keep their feet on our throats. Oh! my colored brethren, all over the world, when shall we arise from this death-like apathy! —and be men!! You will notice, if ever we become men, I mean *respectable* men, such as other people are, we must exert ourselves to the full. For, remember, that it is the greatest desire and object of the greater part of the whites, to keep us ignorant, and make us work to support them and their families.—Here now, in the Southern and Western sections of this country, there are at least three colored persons for one white; why is it, that those few weak, good-for-nothing whites, are able to keep so many able men, one of whom can put to flight a dozen whites, in wretchedness and misery? It shows at once, what the blacks are; we are ignorant, abject, servile and mean—and the whites know it—they know that we are too servile to assert our rights as men—or they would not fool with us as they do. Would they fool with any other people as they do with us? No, they know too well, that they would get themselves ruined. Why do they not bring the inhabitants of Asia to be body servants to them? They know they would get their bodies rent and torn from head to foot. Why do they not get the Aborigines of this country to be slaves to them and their children, to work their farms and dig their mines? They know well that the Aborigines of this country, (or Indians) would tear them from the earth. The Indians would not rest day or night, they would be up all times of night, cutting their cruel throats. But my color, (some, not all,) are willing to stand still and be murdered by the cruel whites. . . .

O! that the coloured people were long since of Moses' excellent disposition, instead of courting favour with, and telling news and lies to our *natural enemies,* against each other —aiding them to keep their hellish chains of slavery upon us. Would we not long before this time, have been respectable men, instead of such wretched victims of oppression as we are? Would they be able to drag our mothers, our fathers, our wives, our children and ourselves, around the world in chains and hand-cuffs as they do, to dig up gold and silver for them and theirs? This question, my brethren, I leave for you to digest; and may God Almighty force it home to your hearts. . . .

Remember that unless you are united, keeping your tongues within your teeth, you will be afraid to trust your secrets to each other, and thus perpetuate our miseries under the *Christians!!* Remember, also, to lay humble at the feet of our Lord and Master Jesus Christ, with prayers and fastings. Let our enemies go on with their butcheries, and at once fill up their cup. Never make an attempt to gain our freedom or *natural right,* from under our cruel oppressors and murderers, until you see your way clear—when that hour arrives and you move, be not afraid or dismayed; for be you assured that Jesus Christ the King of heaven and of earth, who is the God of justice and of armies, will surely go before you. And those enemies who have for hundreds of years stolen our *rights,* and kept us ignorant of Him and His divine worship, He will remove. Millions of whom are, this day, so ignorant and avaricious, that they cannot conceive how God can have an attribute of justice, and show mercy to us because it pleased him to make us black—which color Mr. Jefferson calls unfortunate!! It is not to be understood here, that I mean for us to wait until God shall take us by the hair of our heads and drag us out of abject wretchedness and slavery, nor I do mean to convey the idea for us to wait until our enemies shall make preparations, and call us to seize those preparations, take it away from them, and put every thing before us to death, in order to gain our freedom which God has given us. For you must remember that we are men as well as they. God has been pleased to give us two eyes, two hands, two feet, and some sense in our heads as well as they. They have no more right to hold us in slavery than we have to hold them; we have just as much right, in the sight of God, to hold them and their children in slavery and wretchedness, as they have to hold us, and no more.

They think because they hold us in their infernal chains of slavery, that we wish to be white, or of their color—but they are dreadfully deceived—we wish to be just as it pleased our Creator to have made us. . . .

Now, I ask you, had you not rather be killed than to be a slave to a tyrant, who takes the life of your mother, wife, and dear little children? Look upon your mother, wife, and children, and answer God Almighty; and believe this, that it is no more harm for you to kill a man, who is trying to kill you, than it is for you to take a drink of water when thirsty. . . .

I count my life not dear unto me, but I am ready to be offered at any moment. For what is the use of living, when in fact I am dead. But remember, Americans, that as miserable, wretched, degraded and abject as you have made us in preceding, and in this generation, to support you and your families, that some of you, (whites) on the continent of America, will yet curse the day that you ever were born. You want slaves, and want us for your slaves!!! My colour will yet, root some of you out of the very face of the earth!!!!!

WALKER'S APPEAL CONDEMNED: 1830-31

Abolitionist reaction to Walker's pamphlet

by Benjamin Lundy and William Lloyd Garrison

About The Documents:

How did the abolitionists, the white liberals, respond to David Walker's militancy? The Quaker Benjamin Lundy took the traditional pacifist position that appeals for violence, whether originating from the oppressed or the oppressor, were to be condemned. Lundy's editorial in the April 1830 issue of his newspaper *Genius of Universal Emancipation* is a revealing statement of the position of many white liberals of his time. The editorial appears below.

Equally significant is William Lloyd Garrison's response. Garrison, the famous editor of the abolitionist newspaper *The Liberator,* differed with Lundy on the issues of gradualism. Lundy was the spokesman for Southern Quakers, who felt that slavery was morally wrong, yet also felt that the slaveholders could not be held responsible. The system of slavery was at fault, and the true culprits were the colonial originators of the system. Since the slaveholders were not accountable, the Quakers held, violence against them was untenable. Only moral suasion and education could achieve fundamental changes and bring about emancipation.

Garrison believed in *immediate* emancipation, but he agreed with Lundy that the means to bring it about were persuasion and argument. Garrison was caught up in a terrible dilemma, which—try as he might—he never effectively resolved. He deplored the physical militancy of *Walker's Appeal,* yet in his article of January 8, 1831, in *The Liberator* (which appears below after the Lundy statement) he justified the spirit of the *Appeal,* comparing it with the spirit of 1776.

Garrison's article was ill received by many of his readers,

who felt he should have taken an even more forceful stand. What Garrison did then is fascinating. He published a favorable review of Walker's pamphlet by a writer signing himself "V." The article ran in three parts, each appearing in a subsequent edition of *The Liberator*. When the final line was set in type, Garrison had not only reprinted the *Appeal* practically in its entirety but had also run a review that wholeheartedly endorsed it!

Many articles just as incendiary as the *Appeal* were to appear in *The Liberator*. The abolitionist Wendell Phillips, who was not a pacifist, said that Garrison's protestations of pacifism were really a smokescreen to keep him out of jail. Editorially, according to Phillips, Garrison renounced violence as an instrument of social change; that made his newspaper legal and not guilty of the crime of treason, yet it enabled him to run headlines and articles of the most militant sort. Some have hinted that the contributor "V" was none other than Garrison himself. This is most unlikely, considering Garrison's own personality and style of writing. It is nevertheless a fact that when the South called him a "disturber of the peace" and a "promoter of rebellion," the charges were not entirely unfounded.

The Documents:

Editorial in the *Genius of Universal Emancipation*,
April, 1830
by Benjamin Lundy

I HAD NOT seen this far-famed production until within a few days. A more bold, daring, inflammatory publication, perhaps, never issued from the press, in any country. I can do no less than set the broadest seal of condemnation upon it. Such things can have no other earthly effect than to injure our cause. The writer indulges himself in the wildest strain of reckless fanaticism. He makes a great parade of technical phraseology, purporting to be religious; but religion has nothing at all to do with it. It is a labored attempt to rouse the worst passions of human nature, and inflame the minds of those to whom it is addressed.

Granting that the colored race have as much cause for complaint as this writer intimates (and I readily grant it), yet this is not the way to obtain redress for their wrongs. The *moral,* not the physical, power of this nation must be put in requisition. Any attempt to obtain their liberty and just rights, by force, must for a long time to come end in defeat, if not the extermination of the colored people. It is to avert so direful a catastrophe, that the wise and good are now exerting themselves, in various parts. . . .

Editorial in *The Liberator,* January 8, 1831
by William Lloyd Garrison

BELIEVING, AS WE DO, that men should never do evil that good may come; that a good end does not justify wicked means in the accomplishment of it; and that we ought to suffer, as did our Lord and his apostles, unresistingly—knowing that vengeance belongs to God, and he will certainly repay it where it is due;—believing all this, and that the Almighty will deliver the oppressed in a way which they know not, we deprecate the spirit and tendency of this *Appeal.* Nevertheless, it is not for the American people, as a nation, to denounce it as bloody or monstrous. Mr. Walker but pays them in their own coin, but follows their own creed, but adopts their own language. *We* do not preach rebellion—no, but submission and peace. Our enemies may accuse us of striving to stir up the slaves to revenge; but their accusations are false, and made only to excite the prejudices of the whites, and to destroy our influence. We say, that the possibility of a bloody insurrection at the South fills us with dismay; and we avow, too, as plainly, that if any people were ever justified in throwing off the yoke of their tyrants, the slaves are that people. It is not we, but our guilty countrymen, who put arguments into the mouths, and swords into the hands of the slaves. Every sentence that they write—every word that they speak—every resistance that they make, against foreign oppression, is a call upon their slaves to destroy them. Every Fourth of July celebration must embitter and inflame the minds of the slaves. And the late dinners, and illuminations, and orations, and shoutings, at the south over the downfall of the French tyrant, Charles the Tenth, furnish so many reasons to the slaves why they should obtain their own rights by violence.

Some editors have affected to doubt whether the deceased Walker wrote this pamphlet.—On this point, skepticism need not stumble: the *Appeal* bears the strongest internal evidence of having emanated from his own mind. No white man could have written in language so natural and enthusiastic.

THE CONFESSIONS OF NAT TURNER: 1831

*An account of the South's most
violent slave revolt*

by Nat Turner

About The Document:

The unbelievable cruelty of the colonial slave statutes examined in an earlier section testifies to the pervasive fear that from earliest times tinged the white man's relations with the black man. That fear stalked the white man from the moment blacks were kidnapped from Africa. On the inland march to the coastal slave depots, the black men were lashed to each other by leather thongs and could not escape, but once they were crowded aboard slave ships, enough black men might band together to seize the ship, and records show that they did. Between 1699 and 1845, a total of fifty-five insurrections were reported on slave ships at sea. Fear stalked the white man in every community where there were black slaves, in remote plantation regions and in cities such as Charleston and Richmond. It was fear of black retaliation that brought about in Virginia the first recorded law against blacks—the 1639 prohibition against their carrying guns or ammunition. It was fear of black men rising up against their bondage that made the colonists enact inhuman law after inhuman law for the punishment of insurrection, and still the insurrections continued. Between 1663 and 1864, well over one hundred slave insurrections occurred on land.

The 19th century witnessed three major uprisings, and the men who led them—Gabriel Prosser, Denmark Vesey, Nat Turner—were the martyrs and the heroes of black abolitionists such as Henry Highland Garnet and Frederick Douglass. These and many other black abolitionists invoked the names Prosser, Vesey, and Turner at numerous conventions. And when Frederick Douglass issued his call for black men to join the Union forces in the Civil War, he exhorted them to remember these same three men. After the Civil War, their names were largely ignored, but today they are being called to mind again.

Gabriel Prosser led a three-pronged task force of eleven hundred slaves, moving on Richmond, Virginia, to sack the capitol. The date was September 1, 1800. Summer rain and massive floods kept the slaves from grouping, and two black slaves betrayed them at the last minute. Prosser and thirty-four other black men were executed, but not before they had been interrogated by another one-time revolutionary, James Monroe, then Governor of Virginia.

Denmark Vesey, a former slave of South Carolina, conceived a still larger operation to seize the city of Charleston. Vesey had devoted years to the study of revolutions in various countries, especially the slave revolts of Haiti (which had resulted in the abolition of slavery there in 1791). By 1822, Vesey had perfected his plan and had enlisted thousands of slaves in and around Charleston. As had happened with Gabriel Prosser, the Vesey plot was betrayed by one of his supporters. Vesey and forty-six of his men were executed. Variously fined and jailed were four white men who had helped him.

The third major revolutionist of the 19th century was Nat Turner, leader of the famous Southampton County Insurrection in 1831. Copies of the militant *Walker's Appeal* pamphlet were found in the environs of Southampton just prior to the insurrection, but the influence it had on Nat Turner and his followers was never established.

Nat Turner was born in 1800 (as was John Brown of Harpers Ferry fame). Turner had been visited since childhood by visions, in one of which it had been prophesied that he was intended for some great purpose and that he would know it by a sign. The sign came, an eclipse of the sun, and Nat Turner organized a small band of slaves in Virginia's Southampton County, where he lived. On the night of August 21, 1831, Turner and his group forced their way into the home of his master, killing the entire household. Turner and his band gathered followers, as many as sixty or seventy, while they marched toward the county seat, killing slavemasters and their families along the way. They killed fifty-nine people in all, before the Southampton militia overtook them. Turner escaped and hid out for two months, as he narrates in his account, before he was betrayed by a yelping dog.

Turner's confession, as made to a lawyer named T. R. Gray, follows below in its entirety. The calmness and composure of his manner as he details how he and his band killed ten men, fourteen women, and thirty-five children reveal with shocking clarity the overpowering determination of one black man to achieve freedom.

Turner was among nearly one hundred black men killed in the aftermath of the insurrection. For months afterward the South was panic-stricken by rumors that a full-scale slave uprising would take place.

The Document:

The Confessions of Nat Turner, the leader
of the late insurrection in Southampton, Va.,
as made to T. R. Gray; Baltimore, 1831
by Nat Turner

AGREEABLE to his own appointment, on the evening he was committed to prison, with permission of the Jailer, I visited NAT on Tuesday, the 1st of November, when, without being questioned at all, he commenced his narrative in the following words:

Sir:—You have asked me to give a history of the motives which induced me to undertake the late insurrection, as you call it. To do so I must go back to the days of my infancy, and even before I was born. I was thirty-one years of age the 2nd of October last, and born the property of Benj. Turner, of this county. In my childhood a circumstance occurred which made an indelible impression on my mind, and laid the ground-work of that enthusiasm, which has terminated so fatally to many, both white and black, and for which I am about to atone at the gallows. It is here necessary to relate this circumstance—trifling as it may seem, it was the commencement of that belief which has grown with time, and even now, sir, in this dungeon, helpless and forsaken as I am, I cannot divest myself of. Being at play with other children, when three or four years old, I was telling them something, which, my mother overhearing, said it had happened before I was born. I stuck to my story, however, and related some things which went, in her opinion to confirm it: Others called on were greatly astonished, knowing that these things had happened, and caused them to say in my hearing I surely would be a prophet, as the Lord had shown me things that had happened before my birth. And my father and mother strengthened me in this, my first impression, saying in my presence, I was intended for some great purpose, which they had always thought from certain marks on my head and breast. My grandmother, who was very religious, and to whom I was much attached; my master, who belonged to the church, and other religious persons who visited the house, and whom I often saw at prayers; noticing the singularity of my manners, I suppose, and my uncommon intelligence for a child, remarked I had too much sense to be raised, and if I was, I would never be of any service to any one as a slave. To a mind like mine, restless, inquisitive, and observant of everything that was passing, it is easy to suppose that religion was the subject to which it would be directed, and although this subject principally occupied my thoughts, there was nothing that I saw or heard of to which my attention was not directed. The manner in which I learned to read and write, not only had great influence on my own mind, (as I had acquired it with the most perfect ease, so much so, that I have no recollection whatever of learning the alphabet,) but to the astonishment of the family, one day when a book was shown me to keep me from crying, I began spelling the names of the different objects. This was a source of wonder to all in the neighborhood, particularly the blacks, and this learning was constantly improved at all opportunities. When I got large enough to go to work, while employed, I was reflecting on many things that would present themselves to my imagination, and whenever an opportunity occurred of looking at a book, when the school children were getting their lessons, I would find many things that the fertility of my own imagination had depicted to me before. All my time, not devoted to my master's service, was spent either in prayer, or in making experiments in casting different things in moulds made of earth; in attempting to make paper, gunpowder, and many other experiments, that although I could not perfect, yet convinced me of its practicability if I had the means.* I was not addicted to stealing in my youth, nor have ever been, yet such was the confidence of the Negroes in the neighborhood even at this early period of my life, in my superior judgment that they would often carry me with them when they were going on any roguery, to plan for them. Growing up among them with this confidence in my superior judgment, and when this, in their opinions, was perfected by Divine inspiration, from the circumstances already alluded to in my infancy, and which belief was ever afterwards zealously inculcated by the austerity of my life and manners, which became the subject of remark by white and black, having soon discovered to be great, I must appear so, and therefore studiously avoided mixing in society, and wrapped myself in mystery, devoting my

* When questioned as to the manner of manufacturing those different articles, he was found informed on the subject. [Footnote in original.]

time to fasting and prayer. By this time having arrived to man's estate and hearing the scriptures commented on at meetings, I was struck with that particular passage which says: "Seek ye the Kingdom of Heaven and all things shall be added unto you." I reflected much on this passage, and prayed daily for light on this subject. As I was praying one day at my plough, the Spirit spoke to me, saying: "Seek ye the Kingdom of Heaven and all things shall be added unto you."

Question.—What do you mean by the Spirit?

Answer.—The Spirit that spoke to the Prophets in former days. And I was greatly astonished, and for two years prayed continually, whenever my duty would permit; and then, again, I had the same revelation, which fully confirmed me in the impression that I was ordained for some great purpose in the hands of the Almighty. Several years rolled round, in which many events occurred to strengthen me in this, my belief. At this time I reverted in my mind to the remarks made of me in my childhood, and the things that had been shown me, and as it had been said of me in my childhood by those by whom I had been taught to pray, both white and black, and in whom I had the greatest confidence, that I had too much sense to be raised, and if I was, I would never be of any use as a slave. Now, finding that I had arrived to man's estate, and was a slave, and these revelations being known to me, I began to direct my attention to this great object, to fulfill the purpose for which, by this time, I felt assured I was intended. Knowing the influence I had obtained over the minds of my fellow-servants, (not by the means of conjuring and such like tricks, for to them I always spoke of such things with contempt,) but by the communion of the Spirit, whose revelation I often communicated to them, and they believed and said my wisdom came from God. I now began to prepare them for my purpose by telling them something was about to happen that would terminate in fulfilling the great promise that had been made to me. About this time I was placed under an overseer, from whom I ran away and after remaining in the woods thirty days I returned, to the astonishment of the Negroes on the plantation who thought I had made my escape to some other part of the country, as my father had done before. But the reason of my return was, that the Spirit appeared to me and said I had my wishes directed to the things of this world, and not to the Kingdom of Heaven, and that I should return to the service of my earthly master—"For he who knoweth his Master's will, and doeth it not, shall be beaten with many stripes, and thus have I chastened you." And the Negroes found fault and murmured against me, saying if they had my sense they would not serve any master in the world. And about this time I had a vision, and I saw white spirits and black spirits engaged in battle, and the sun was darkened—the thunder rolled in the Heavens, and blood flowed in streams—and I heard a voice saying, "Such is your luck, such you are called to see, and let it come rough or smooth, you must surely bear it." I now withdrew myself as much as my situation would permit, from the intercourse of my fellow-servants, for the avowed purpose of serving the Spirit more fully; and it appeared to me and reminded me of the things it had already shown me, and that it would then reveal to me the knowledge of the elements, the revolution of the planets, the operation of tides, and the changes of the seasons. After this revelation of the year 1825, and the knowledge of the elements being made known to me I sought more than ever to obtain true holiness before the great day of judgment should appear; and then I began to receive the true knowledge of faith. And from the first steps of righteousness until the last, was I made perfect; and the Holy Ghost was with me and said, "Behold me as I stand in the Heavens;" and I looked and saw the forms of men in different attitudes, and there were lights in the sky to which the children of darkness gave other names than what they really were, for they were the lights of the Saviour's hands, stretched forth from east to west, even as they were extended on the cross on Calvary for the redemption of sinners. And I wondered greatly at these miracles, and prayed to be informed of a certainty of the meaning thereof, and shortly afterwards, while labouring in the field, I discovered drops of blood on the corn, as though it was dew from heaven, and I communicated it to many, both white and black, in the neighborhood; and then I found on the leaves in the woods hieroglyphic characters and numbers, with the forms of men in different attitudes, portrayed in the blood, and representing the figures I had seen before in the Heavens. And now the Holy Ghost had revealed itself to me, for as the blood of Christ had been shed on this earth, and had ascended to Heaven for the salvation of sinners, and was now returning to earth again in the form of dew; and as the leaves on the trees bore the impression of figures I had seen in the Heavens, it was plain to me that the Saviour was about to lay down the yoke he had borne for the sins of men, and the great day of judgment was at hand. About this time I told these things to a white man (Etheldred T. Brantley) on whom it had a wonderful effect, and he ceased from his wickedness and was attacked immediately with a cutaneous eruption, and blood oozed from the pores of his skin, and after praying and fasting nine days, he was healed; and the Spirit appeared to me again and said, "As the Saviour had been baptized so should we be also;"—and when the white people would not let us be baptized by the church, we went down into water together, in the sight of many who reviled us, and were baptized by the Spirit. After this I rejoiced greatly, and gave thanks to God. And on the 12th of May, 1828, I heard a loud noise in the Heavens, and the Spirit instantly appeared to me and said the Serpent was loosened, and Christ had laid down the yoke he had borne for the sins of men, and that I should take it on and fight against the Serpent, for the time was fast approaching when the first should be last and the last should be first.

Question.—Do you not find yourself mistaken now?

Answer.—Was not Christ crucified?

And by signs in the Heavens that it would make known to me when I should commence the great work, and until the first sign appeared I should conceal it from the knowledge of men; and on the appearance of the sign (the eclipse of the sun last February,) I should arise and prepare myself and slay my enemies with their own weapons. And immediately on the sign appearing in the Heavens the seal was removed from my lips, and I communicated the great work laid out for me to do, to four, in whom I had the greatest confidence, (Henry, Hark, Nelson, and Sam.) It was intended by us to have begun the work of death on the 4th of July last. Many were the plans formed and rejected by us, and it affected my mind to such a degree that I felt sick, and the time passed without our coming to any determination how to commence. Still forming new schemes and rejecting them, when the sign appeared again, which determined me not to wait longer.

Since the commencement of 1830, I had been living with Mr. Joseph Travis, who was to me a kind master and placed the greatest confidence in me; in fact, I had no cause to complain of his treatment of me. On Saturday evening, the 20th of August, it was agreed between Henry, Hark, and myself, to prepare a dinner the next day for the men we expected, and then to concert a plan, as we had not yet determined on any. Hark, on the following morning, brought a pig, and Henry, brandy, and being joined by Sam, Nelson, Will, and Jack, they prepared in the woods a dinner where about three o'clock, I joined them.

Question.—Why were you so backward in joining them?

Answer.—The same reason that had caused me not to mix with them for years before.

I saluted them on coming up, and asked Will how came he there. He answered, his life was worth no more than others, and his liberty as dear to him. I asked him if he thought to obtain it. He said he would, or lose his life. This was enough to put him in full confidence. Jack, I knew, was only a tool in the hands of Hark. It was quickly agreed we should commence at home (Mr. J. Travis') on that night, and until we had armed and equipped ourselves, and gathered sufficient force, neither age nor sex was to be spared, (which was invariably adhered to.) We remained at the feast until about two hours in the night, when we went to the house and found Austin; they all went to the cider press and drank except myself. On returning to the house, Hark went to the door with an axe for the purpose of breaking it open, as we knew we were strong enough to murder the family if they were awaked by the noise; but reflecting that it might create an alarm in the neighborhood, we determined to enter the house secretly and murder them whilst sleeping. Hark got a ladder and set it against the chimney, on which I ascended, and hoisting a window, entered and came down stairs, unbarred the door, and removed the guns from their places. It was then observed that I must spill the first blood, on which, armed with a hatchet, and accompanied by Will, I entered my Master's chamber. It being dark I could not give a death blow; the hatchet glanced from his head; he sprang from the bed and called his wife; it was his last word; Will laid him dead with a blow of his axe, and Mrs. Travis shared the same fate, as she lay in bed. The murder of this family, five in number, was the work of a moment, not one of them awoke. There was a little infant sleeping in a cradle that was forgotten until we had left the house and gone some distance, when Henry and Will returned and killed it. We got here four guns that would shoot and several old muskets, with a pound or two of powder. We remained some time at the barn, where we paraded. I formed them in line as soldiers, and after carrying them through all the manoeuvres I was master of, marched them off to Mr. Salathul Francis', about six hundred yards distant. Sam and Will went to the door and knocked. Mr. Francis asked who was there. Sam replied it was him, and he had a letter for him; on which he got up and came to the door. They immediately seized him, and dragging him out a little from the door, he was despatched by repeated blows on the head. There was no other white person in the family. We started from there for Mrs. Reese's, maintaining the most perfect silence on our march, where, finding the door unlocked, we entered, and murdered Mrs. Reese in her bed while sleeping. Her son awoke, but it was only to sleep the sleep of death; he had only time to say who is that, and he was no more. From Mrs. Reese's we went to Mrs. Turner's, a mile distant, which we reached about sun rise, on

Monday morning. Henry, Austin, and Sam, went to the still, where, finding Mr. Peebles, Austin shot him, and the rest of us went to the house. As we approached the family discovered us and shut the door. Vain hope! Will, with one stroke of his axe, opened it, and entered and found Mrs. Turner and Mrs. Newsome in the middle of the room, almost frightened to death. Will immediately killed Mrs. Turner with one blow of his axe. I took Mrs. Newsome by the hand, and with the sword I had when I was apprehended, I struck her several blows over the head, but not being able to kill her, as the sword was dull, Will turning around and discovered it, despatched her also. A general destruction of property and search for ammunition, always succeeded the murders. By this time my company amounted to fifteen, and nine men mounted, who started for Mrs. Whitehead's, (the other six were to go through a by-way to Mr. Bryant's, and rejoin us at Mrs. Whitehead's.) As we approached the house we discovered Mr. Richard Whitehead standing in the cotton patch, near the lane fence. We called him over into the lane, and Will, the executioner, was near at hand, with his fatal axe, to send him to an untimely grave. As we pushed on to the house I discovered some one running around the garden, and thinking it was some of the white family, I pursued them, but finding it was a servant girl belonging to the house, I returned to commence the work of death, but they whom I left had not been idle. All the family were already murdered but Mrs. Whitehead and her daughter Margaret. As I came round to the door I saw Will pulling Mrs. Whitehead out of the house, and at the step he nearly severed her head from her body with his broad axe. Miss Margaret, when I discovered her, had concealed herself in the corner, formed by the projection of the cellar cap from the house. On my approach she fled, but was soon overtaken, and after repeated blows with a sword, I killed her by a blow on the head with a fence rail. By this time the six who had gone by Mr. Bryant's rejoined us, and informed me that they had done the work of death assigned them. We again divided, part going to Mr. Richard Porters', and from thence to Nathaniel Francis'; the others to Mr. Howell Harris' and Mr. T. Doyle's. On my reaching Mr. Porters' he had escaped with his family. I understood there that the alarm had already spread, and I immediately returned to bring up those sent to Mr. Doyle's and Mr. Howell Harris'—the party I left going on to Mr. Francis' having told them I would join them in that neighborhood. I met those sent to Mr. Doyle's and Mr. Harris' returning, having met Mr. Doyle on the road and killed him; and learning from some who joined them that Mr. Harris was from home, I immediately pursued the course taken by the party gone on before, but knowing they would complete the work of death and pillage at Mr. Francis' before I could get there, I went to Mr. Peter Edwards' expecting to find them there, but they had been here also. I then went to Mr. John T. Barrow's; they had been here and murdered him. I pursued on their track to Capt. Newit Harris', where I found the greater part mounted and ready to start. The men now amounting to about forty, shouted and hurrahed as I rode up. Some were in the yard loading their guns, others drinking. They said Captain Harris and his family had escaped; the property in the house they destroyed, robbing him of money and other valuables. I ordered them to mount and march instantly. This was about nine or ten o'clock Monday morning. I proceeded to Mr. Levi Waller's, two or three miles distant. I took my station in the rear, and as it was my object to carry terror and devastation wherever we went, I placed fifteen or twenty of the best armed and most to be relied on in front, who generally approached the houses as fast as their horses could run. This was for two purposes—to prevent the escape and strike terror to the inhabitants. On this account I never got to the houses after leaving Mrs. Whitehead's until after the murders were committed, except in one case. I some times got in sight in time to see the work of death completed, viewed the mangled bodies as they lay, in silent satisfaction, and immediately started in quest of other victims. Having murdered Mrs. Waller and ten children, we started for Mr. William Williams', having killed him and two little boys that were there. While engaged in this, Mrs. Williams fled and got some distance from the house, but she was pursued, overtaken, and compelled to get up behind one of the company, who brought her back, and after showing her the mangled body of her lifeless husband, she was told to get down and lay by his side, where she was shot dead. I then started for Mr. Jacob Williams', where the family were murdered. Here we found a young man named Drury, who had come on business with Mr. Williams; he was pursued, overtaken and shot. Mrs. Vaughan's was the next place we visited, and, after murdering the family here, I determined on starting for Jerusalem. Our number now amounting to fifty or sixty, all mounted and armed with guns, axes, swords and clubs. On reaching Mr. James W. Parker's gate, immediately on the road leading to Jerusalem, and about three miles distant, it was proposed to me to call there, but I objected, as I knew he was gone to Jerusalem, and my object was to reach there as soon as possible; but some of the men having relations at Mr. Parker's, it was agreed that they might call and get his people. I re-

mained at the gate on the road with seven or eight, the others
going across the field to the house, about half a mile off.
After waiting some time for them, I became impatient,
started to the house for them, and on our return we were met
by a party of white men, who had pursued our blood-stained
track, and who had fired on those at the gate and dispersed
them, which I knew nothing of, not having been at that time
rejoined by any of them. Immediately on discovering the
whites I ordered my men to halt and form, as they appeared
to be alarmed. The white men, eighteen in number, approached us with in about one hundred yards, when one of
them fired, (this was against the positive orders of Capt. Alexander P. Peete, who commanded, and who had directed the
men to reserve their fire until within thirty paces,) and discovered about half of them retreating. I then ordered my
men to fire and rush on them. The few remaining stood their
ground until we approached within fifty yards, when they
fired and retreated. We pursued and overtook some of them,
who, we thought, we left dead, (they were not killed;) after
pursuing them about two hundred yards, and rising a little
hill, I discovered they were met by another party and had
halted, and were reloading their guns, thinking that those
who retreated first, and the party who fired on us at fifty or
sixty yards distant, had all only fallen back to meet others
with ammunition. As I saw them reloading their guns and
more coming up than I saw at first, and several of my bravest
men being wounded, the others became panic-struck and
squandered over the field; the white men pursued and fired
on us several times. Hark had his horse shot under him and I
caught another for him as it was running by me; five or six
of my men were wounded, but none left on the field. Finding
myself defeated here, I instantly determined to go through a
private way, and cross the Nottoway River at the Cypress
Bridge, three miles below Jerusalem, and attack that place in
the rear, as I expected they would look for me on the road,
and I had a great desire to get there to procure arms and ammunition. After going a short distance in this private way, accompanied by about twenty men, I overtook two or three
who told me the others were dispersed in every direction.
After trying in vain to collect a sufficient force to proceed to
Jerusalem, I determined to return, as I was sure they would
make back to their old neighborhood, where they would rejoin me, make new recruits, and come down again. On my
way back I called at Mrs. Thomas', Mrs. Spencer's, and several other places; the white families having fled we found no
more victims to gratify our thirst for blood. We stopped at
Maj. Ridley's quarters for the night, and being joined by four

of his men, with the recruits made since my defeat, we mustered now about forty strong. After placing out sentinels, I laid down to sleep, but was quickly roused by a great racket. Starting up I found some mounted, and others in great confusion. One of the sentinels having given the alarm that we were about to be attacked, I ordered some to ride round and reconnoitre, and on their return, the others being more alarmed, not knowing who they were, fled in different ways, so that I was reduced to about twenty again. With this I determined to attempt to recruit, and proceed to rally in the neighborhood I had left. Dr. Blunt's was the nearest house, which we reached just before day. On riding up the yard Hark fired a gun. We expected Dr. Blunt and his family were at Maj. Riley's, as I knew there was a company of men there, the gun was fired to ascertain if any of the family were at home. We were immediately fired upon, and retreated, leaving several of my men. I do not know what became of them, as I never saw them afterwards. Pursuing our course back, and coming in sight of Captain Harris', where we had been the day before, we discovered a party of white men at the house, on which all deserted but two, (Jacob and Nat.) We concealed ourselves in the woods until near night, when I sent them in search of Henry, Sam, Nelson, and Hark, and directed them to rally all they could at the place we had had our dinner the Sunday before, where they would find me, and I, accordingly, returned there as soon as it was dark and remained until Wednesday evening, when discovering white men riding around the place as though they were looking for some one, and none of my men joining me, I concluded Jacob and Nat had been taken and compelled to betray me. On this I gave up all hope for the present, and on Thursday night, after having supplied myself with provisions from Mr. Travis', I scratched a hole under a pile of fence rails in a field, where I concealed myself for six weeks, never leaving my hiding place but for a few minutes in the dead of night to get water, which was very near. Thinking by this time I could venture out, I began to go about in the night and eavesdrop the houses in the neighborhood; pursuing this course for about a fortnight and gathering little or no intelligence, afraid of speaking to any human being, and returning every morning to my cave before the dawn of day. I know not how long I might have led this life if accident had not betrayed me. A dog in the neighborhood passing by my hiding-place one night while I was out, was attracted by some meat I had in my cave, and crawled in and stole it, and was coming out just as I returned. A few nights after, two Negroes having started to go hunting with the same dog, and passing that way, the dog came again to the place, and having just gone out to walk about, discovered me and barked, on which, thinking myself discovered, I spoke to them to beg concealment. On making myself known they fled from me. Knowing then they would betray me, I immediately left my hiding place, and was pursued almost incessantly until I was taken a fortnight afterwards by Mr. Benjamin Phipps, in a little hole I had dug out with my sword, for the purpose of concealment, under the top of a fallen tree. On Mr. Phipps' discovering the place of my concealment, he cocked his gun and aimed at me. I requested him not to shoot, and I would give up, upon which he demanded my sword. I delivered it to him and he brought me to prison. During the time I was pursued I had many hair-breadth escapes, which your time will not permit me to relate. I am here loaded with chains, and willing to suffer the fate that awaits me.

"LET SOUTHERN OPPRESSORS TREMBLE!": 1831

*Garrison's editorial comment on the
Nat Turner rebellion*

by William Lloyd Garrison

About The Document:

William Lloyd Garrison was born in 1805, the son of a New England sea captain, a prodigious drinker who, when William was three years old, deserted his family in Newburyport, Massachusetts. Young Garrison was apprenticed to a shoemaker, then to a cabinetmaker. He ran away. Apprenticed at twelve to a printer, he had found his niche, he soon became an expert type compositor and began writing on the side anonymously. As a journeyman printer he went to Boston when he was twenty-two and became the editor of the *National Philanthropist,* the first American newspaper devoted to promoting the prohibition of alcohol.

In those days there were no wire services, and, to obtain new material, editors engaged in "exchanges," sending their papers all over the country in return for the papers of other editors. In this manner there came to Garrison a newspaper from Baltimore with the imposing title *Genius of Universal Emancipation.* Carrying primarily antislavery articles, it was the only periodical in this country at that time concerned with the slavery issue. Its owner was a Quaker, Benjamin Lundy, who published it as a monthly, often at irregular intervals when he could afford it. The paper's editorial policy followed the Quaker position that emancipation of the slaves must come about gradually, and it advocated colonization of all black men.

Garrison became a devoted and enthusiastic admirer of Lundy and in 1829 accepted his offer to be the paper's co-editor. When Garrison arrived in Baltimore, however, he told

Lundy that he had had sound thoughts about editorial policy: he could not go along with the gradualist concept and insisted on immediate freedom for the slaves and their assimilation into American society. To this Lundy answered with stolid Quaker compromise: "Thee may put thy initials to thy articles, and I will put my initials to mine, and each will bear his own burden."

It is difficult to believe that Lundy could have been so naive. His readers, after all, were Southern Quakers who, though well meaning, could not possibly accept Garrison's militant immediacy. Every article by Garrison brought subscription cancellations.

When in one issue he attacked the owner of a slave-carrying vessel as a "highway robber and murderer," Garrison was prosecuted for libel and jailed because he refused to pay the $50 fine. Through the intercession of the poet John Greenleaf Whittier and the New York philanthropist Arthur Tappan, the fine was paid for him, and Garrison was released after serving seven weeks in jail.

Libel suits and jail sentences were too much for Lundy, however; he dissolved his partnership with Garrison and moved the paper to Washington, D.C.

Garrison thereupon took the antislavery crusade to New England, expecting to enlist the support of such powerful church leaders and moralists as Lyman Beecher and William Ellery Channing, but he found no support.

Instead of returning to a border state to start a newspaper of his own, as he had planned, Garrison determined that little could be done as long as the North was a silent partner with the slaveholding South. Had not the New England ships been competing with the ships of England to supply the slave markets in the South? And now were not the same ships bringing contraband slaves from Africa to the same markets? Yet even those Northerners who were not making fortunes in the slave trade were silent partners, in Garrison's view. He condemned their silence in the same way that America condemned the silence of the Germans in the face of Nazi atrocities.

In Boston, on January 1, 1831, without capital, Garrison and his new partner Isaac Knapp published the first issue of *The Liberator,* a four-page weekly. For many months Garrison and Knapp slept on the floor of the room in which they printed the paper. During the first year they had six paid subscribers; in the following year, fifty-three. The paper gradually increased in circulation but never exceeded—in thirty-five years of publication—2,700 copies.

Yet *The Liberator* was to exert an enormous influence and

become the most important reform journal of its time in the United States.

In his inaugural editorial Garrison took to task critics of his style of writing, which they claimed was inflammatory:

> I am aware, that many object to the severity of my language; but is there not cause for severity? I *will* be as harsh as truth, and as uncompromising as justice. On this subject, I do not wish to think, or speak, or write, with moderation. No! No! Tell a man whose house is on fire, to give a moderate alarm; tell him to moderately rescue his wife from the hands of the ravisher; tell the mother to gradually extricate her babe from the fire into which it has fallen—but urge me not to use moderation in a cause like the present. I am in earnest—I will not equivocate—I will not excuse—I will not retreat a single inch—AND I WILL BE HEARD.

That inaugural editorial is oft repeated as evidence of Garrison's strong abolitionist leanings. Perhaps more pertinent to the problems facing us today is the editorial Garrison wrote five months after the revolt of Nat Turner. Garrison, incidentally, had been accused by the South of instigating the revolt, because it had happened within a matter of months after the founding of Garrison's newspaper.

The Document:

Editorial in *The Liberator,*
September 3, 1831

WHAT WE HAVE long predicted,—at the peril of being stigmatized as an alarmist and declaimer,—has commenced its fulfilment. The first step of the earthquake, which is ultimately to shake down the fabric of oppression, leaving not one stone upon the other, has been made. The first drops of blood, which are but the prelude to a deluge from the gathering clouds, have fallen. The first flash of lightning, which is to ignite and consume, has been felt. The first wailings of a bereavement, which is to clothe the earth in sackcloth, have broken upon our ears.

In the first number of the Liberator, we alluded to the hour of vengeance in the following lines:

> Wo if it come with storm, and blood, and fire,
>   When midnight darkness veils the earth and sky!
> *Wo to the innocent babe*—the guilty sire—
>   *Mother and daughter*—friends of kindred tie!
>   *Stranger and citizen alike shall die!*

Red-handed Slaughter his revenge shall feed,
    And Havoc yell his ominous death-cry,
And wild Despair in vain for mercy plead—
    While hell itself shall shrink and sicken at the deed!

Read the account of the insurrection in Virginia, and say whether our prophecy be not fulfilled. What was poetry—imagination—in January, is now bloody reality. 'Wo to the innocent babe—to mother and daughter!' Is it not true? Turn again to the record of slaughter! Whole families have been cut off—not a mother, not a daughter, not a babe left. Dreadful retaliation! 'The dead bodies of white and black lying just as they were slain, unburied'—the oppressor and the oppressed equal at last in death—what a spectacle!

True, the rebellion is quelled. Those of the slaves who were not killed in combat, have been secured, and the prison is crowded with victims destined for the gallows!

Yet laugh not in your carnival of crime
Too proudly, ye oppressors!

You have seen, it is to be feared, but the beginning of sorrows. All the blood which has been shed will be required at your hands. At your hands alone? No—but at the hands of the people of New-England and of all the free states. The crime of oppression is national. The south is only the agent in this guilty traffic. But, remember! the same causes are at work which must inevitably produce the same effects; and when the contest shall have again begun, it must be again a war of extermination. In the present instance, no quarters have been asked or given.

But we have killed and routed them now—we can do it again and again—we are invincible! A dastardly triumph well becoming a nation of oppressors. Detestable complacency, that can think, without emotion, of the extermination of the blacks! We have the power to kill *all*—let us, therefore, continue to apply the whip and forge new fetters!

In his fury against the revolters, who will remember their wrongs? What will it avail them, though the catalogue of their sufferings, dripping with blood fresh from their lacerated bodies, be held up to extenuate their conduct? It is enough that the victims were black—that circumstance makes them less precious than the dogs which have been slain in our streets! They were black—brutes, pretending to be men—legions of curses on their memories! They were black—God made them to serve us!

Ye patriotic hypocrites! ye panegyrists of Frenchmen,

Greeks, and Poles! ye fustian declaimers for liberty! yet haters of aristocracy! ye assailants of monarchies! ye republican nullifiers! ye treasonable disunionists! be dumb! Cast no reproach upon the conduct of the slaves, but let your lips and cheeks wear the blisters of condemnation!

Ye accuse the pacific friends of emancipation of instigating the slaves to revolt. Take back the charge as a foul slander. The slaves need no incentives at our hands. They will find them in their stripes—in their emaciated bodies—in their ceaseless toil—in their ignorant minds—in every field, in every valley, on every hill-top and mountain, wherever you and your fathers have fought for liberty—in your speeches, your conversations, your celebrations, your pamphlets, your newspapers—voices in the air, sounds from across the ocean, invitations to resistance above, below, around them! What more do they need? Surrounded by such influences, and smarting under their newly made wounds, is it wonderful that they should rise to contend—as other 'heroes' have contended —for their lost rights? It is *not* wonderful.

In all that we have written, is there aught to justify the excesses of the slaves? No. Nevertheless, they deserve no more censure than the Greeks in destroying the Turks, or the Poles in exterminating the Russians, or our fathers in slaughtering the British. Dreadful, indeed, is the standard erected by worldly patriotism!

For ourselves, we are horror-struck at the late tidings. We have exerted our utmost efforts to avert the calamity. We have warned our countrymen of the danger of persisting in their unrighteous conduct. We have preached to the slaves the pacific precepts of Jesus Christ. We have appealed to christians, philanthropists and patriots, for their assistance to accomplish the great work of national redemption through the agency of moral power—of public opinion—of individual duty. How have we been received? We have been threatened, proscribed, vilified and imprisoned—a laughing-stock and a reproach. Do we falter, in view of these things? Let time answer. If we have been hitherto urgent, and bold, and denunciatory in our efforts,—hereafter we shall grow vehement and active with the increase of danger. We shall cry, in trumpet tones, night and day,—Wo to this guilty land, unless she speedily repents of her evil doings! The blood of millions of her sons cries aloud for redress! IMMEDIATE EMANCIPATION can alone save her from the vengeance of Heaven, and cancel the debt of ages!

THE UNDERGROUND RAILROAD: 1836

First-hand account of a "station agent"

by Levi Coffin

About The Document:

The Underground Railroad was neither underground nor a railroad. It was a network of secret routes by land and by sea, over which black men escaped to free states and to Canada. It took its name from the then new industrial invention, the locomotive. The escaping slaves were called passengers; the people who sheltered them, station agents; and those who guided them, conductors.

The term "Underground Railroad" (later shortened to "U.R.") first appeared in print in the early 1840's, but slave escapes were nothing new. In the 1780's, George Washington had complained in letters to friends of escaping slaves; and in the early colonial period, the harsh penalties meted out to fleeing slaves by the colonial statutes attest to the frequency of escapes.

The U.R. was most active from the 1840's to the 1860's, and during that period several thousand slaves each year made successful flights to freedom. There were two main routes: One was the Middle Western line, leading from the South through Ohio and Indiana and terminating in Canada. The other was the Eastern line or Seaboard route, running through Maryland, Delaware, and Pennsylvania.

The Middle Western line was directed from Cincinnati by the Quaker Levi Coffin, who served as a station agent. Coffin wrote a book about his experiences in the U.R., titled *Reminiscences*, published in 1876. The document that appears below, an excerpt from this book, shows that the operation was not as tightly organized as many glorified reports claimed. Most of the help given the fleeing black men was, in fact, spontaneous, motivated by sympathy for their plight. There was organization, to be sure, but it is a mistake to assume that the operation boasted conductors and station agents in every town along the route. One feature of the U.R.

was that the actual details of operation, far from being kept underground, were widely publicized both in the North and the South. Northern abolitionists exploited the feats of the U.R. to dramatize the evils of slavery. Southerners did the same—to dramatize the North's lack of sincerity in enforcing the Fugitive Slave Law.

This law, passed by the Congress in 1851, decreed that every American, even in states where slavery had been abolished, be responsible for returning runaway slaves. It fomented intense feeling among the abolitionists, especially in New England. "This is a law," cried Ralph Waldo Emerson to a Concord audience, "which every one of you will break on the earliest occasion." And Henry David Thoreau, but recently a man who had prided himself on aloofness from politics, invoked all his powers of sarcasm and invective against the law. Thoreau was a station agent in the U.R., and he and Emerson both contributed substantial help to another famous station agent, John Brown.

Levi Coffin's account of his role as a receiver and forwarder of slaves comes about as close to summarizing the realities of the U.R. as any that survives. Particularly interesting is the light it throws on the thinking of persons who felt they could not break the law even to further a cause they knew was morally right; yet by the end of Coffin's story, some years later, many of these same people had come to believe that commitment to the U.R. movement was in itself a mark of responsible citizenship.

Another feature of the U.R. that has received insufficient recognition is the role black men played in it. Records indicate that although most of the station agents were white men, by far the majority of conductors were black men. It is logical that this would be so, since white Northerners were easily identifiable by their manners and speech, and all Southern states offered a bounty for the capture of white men aiding escaping slaves. Further, white men could not know the details of geography and the hideout locations in swamps and other places, as did the black men who lived there.

The most famous conductor was Harriet Tubman, herself a fugitive slave from Maryland. She made regular trips back and forth, bringing slaves out of the South and escorting them to Canada. Harriet Tubman made at least nineteen forays into the South, with a price upon her head, and she singlehandedly effected the escape of more than three hundred slaves.

The Document:

From the autobiography of Levi Coffin
titled *Reminiscences,* Cincinnati, Weslin Tract Society, 1876

IN THE EARLY part of the ninth month, 1826, we took a final
leave of North Carolina. My parents had emigrated to Indiana the previous year, and I was the last one of our family to
go. My family at this time consisted of myself, my wife, and
our son Jessie, about a year old. . . .

We made the journey in light wagons, with good teams,
and had a pleasant trip. We took the shortest route, called the
Kanawha road, and arrived at our destination in four weeks
from the time of starting. We located at Newport, Wayne
County, Indiana, where we lived for more than twenty years.
This village was in the midst of a large settlement of Friends,
and a Quarterly Meeting was then established at New Garden
Meeting-House, about a half mile from the village. I bought
property in Newport, and finding that there was a good opening there for a mercantile business, I concluded to engage in
it. I went to Cincinnati and purchased a small stock of goods
and opened a store. This venture was successful, and I increased my stock and varied my assortment of goods until a
large retail business was established.

The next year I commenced cutting pork in a small way,
besides carrying on my other business. This I continued to
do, enlarging my operations every year, and kept it up as
long as I remained in Newport.

In the year 1836, I built an oil mill and manufactured lin-
seed oil. Notwithstanding all this multiplicity of business, I
was never too busy to engage in Underground Railroad
affairs. Soon after we located at Newport, I found that we
were on a line of the U.G.R.R. Fugitives often passed
through that place, and generally stopped among the colored
people. There was in that neighborhood a number of families
of free colored people, mostly from North Carolina, who
were the descendants of slaves who had been liberated by
Friends many years before, and sent to free states at the expense of North Carolina Yearly Meeting. I learned that the
fugitive slaves who took refuge with these people were often
pursued and captured, the colored people not being very
skillful in concealing them, or shrewd in making arrangements to forward them to Canada. I was pained to hear of
the capture of these fugitives, and inquired of some of the
Friends in our village why they did not take them in and se-

crete them, when they were pursued, and then aid them on their way to Canada? I found that they were afraid of the penalty of the law. I told them that I read in the Bible when I was a boy that it was right to take in the stranger and administer to those in distress, and that I thought it was always safe to do right. The Bible, in bidding us to feed the hungry and clothe the naked, said nothing about color, and I should try to follow out the teachings of that good book. I was willing to receive and aid as many fugitives as were disposed to come to my house. I knew that my wife's feelings and sympathies regarding this matter were the same as mine, and that she was willing to do her part. It soon became known to the colored people in our neighborhood and others, that our house was a depot where the hunted and harassed fugitive journeying northward, on the Underground Railroad, could find succor and sympathy. It also became known at other depots on the various lines that converged at Newport.

In the winter of 1826–27, fugitives began to come to our house, and as it became more widely known on different routes that the slaves fleeing from bondage would find a welcome and shelter at our house, and be forwarded safely on their journey, the number increased. Friends in the neighborhood, who had formerly stood aloof from the work, fearful of the penalty of the law, were encouraged to engage in it when they saw the fearless manner in which I acted, and the success that attended my efforts. They would contribute to clothe the fugitives, and would aid in forwarding them on their way, but were timid about sheltering them under their roof so that part of the work devolved on us. Some seemed really glad to see the work go on if somebody else would do it. Others doubted the propriety of it, and tried to discourage me, and dissuade me from running such risks. They manifested great concern for my safety and pecuniary interests, telling me that such a course of action would injure my business and perhaps ruin me; that I ought to consider the welfare of my family; and warning me that my life was in danger, as there were many threats made against me by the slave-hunters and those who sympathized with them.

After listening quietly to these counselors, I told them that I felt no condemnation for anything that I had done for the fugitive slaves. If by doing my duty and endeavoring to fulfill the injunctions of the Bible, I injured my business, then let my business go. . . .

Many of my pro-slavery customers left me for a time, my sales were diminished, and for a while my business prospects were discouraging, yet my faith was not shaken, nor my efforts for the slaves lessened. New customers soon came in to fill the places of those who had left me. New settlements were rapidly forming to the north of us, and our own was filling up with emigrants from North Carolina, and other States. My trade increased, and I enlarged my business. I was blessed in all my efforts and succeeded beyond my expectations. The Underground Railroad business increased as time advanced, and it was attended with heavy expenses, which I could not have borne had not my affairs been prosperous. I found it necessary to keep a team and a wagon always at command, to convey the fugitive slaves on their journey. Sometimes, when we had large companies, one or two other teams and wagons were required. These journeys had to be made at night, often through deep mud and bad roads, and along by-ways that were seldom traveled. Every precaution to evade pursuit had to be used, as the hunters were often on the track, and sometimes ahead of the slaves. We had different routes for sending the fugitives to depots, ten, fifteen, or twenty miles distant, and when we heard of slave-hunters having passed on one road, we forwarded our passengers by another.

In some instances where we learned that the pursuers were ahead of them, we sent a messenger and had the fugitives brought back to my house to remain in concealment until the bloodhounds in human shape had lost the trail and given up the pursuit.

I soon became extensively known to the friends of the slaves, at different points on the Ohio River, where fugitives generally crossed, and to those northward of us on the various routes leading to Canada. Depots were established on the different lines of the Underground Railroad, south and north of Newport, and a perfect understanding was maintained between those who kept them. Three principal lines from the South converged at my house; one from Cincinnati, one from Madison, and one from Jeffersonville, Indiana. The roads were always in running order, the connections were good, the conductors active and zealous, and there was no lack of passengers. Seldom a week passed without our receiving passengers by this mysterious road. We found it necessary to be always prepared to receive such company and properly care for them. We knew not what night or what hour of the night we would be roused from slumber by a gentle rap at the door. That was the signal announcing the arrival of a train of the Underground Railroad, for the locomotive did not whistle, nor make any unnecessary noise. I have often been awakened by this signal, and sprang out of bed in the dark and opened the door. Outside in the cold or rain, there would be a two-horse wagon loaded with fugitives, perhaps the greater part of them women and children. I would invite them, in a low tone, to come in, and they would follow me into the darkened house without a word, for we knew not who might be watching and listening. When they were all safely inside and the door fastened, I would cover the windows, strike a light and build a good fire. By this time my wife would be up and preparing victuals for them, and in a short time the cold and hungry fugitives would be made comfortable. I would accompany the conductor of the train to the stable, and care for the horses, that had, perhaps, been driven twenty-five or thirty miles that night, through the cold and rain. The fugitives would rest on pallets before the fire the rest of the night. Frequently, wagon-loads of passengers from the different lines have met at our house, having no previous knowledge of each other. The companies varied in number, from two or three fugitives to seventeen.

The care of so many necessitated much work and anxiety on our part, but we assumed the burden of our own will and bore it cheerfully. It was never too cold or stormy, or the hour of night too late, for my wife to rise from sleep, and provide food and comfortable lodging for the fugitives. Her sympathy for those in distress never tired, and her efforts in their behalf never abated. This work was kept up during the time we lived at Newport, a period of more than twenty years. The number of fugitives varied considerably in different years, but the annual average was more than one hundred. They generally came to us destitute of clothing, and were often barefooted. Clothing must be collected and kept on hand, if possible, and money must be raised to buy shoes, and purchase goods to make garments for women and children. The young ladies in the neighborhood organized a sewing society, and met at our house frequently, to make clothes for the fugitives. . . .

"YOU ARE EMPANELLED AS A JUROR": 1839

The Introduction of a documentary book on the living and working conditions of slaves in the South

by Theodore D. Weld

About The Document:

Below appears the text of the Introduction to *American Slavery As It Is,* a book published in 1839 by the American Anti-Slavery Society. The complete volume, consisting of 210 double-column pages printed in small type, details the ugly realities of the life of plantation slaves. Taken primarily from Southern sources—court records, medical reports, letters, eyewitness accounts, etc., it remains to this day an excellent source book that gives the lie to the Southern myth of the "happy, loyal" slave.

The Introduction is presented in the style of a district attorney building up a case against a defendant. *American Slavery As It Is,* incidentally, was Harriet Beecher Stowe's basic source book when writing *Uncle Tom's Cabin.*

The Document:

From *American Slavery As It Is.*
Written by Theodore D. Weld, New York
American Anti-Slavery Society, 1839

READER, YOU ARE empanelled as a juror to try a plain case and bring in an honest verdict. The question at issue is not one of law, but of fact—"What is the actual condition of slaves in the United States?"

A plainer case never went to a jury. Look at it. TWENTY-SEVEN HUNDRED THOUSAND PERSONS in this country, men, women, and children, are in SLAVERY. Is slavery, as a condition for human beings, good, bad, or indifferent?

We submit the question without argument. You have common sense, and conscience, and a human heart—pronounce upon it. You have a wife, or a husband, a child, a father, a mother, a brother or a sister—make the case your own, make it theirs, and bring in your verdict.

The case of Human Rights against Slavery has been adjudicated in the court of conscience times innumerable. The same verdict has always been rendered—"Guilty;" the same sentence has always been pronounced "Let it be accursed;" and human nature, with her million echoes, has rung it round the world in every language under heaven. "Let it be accursed. . . ."

As slaveholders and their apologists are volunteer witnesses in their own cause, and are flooding the world with testimony that their slaves are kindly treated; that they are well fed, well clothed, well housed, well lodged, moderately worked, and bountifully provided with all things needful for their comfort, we propose,—first, to disprove their assertions by the testimony of a multitude of impartial witnesses, and then to put slaveholders themselves through a course of cross-questioning which will draw their condemnation out of their own mouths.

We will prove that the slaves in the United States are treated with barbarous inhumanity; that they are overworked, underfed, wretchedly clad and lodged, and have insufficient sleep; that they are often made to wear round their necks iron collars armed with prongs, to drag heavy chains and weights at their feet while working in the field, and to wear yokes and bells, and iron horns; that they are often kept confined in the stocks day and night for weeks together, made to wear gags in their mouths for hours or days, have some of their front teeth torn out or broken off, that they may be easily detected when they run away; that they are frequently flogged with terrible severity, have red pepper rubbed into their lacerated flesh, and hot brine, spirits of turpentine, &c., poured over the gashes to increase the torture; that they are often stripped naked, their backs and limbs cut with knives, bruised and mangled by scores and hundreds of blows with the paddle, and terribly torn by the claws of cats, drawn over them by their tormentors; that they are often hunted with bloodhounds and shot down like beasts, or torn in pieces by dogs; that they are often suspended by the arms and whipped and beaten till they faint, and when revived by restoratives, beaten again till they faint, and sometimes till they die; that their ears are often cut off, their eyes knocked out, their bones broken, their flesh branded with red hot irons; that they are maimed, mutilated and burned to death, over slow fires. All these things, and more, and worse, we shall *prove.* . . .

We shall show, not merely that such deeds are committed, but that they are frequent; not done in corners, but before the sun; not in one of the slave states, but in all of them; not perpetrated by brutal overseers and drivers merely, but by magistrates, by legislators, by professors of religion, by preachers of the gospel, by governors of states, by "gentlemen of property and standing," and by delicate females moving in the "highest circles of society."

We know, full well, the outcry that will be made by multitudes, at these declarations; the multiform cavils, the flat denials, the charges of "exaggeration" and "falsehood" so often bandied, the sneers of affected contempt at the credulity that can believe such things, and the rage and imprecations against those who give them currency. We know, too, the threadbare sophistries by which slaveholders and their apologists seek to evade such testimony. If they admit that such deeds are committed, they tell us that they are exceedingly rare, and therefore furnish no grounds for judging of the general treatment of slaves; that occasionally a brutal wretch in the *free* states barbarously butchers his wife, but that no one thinks of inferring from that, the general treatment of wives at the North and West.

They tell us, also, that the slaveholders of the South are proverbially hospitable, kind, and generous, and it is incredible that they can perpetrate such enormities upon human beings; further, that it is absurd to suppose that they would thus injure their own property, that self-interest would prompt them to treat their slaves with kindness, as none but fools and madmen wantonly destroy their own property; further, that Northern visitors at the South come back testifying to the kind treatment of the slaves, and that the slaves themselves corroborate such representations. All these pleas, and scores of others, are bruited in every corner of the free States; and who that hath eyes to see, has not sickened at the blindness that saw not, at the palsy of heart that felt not, or at the cowardice and sycophancy that dared not expose such shallow fallacies. We are not to be turned from our purpose by such vapid babblings. In their appropriate places, we propose to consider these objections and various others, and to show their emptiness and folly.

A CALL TO REBELLION: 1843

A passionate appeal to the slaves
of the South to rise up in arms

by Henry Highland Garnet

About The Document:

Henry Highland Garnet has been called the "Thomas Paine of the abolitionist movement." He was the grandson, according to tradition, of an African chieftain. At ten he escaped with his family from Maryland by way of the Underground Railroad to New York City.

In 1831 Garnet entered a New York African Free School —one of the first public schools for blacks in the United States. At the age of nineteen, he journeyed to Canaan, New Hampshire, to study at a summer session of the Canaan Academy. He and two friends had been invited by the principal, who wanted to make the Academy interracial. Garnet's studies were cut short by the violent reaction of the Canaan townspeople against the new school policy. How Garnet handled the violence is described by Alexander Crummell, one of the students who had accompanied him to Canaan, in *The Eulogy of Henry Highland Garnet* (1882):

It was a long and wearisome journey, of some four hundred and more miles; and rarely would an inn or a hotel give us food, and nowhere could we get shelter. . . . The sight of three black youths, in gentlemanly garb, traveling through New England was, *in those days, a most unusual sight;* started not only surprise, but brought out universal sneers and ridicule. We met a most cordial reception at Canaan from two score white students, and began, with the highest hopes, our studies. But our stay was the briefest. . . . On the 4th of July, with wonderful taste and felicity, the farmers, from a wide region around, assembled at Canaan and resolved to remove the academy as a public nuisance. On the

10th of August they gathered together from the neighboring towns, seized the building, and with ninety yoke of oxen carried it off into a swamp about a half mile from its site. They were two days in accomplishing this miserable work.

Meanwhile, under Garnet, as our leader, the boys in our boarding house were moulding bullets, expecting an attack upon our dwelling. About eleven o'clock at night the tramp of horses was heard approaching, and as one rapid rider passed the house and fired at it, Garnet quickly replied by a discharge from a double-barrelled shotgun which blazed away through the window. At once the hills, from many miles around, reverberated with the sound. Lights were seen in scores of houses on every side, and the towns and villages far and near were in a state of great excitement. But that musket shot by Garnet doubtless saved our lives. The cowardly ruffians dared not attack us. . . .

Garnet became a schoolteacher—he taught at the first public school for blacks in Troy, New York, in 1840. That same year he gained prominence for a hard-hitting anti-slavery address he delivered before the American Anti-Slavery Convention. He was then twenty-five years old. He went on to become a Presbyterian minister and an eloquent, fiery orator. He also edited the abolitionist newspaper the *National Watchman*.

Garnet was one of a number of young men who attended the National Convention of Colored Citizens, held in Buffalo, August 21–24, 1843. His speech to the delegates calling for a slave revolt and a general strike had all the militancy of David Walker, but it also had Garnet's own eloquence of style. As a pastor and an editor, he carried tremendous weight. When he had finished, shouts from the floor called for the adoption of the speech as the sentiment of the Convention. A resolution to that effect was duly introduced. It lost by a single vote! (The speech, which appears below, was published and circulated by John Brown.)

Two decades later, on February 12, 1865, before an overflow audience in the House of Representatives in the Capitol, Garnet delivered a stirring sermon to commemorate the abolition of slavery. It was the first time a black man had set foot in the hall of the House of Representatives in a role other than that of a menial.

The Document:

From "An address to the Slaves of the United States," delivered at the National Negro Convention held in Buffalo, New York, August, 1843, and later as a

"Memorial Discourse," delivered in the Hall of the
House of Representatives, Washington, D. C., on
Sabbath, February, 1865. Philadelphia: Joseph M. Wilson, 1865

BRETHREN AND FELLOW-CITIZENS:—Your brethren of the
North, East, and West have been accustomed to meet together in National Conventions, to sympathize with each
other, and to weep over your unhappy condition. In these
meetings we have addressed all classes of the free, but we
have never, until this time, sent a word of consolation and
advice to you. We have been contented in sitting still and
mourning over your sorrows, earnestly hoping that before
this day your sacred liberties would have been restored. But,
we have hoped in vain. Years have rolled on, and tens of
thousands have been borne on streams of blood and tears, to
the shores of eternity. While you have been oppressed, we
have also been partakers with you; nor can we be free while
you are enslaved. We, therefore, write to you as being bound
with you. . . .

SLAVERY! How much misery is comprehended in that single word. What mind is there that does not shrink from its
direful effects? Unless the image of God be obliterated from
the soul, all men cherish the love of Liberty. The nice dis-
cerning political economist does not regard the sacred right
more than the untutored African who roams in the wilds of
Congo. Nor has the one more right to the full enjoyment of
his freedom than the other. In every man's mind the good
seeds of liberty are planted, and he who brings his fellow
down so low, as to make him contented with a condition of
slavery, commits the highest crime against God and man.
Brethren, your oppressors aim to do this. They endeavor to
make you as much like brutes as possible. When they have
blinded the eyes of your mind—when they have embittered
the sweet waters of life—when they have shut out the light
which shines from the word of God—then, and not till then,
has American slavery done its perfect work.

TO SUCH DEGRADATION IT IS SINFUL IN THE EXTREME FOR
YOU TO MAKE VOLUNTARY SUBMISSION. The divine commandments you are in duty bound to reverence and obey. If you
do not obey them, you will surely meet with the displeasure
of the Almighty. He requires you to love him supremely, and
your neighbor as yourself—to keep the Sabbath day holy—to
search the Scriptures—and bring up your children with respect for his laws, and to worship no other God but him. But
slavery sets all these at nought, and hurls defiance in the face
of Jehovah. The forlorn condition in which you are placed,
does not destroy your moral obligation to God. You are not

certain of heaven, because you suffer yourselves to remain in a state of slavery, where you cannot obey the commandments of the Sovereign of the universe. If the ignorance of slavery is a passport to heaven, then it is a blessing, and no curse, and you should rather desire its perpetuity than its abolition. God will not receive slavery, nor ignorance, nor any other state of mind, for love and obedience to him. Your condition does not absolve you from your moral obligation. The diabolical injustice by which your liberties are cloven down, NEITHER GOD, NOR ANGELS, OR JUST MEN, COMMAND YOU TO SUFFER FOR A SINGLE MOMENT. THEREFORE IT IS YOUR SOLEMN AND IMPERATIVE DUTY TO USE EVERY MEANS, BOTH MORAL, INTELLECTUAL, AND PHYSICAL, THAT PROMISES SUCCESS. If a band of heathen men should attempt to enslave a race of Christians, and to place their children under the influence of some false religion, surely, Heaven would frown upon the men who would not resist such aggression, even to death. If, on the other hand, a band of Christians should attempt to enslave a race of heathen men, and to entail slavery upon them, and to keep them in heathenism in the midst of Christianity, the God of heaven would smile upon every effort which the injured might make to disenthrall themselves. . . .

Brethren, the time has come when you must act for yourselves. It is an old and true saying that, "if hereditary bondsmen would be free, they must themselves strike the blow." You can plead your own cause, and do the work of emancipation better than any others. The nations of the old world are moving in the great cause of universal freedom, and some of them at least will, ere long, do you justice. The combined powers of Europe have placed their broad seal of disapprobation upon the African slave-trade. But in the slaveholding parts of the United States, the trade is as brisk as ever. They buy and sell you as though you were brute beasts. The North has done much—her opinion of slavery in the abstract is known. But in regard to the South, we adopt the opinion of the *New York Evangelist*—"We have advanced so far, that the cause apparently waits for a more effectual door to be thrown open than has been yet." We are about to point you to that more effectual door. Look around you, and behold the bosoms of your loving wives heaving with untold agonies! Hear the cries of your poor children! Remember the stripes your fathers bore. Think of the torture and disgrace of your noble mothers. Think of your wretched sisters, loving virtue and purity, as they are driven into concubinage and are exposed to the unbridled lusts of incarnate devils. Think of the undying glory that hangs around the ancient name of Africa:

—and forget not that you are native-born American citizens, and as such, you are justly entitled to all the rights that are granted to the freest. Think how many tears you have poured out upon the soil which you have cultivated with unrequited toil and enriched with your blood; and then go to your lordly enslavers and tell them plainly, that you *are determined to be free*. Appeal to their sense of justice, and tell them that they have no more right to oppress you, than you have to enslave them. Entreat them to remove the grievous burdens which they have imposed upon you, and to remunerate you for your labor. Promise them renewed diligence in the cultivation of the soil, if they will render to you an equivalent for your services. Point them to the increase of happiness and prosperity in the British West-Indies since the Act of Emancipation. Tell them in language which they cannot misunderstand, of the exceeding sinfulness of slavery, and of a future judgment, and of the righteous retributions of an indignant God. Inform them that all you desire is FREEDOM, and that nothing else will suffice. Do this, and for ever after cease to toil for the heartless tyrants, who give you no other reward but stripes and abuse. If they then commence the work of death, they, and not you, will be responsible for the consequences. You had far better all die—*die immediately,* than live slaves, and entail your wretchedness upon your posterity. If you would be free in this generation, here is your only hope. However much you and all of us may desire it, there is not much hope of redemption without the shedding of blood. If you must bleed, let it all come at once—rather *die freemen, than live to be slaves*. It is impossible, like the children of Israel, to make a grand exodus from the land of bondage. The Pharaohs are on both sides of the blood-red waters! You cannot move *en masse,* to the dominions of the British Queen—nor can you pass through Florida and overrun Texas, and at last find peace in Mexico. . . . The propagators of American slavery are spending their blood and treasure, that they may plant the black flag in the heart of Mexico and riot in the halls of the Montezumas.

"THE NORTH STAR SHALL LIVE": 1847

The two inaugural editorials
in Frederick Douglass' newspaper

by Frederick Douglass

About The Document:

Escaping slaves usually traveled at night, and when they were unsure of the roads that would lead them to freedom, they guided themselves by the North Star. Frederick Douglass, the greatest black leader of the 19th century, could not have chosen a more appropriate title for his militant newspaper, the *North Star*. From his headquarters in Rochester, New York, Douglass edited the *North Star* for seventeen years. It is worth noting that for most of this time he also operated— with the Quaker Susan B. Anthony—a station on the Underground Railroad.

Douglass was nineteen when he effected his escape from a Baltimore shipyard, where he labored as the slave of one Thomas Auld. When Douglass was sixteen, he beat in a fist fight a professional "Negro-breaker," in whose care he had been placed. He wrote:

> I was a changed being after that fight. I was nothing before,
> I was a man now.

He made his way to New Bedford, Massachusetts, hoping to get employment as a ship's caulker. Barred by the opposition of white workmen in the shipyards, he obtained menial work digging cellars and carting rubbish. Some weeks after his arrival in New Bedford he attended a black abolitionist meeting, where William Lloyd Garrison was the featured speaker. After the speech Douglass joined in the discussion. His comments and his manner of delivery impressed Garrison, who invited him to become a full-time agent of the Masɔachusetts Anti-Slavery Society. Within the year, in the company of Society leaders, Douglass lectured in sixty villages and towns. In 1843 he joined the Hundred Conventions, appearing at antislavery meetings from New Hampshire to Indiana. At the National Convention of Colored Citizens, in Buffalo, he met other black leaders, in particular the ex-slave Henry Highland Garnet. It was at this Convention that Garnet's "Call for Rebellion" failed of adoption by one vote. The resolution that passed in its stead called for "moral suasion" as the best means to achieve emancipation of the slaves. The delegate who introduced the resolution was Frederick Douglass.

Douglass was eventually to change his ideas about the tactics of moderation, but it must be kept in mind that in 1843 he had been in the abolition movement only about two years, and he was still very much under Garrison's influence. Actually, Garrison's views were also undergoing a change. He was coming to believe in Northern secession under the slogan "No union with the slaveholders," but he still was insisting that the best weapons of the abolitionists were "spiritual."

Like all abolitionist agents, Douglass suffered incessant attacks from hoodlums hired by proslavery forces. Being a black man in the largely white-dominated Anti-Slavery Society, he was especially subject to abuse, and on the same tour in which he confronted Henry Garnet, he was almost killed by a mob in Newcastle, Indiana. In a letter to *The Liberator* of October 13, 1843, agent William A. White described the attacks:

> Frederick Douglass who, at the time, was safe among the friends, not seeing me, thought I was knocked down, and seizing a club, rushed into the crowd. His weapon was immediately snatched from him. . . . [He] fled for his life, and ten or more of the mob followed crying, "Kill the nigger, kill the damn nigger. . . ." The leader of the mob soon overtook him, and knocked him down and struck him once with his club, and was raising it the second time to level a blow which must have been fatal had it fallen, but I, by dint of hard running, came up in time to throw myself upon him, and stop him in his murderous purpose. . . . Frederick was taken up, and though at first he seemed to have been severely injured, he soon recovered and was able to lecture the next day.

Douglass' abilities as an orator grew steadily, and his platform bearing became so perfect that his friends feared lest his audiences disbelieve that he really had been a slave. To set the record straight, Douglass wrote his autobiography,

Narrative of the Life of Frederick Douglass. It was publishe
in 1845, with prefaces by Garrison and the other leading abolitionist, Wendell Phillips. The book sold well, but it named
names and specified places, and slave agents came North
seeking to capture Douglass. He eluded them by sailing to
Europe.

Douglass traveled in England, Scotland, and Ireland for
two years, and his experiences abroad are summed up in the
following letter he wrote to *The Liberator* on January 1,
1846:

> The warm and generous cooperation extended to me by the
> friends of my despised race—the prompt and liberal manner
> with which the press has rendered me its aid—the glorious
> enthusiasm with which thousands have flocked to hear the
> cruel wrongs of my down-trodden and long enslaved coun-
> trymen portrayed—the deep sympathy of the slave, and the
> strong abhorrence of the slave-holder, everywhere evinced—
> the cordiality with which members and ministers of various
> religious bodies, and of various shades of religious opinion,
> have embraced me and lent me their aid—the kind hospital-
> ity constantly proferred to me by persons of the highest rank
> in society—the spirit of freedom that seems to animate all
> with whom I come in contact—and the entire absence of
> everything that looked like prejudice against me, on account
> of the color of my skin—contrasting so strongly with my
> long and bitter experience in the United States, that I look
> with wonder and amazement on the transition.

Douglass' friends in England raised $750 to purchase his
freedom, a gesture that some American abolitionists denounced on the grounds that it "conceded the right of property in man" and was "a wasteful expenditure of money."
Douglass answered simply that if his freedom were not
bought, he would be seized by his master and returned to
slavery the moment he set foot on U.S. soil. Douglass received the bill of sale for his life in December 1846.

In addition to buying his freedom, Englishmen had sub-
scribed $2,000 for a newspaper Douglass wanted to launch.
On his return to the U.S., however, Garrison and Phillips
temporarily dissuaded him from this venture, arguing that he
was "more serviceable as a public speaker than . . . as an editor."

For some time, Douglass complained that, in Garrison's
employ, he was an "exhibit, not an advocate." He questioned
the appropriateness of white men leading the black crusade.
Finally he demanded a share in its "generalship," then, lash-
ing out at the "colored mail-wrappers" in the predominantly
white Anti-Slavery Society, Douglass exclaimed: "Our op-

pressed people are wholly ignored in one sense, in the general-ship of the movement."

At this time Douglass was living in Rochester, New York. There, with the aid of the woman suffrage leader Susan B. Anthony, he served as a station master and conductor for the Underground Railroad. During the day he hid fugitive slaves in his home and at night he put them on the train to Canada. In the Samuel D. Porter Manuscripts at the University of Rochester Library is this hastily scribbled, undated note from Douglass to Porter: "Three men in peril. Am unwell. Need your help. Come at once."

In 1847, several months before his decision to become an "advocate" in his own right, as an editor, Douglass visited John Brown in Springfield, Massachusetts. In an after-dinner conversation, Brown explained why he believed that neither moral suasion nor political action would ever abolish the slave system, and he confided to Douglass his plan to estab-lish bands of armed men in the Allegheny Mountains to help the slaves in Virginia escape. Douglass wrote later that he thought Brown's plan had "much to commend it," but he still could not accept violent means.

Twelve years later, in 1859, the U.S. District Attorney for Western New York was to board a train for Rochester with a warrant for Douglass' arrest as a conspirator with John Brown in the Harpers Ferry plot. To this day it is not known how deeply Douglass was implicated with Brown. It is estab-lished, however, that Douglass was closely associated with him, and—regardless of his possible involvement at Harpers Ferry—he later credited Brown with being the man most re-sponsible for starting the war that ended slavery.

On July 28, 1848, Douglass finally asserted his right to a part in the "generalship" of the abolition movement with the first edition of the *North Star*. The paper carried two edito-rials, the first addressed to white abolitionists, the second to black men. The issues Douglass raised in these editorials are of absorbing interest, since similar issues are being debated today. The editorials appear below in the sequence of the orig-inal edition of the *North Star*.

The Document:

Inaugural editorials in the *North Star*
Rochester, New York, December 3, 1847

To Our Friends and Fellow-Laborers:

IT IS SCARCELY necessary for us to say that our desire to occupy our present position at the head of an Anti-Slavery
Journal, has resulted from no unworthy distrust or ungrateful
want of appreciation of the zeal, integrity, or ability of the
noble band of white laborers in this department of our cause;
but, from the sincere and settled conviction that such a Journal, if conducted with only moderate skill and ability, would
do a most important and indispensable work, which it would
be wholly impossible for our white friends to do for us.

It is neither a reflection on the fidelity, nor a disparage-
ment of the ability of our friends and fellow-laborers, to assert what "common sense affirms and only folly denies," that
the man who has *suffered the wrong* is the man to *demand
redress*—that the man STRUCK is the man to CRY OUT—and
that he who has *endured the cruel pangs of Slavery* is the
man to *advocate Liberty*. It is evident we must be our own
representatives and advocates, not exclusively, but peculiarly
—not distinct from, but in connection with our white friends.
In the grand struggle for liberty and equality now waging, it
is meet, right and essential that there should arise in our
ranks authors and editors, as well as orators, for it is in these
capacities that the most permanent good can be rendered to
our cause. . . .

To Our Oppressed Countrymen:

WE SOLEMNLY dedicate the *North Star* to the cause of our
long oppressed and plundered fellow countrymen. May God
bless the offering to your good! It shall fearlessly assert your
rights, faithfully proclaim your wrongs, and earnestly demand
for you instant and even-handed justice. Giving no quarter to
slavery at the South, it will hold no truce with oppressors at
the North. While it shall boldly advocate emancipation for
our enslaved brethren, it will omit no opportunity to gain for
the nominally free, complete enfranchisement. Every effort to
injure or degrade you or your cause—originating where-

soever, or with whomsoever—shall find in it a constant, unswerving and inflexible foe. . . .

Remember that we are one, that our cause is one, and that we must help each other, if we would succeed. We have drunk to the dregs the bitter cup of slavery; we have worn the heavy yoke; we have sighed beneath our bonds, and writhed beneath the bloody lash;—cruel mementoes of our oneness are indelibly marked in our living flesh. We are one with you under the ban of prejudice and proscription—one with you under the slander of inferiority—one with you in social and political disfranchisement. What you suffer, we suffer; what you endure, we endure. We are indissolubly united, and must fall or flourish together. . . .

Brethren, the first number of the paper is before you. It is dedicated to your cause. Through the kindness of our friends in England, we are in possession of an excellent printing press, types, and all other materials necessary for printing a paper. Shall this gift be blest to our good, or shall it result in our injury? It is for you to say. With your aid, co-operation and assistance, our enterprise will be entirely successful. We pledge ourselves that no effort on our part shall be wanting, and that no subscriber shall lose his subscription—"The *North Star* Shall Live."

"PLEA FOR CAPTAIN JOHN BROWN": 1860

Henry David Thoreau,
advocate of nonviolence,
praises John Brown's raid

by Henry David Thoreau

About The Document:

Northerners tried to save John Brown by having him declared insane at his trial. This legal maneuver failed, and the state of Virginia convicted Brown of murder, treason, and conspiracy. History books have generally labeled him a "religious fanatic," yet to the Northern abolitionists he was a martyr and a hero. On the day of his hanging, Ralph Waldo Emerson declared that John Brown would make the gibbet as "glorious as the cross." What manner of man was John Brown?

Brown came of Puritan stock and was born in Torrington, Connecticut, in 1800. His family moved to the Midwest, to Ohio, when he was a young boy, and like many other New Englanders took with them the Puritan code of individual morality and unquestioning faith in the vengeful god of the Old Testament.

John Brown married twice and fathered twenty children. As a businessman, he was unsuccessful; a series of small businesses he founded in Ohio, Pennsylvania, Massachusetts, and New York ended in bankruptcy. He was a station agent for the Underground Railroad when he was still in Richmond, Virginia. In 1855 he followed five of his sons to Kansas, avowedly to help keep the territory free from slavery.

The Kansas-Nebraska Act of 1854 had created the Territory of Kansas, which included part of Colorado and was far larger than the present state. The Act also repealed the Missouri Compromise of 1820 and provided that the settlers of the new territory should decide whether it would become a slaveholding or a free state. Slavery advocates won the first elections, but the Free Staters cried that more votes had been cast than there were people. The antislavery forces thereupon set up their own state government, which Washington refused to recognize. Then came the brutal attack against the town of Lawrence in 1856. Proslavery men wrecked a newspaper office, burned a number of buildings, and killed several Free Staters. This, in brief, is the background of an act of John Brown's that has always baffled even his most ardent supporters.

On May 24, three days after the Lawrence attack, Brown led four of his sons and two other men in a raid on a small settlement on Pottawatomie Creek, murdering five proslavery men. Despite frequent charges, no women or children were killed in this action. Brown said that he deliberately killed the men to create "a restraining fear," and that he acted as an instrument in the hand of God. In another move he crossed to Missouri and liberated eleven slaves; one slaveholder was killed in this action.

Late in 1857 Brown started enlisting support for a campaign that took shape at a convention of his followers held in Chatham, Ontario, in the following spring. His plan was to establish a stronghold in the Blue Ridge Mountains, in which slaves and free blacks could take refuge, and which would serve as a base of operations for fomenting slave insurrections. The key to the abolition of slavery, he believed, was guerrilla warfare. Through small forces of volunteer soldiers making surprise raids against slave-operating plantations, he hoped to weaken the market value of the slave and eventually force the collapse of the slave system. Small-scale surprise operations would keep bloodshed to a minimum.

At Harpers Ferry, which is a day's march from Washington, D.C., the Potomac River breaks through the Blue Ridge Mountains and meets the Shenandoah River in a wide, sweeping curve between tree-covered hills. From a farm he had rented on the opposite side of the Potomac, Brown, on Sunday, October 16, 1859, crossed the river with twenty-two followers, five of whom were black men, just after sundown. Their objective was the capture of the federal arsenal at Harpers Ferry, from which they planned to distribute munitions to slaves in the surrounding region. Brown and his men marched through the night in a heavy rain, which kept their passage unobserved. They reached Harpers Ferry at 4 A.M. and took the town and the arsenal without incident. Authorities agree that at any time between 4 A.M. and 9 A.M. Monday morning they could have taken all the munitions they could carry and left without hindrance. Probably they could have left at any time up to noon. Brown's stated reason for staying was:

> A lenient feeling towards the citizens led me to parley with them as to a compromise; and by prevarication on their part I was delayed until attacked, and then in self-defense was compelled to entrench myself.

By noon the militiamen of Harpers Ferry had organized themselves and were able to force Brown into the locomotive roundhouse, where they kept him at bay. Meanwhile, Washington had been alerted, and Colonel Robert E. Lee had been dispatched with a company of one hundred Marines. Lee arrived at midnight and surrounded the roundhouse. On Tuesday morning he attacked. Ten of Brown's men, including two of his sons, were killed in the ensuing fight. Brown himself was wounded.

The South was consumed by the fear that other Northerners would undertake similar invasions. Most Northerners were profoundly shocked by Brown's action, but as the weeks passed—largely as a result of Brown's dignified conduct and calm defense during his trial—he came to be regarded by abolitionists in the North as a martyr.

The document that appears below is Henry David Thoreau's impassioned "Plea for Captain John Brown," made in an address at the Concord, New Hampshire, church on the evening of Brown's execution—December 2, 1859.

The text will surprise many. Thoreau is known, after all, for his advocacy of passive resistance. His great essay "On the Duty of Civil Disobedience" influenced Mohandas Gandhi, and through Gandhi, leaders such as Martin Luther King. The "Civil Disobedience" essay was written in 1849, ten years *before* his militant plea for John Brown. The drastic change in his thinking is clearly shown in his words that follow.

The Document:

Speech reprinted from
Echoes of Harpers Ferry,
James Redpath, Boston, 1860

. . . IT WAS HIS peculiar doctrine that a man has a perfect right to interfere by force with the slaveholder, in order to rescue the slave. I agree with him. They who are continually shocked by slavery have some right to be shocked by the violent death of the slaveholder, but no others. Such will be more shocked by his life than by his death. I shall not be forward to think him mistaken in his method who quickest succeeds to liberate the slave. I speak for the slave when I say, that I prefer the philanthropy of Captain Brown to that philanthropy which neither shoots me nor liberates me. At any rate, I do not think it is quite sane for one to spend his whole life in talking or writing about this matter, unless he is continuously inspired, and I have not done so. A man may have other affairs to attend to. I do not wish to kill nor to be killed, but I can foresee circumstances in which both these things would be by me unavoidable. We preserve the so-called peace of our community by deeds of petty violence every day. Look at the policeman's billy and handcuffs! Look at the jail! Look at the gallows! Look at the chaplain of the regiment! We are hoping only to live safely on the outskirts of *this* provisional army. So we defend ourselves and our hen-roosts, and maintain slavery. I know that the mass of my countrymen think that the only righteous use that can be made of Sharpe's rifles and revolvers is to fight duels with them, when we are insulted by other nations, or to hunt Indians, or shoot fugitive slaves with them, or the like. I think that for once the Sharpe's rifles and the revolvers were employed in a righteous cause. The tools were in the hands of one who could use them. . . .

This event advertises me that there is such a fact as death —the possibility of a man's dying. It seems as if no man had ever died in America before; for in order to die you must first have lived. I don't believe in the hearses, and palls, and funerals that they have had. There was no death in the case, because there had been no life; they merely rotted or sloughed off, pretty much as they had rotted or sloughed along. No temple's veil was rent, only a hole dug somewhere. Let the dead bury their dead. The best of them fairly ran down like a clock. Franklin,—Washington,—they were let off without dying; they were merely missing one day. I hear a good many pretend that they are going to die; or that they have died, for aught that I know. Nonsense! I'll defy them to do it. They haven't got life enough in them. They'll deliquesce like fungi, and keep a hundred eulogists mopping the spot where they left off. Only half a dozen or so have died since the world began. . . .

Any man knows when he is justified, and all the wits in the world cannot enlighten him on that point. The murderer always knows that he is justly punished; but when a government takes the life of a man without the consent of his conscience, it is an audacious government, and is taking a step towards its own dissolution. Is it not possible that an individual may be right and a government wrong? Are laws to be enforced simply because they were made? or declared by any number of men to be good, if they are *not* good? Is there any necessity for a man's being a tool to perform a deed of which his better nature disapproves? Is it the intention of law-makers that *good* men shall be hung ever? Are judges to interpret the law according to the letter, and not the spirit? What right have *you* to enter into a compact with yourself that you *will* do thus or so, against the light within you? Is it for *you* to *make up* your mind,—to form any resolution whatever,—and not accept the convictions that are forced upon you, and which ever pass your understanding? I do not believe in lawyers, in that mode of attacking or defending a man, because you descend to meet the judge on his own ground, and, in cases of the highest importance, it is of no consequence whether a man breaks a human law or not. Let lawyers decide trivial cases. Business men may arrange that among themselves. If they were the interpreters of the everlasting laws which rightfully bind man, that would be another thing. A counterfeiting law-factory, standing half in a slave land and half in a free! What kind of laws for free men can you expect from that?

I am here to plead his cause with you. I plead not for his life, but for his character,—his immortal life; and so it becomes your cause wholly, and is not his in the least. Some eighteen hundred years ago Christ was crucified; this morning, perchance, Captain Brown was hung. These are the two ends of a chain which is not without its links. He is not Old Brown any longer; he is an angel of light.

I see now that it was necessary that the bravest and humanest man in all the country should be hung. Perhaps he saw it himself. I *almost fear* that I may yet hear of his deliverance, doubting if a prolonged life, if *any* life, can do as much good as his death. . . .

SECTION II

Not In Mercy, But In Wrath

*"Liberty came to the freedman
not in mercy, but in wrath, not
by word choice, but by military
necessity, not by the generous
action of the people among whom
they were to live, and whose good-
will was essential to the success
of the measure, but by strangers . . ."*

Frederick Douglass

"MEN OF COLOR, TO ARMS!": 1863

*An appeal to black men
to join the Union army*

by Frederick Douglass

About The Document:

"In my opinion, the biggest things that are happening in the world today are on the one hand the movement of the slaves in America started by the death of John Brown, and on the other the movement of the serfs in Russia."

So wrote the economic theorist Karl Marx to his friend Frederick Engels early in 1860. A year later, in March 1861, Alexander II signed the Edict of Emancipation, freeing 15,000,000 Russian serfs from bondage. The Edict of Emancipation won the czar the title of "Liberator," but his reforms did not satisfy Russian revolutionists, and he was assassinated.

Abraham Lincoln in 1863 issued the Proclamation of Emancipation, and although at the time of its signing, the Proclamation freed not a single slave, its long-term effect was the abolition of slavery in the United States. Because of it, Lincoln was called the "Great Emancipator," and he too was assassinated.

Political scientists and sociologists agree that the tragedy of the Russian Edict of Emancipation was its failure to provide the serfs with the economic means to achieve freedom. Frederick Douglass and other black leaders were to make the same criticism of the American Emancipation Proclamation.

Today, a consideration of what the Proclamation *might* have achieved is not at issue. The questions—asked increasingly by American black men—are rather: Was the Proclamation of Emancipation a declaration of humanitarian principles? Was the Civil War, in truth, a war to end slavery?

Frederick Douglass was the acknowledged black leader of

his time, and long before John Brown he had believed strongly in the inevitability of slave emancipation. An outspoken critic of African colonization schemes, he had consistently urged free black men to remain in America to fight for liberation.

Douglass' confidence that emancipation would come about fell precipitously in the months following Lincoln's election as President. Disenchantment began with the inaugural address. In that address Lincoln announced his intention to keep out of the affairs of states that permitted slavery, although he had previously opposed the extension of slavery in the new states being formed in the West.

In his disillusionment Douglass wrote in his *Monthly* that he planned to visit Haiti to consider it as a haven for black Americans. Haiti—the only place in the New World where black slaves had successfully revolted and formed their own country. Douglass was scheduled to sail on April 25, 1861. Then on April 12 Confederate guns fired on Fort Sumter, and the Civil War began. Wrote Douglass in his May issue:

> Since this article upon Haiti was put into type, we find ourselves in circumstances which induce us to forego our much desired trip to Haiti, for the present. The last ten days have made a tremendous revolution in all things pertaining to the possible future of the colored people in the United States. We shall stay here and watch the current of events, and serve the cause of freedom and humanity in any way that shall be open to us during the struggle now going on between the slave power and the government. When the Northern people have been made to experience a little more of the savage barbarism of slavery, they may be willing to make war upon it, and in that case we stand ready to lend a hand in any way we can be of service. At any rate, this is no time for us to leave the country.

Douglass and other black leaders immediately began a campaign to convince Lincoln that, in Douglass' words, "the Union could never prosper until the war assumed an antislavery attitude, and the Negro was enlisted on the loyal side."

For a year and a half after Fort Sumter, Lincoln strove against this course. Time and time again he declared that the purpose of the war was to save the Union, and not, as he wrote to the newspaper editor Horace Greeley, "either to save or destroy slavery." When Southern slaves fled toward the advancing Union armies, Lincoln ordered that they be returned to their owners. He barred even free black men from the Union army.

What then was the Proclamation of Emancipation all

about? It was a threat, actually, serving notice on the Confederate states that they had one hundred days to lay down their arms, or have their slaves declared "forever free." This threat was made public in the Preliminary Proclamation of September 1862. The South was given until midnight, January 1, to comply. When the appointed time came and passed Lincoln signed the Proclamation—after eighteen months of warfare.

Even then the Proclamation did little emancipating. It freed slaves only in states that were found as of January 1 to be in open rebellion against the Union—not in the loyal border states, not in the states that hadn't seceded, not in regions within the rebellious states occupied by the Union army.

That the Proclamation was a military measure rather than an idealistic gesture is evident from the reasons Lincoln himself gave for issuing it:

Things have gone from bad to worse, until I felt we had reached the end of our rope in the plan of operations we had been pushing; that we had about played our last card.

What was the "last card" designed to accomplish? Its primary objective was to pressure the Southern states into submission by threatening to deprive them of their slaves and at the same time to create a fifth column of freed slaves behind enemy lines. There were other objectives, however. Within Lincoln's Republican Party were men uncompromisingly opposed to slavery—men such as Charles Sumner, Senator from Massachusetts, and Thaddeus Stevens, Representative from Pennsylvania. They were militant abolitionists all and, though decidedly a minority, they were powerful and highly vocal. These men had been castigating Lincoln for placating the South. They demanded, with Frederick Douglass, that slavery in all parts of the country be abolished and that blacks be permitted to join the army. Lincoln's Proclamation of Emancipation was intended to still this minority.

Fully as important was the international objective. By adding as an aim of the Civil War the abolition of slavery, the Proclamation swung international opinion against the South and crushed its hope—a very real hope—that Great Britain and France would intervene in its behalf. Manufacturing interests in both these countries, deprived of cotton imports by the Union blockade of Southern ports, were urging their governments to declare in favor of the South. The Proclamation of Emancipation rallied the workers in Britain and France in defense of the North. Czar Alexander of Russia sent his fleet across the sea to anchor off the coast of New York, ready to do battle if England and France tried to break the blockade of the South.

How did black men regard the Civil War? It was not until six months after the Emancipation Proclamation that they were allowed to enlist in the Union Army; when permission finally came, they enlisted eagerly. Douglass established enlistment posts from Boston to St. Louis, and he personally enrolled two companies of recruits—including two of his three sons. In New Orleans an ex-river boat gambler named P. B. S. Pinchback raised a company in a week. Though they were paid only about half as much as white soldiers until 1864, and were treated more brutally when captured by the Confederates, more than 180,000 black soldiers served the Union in the Civil War. The 54th Massachusetts Regiment fought for a year and refused to accept any pay at all in protest against the discriminatory pay scale.

Even before Lincoln gave them permission to join the army, black men had formed to fight. The First South Carolina Volunteer Regiment, the First Regiment of Kansas Colored Volunteers, and the First Regiment of Louisiana Native Guards were all formed without official consent of the War Department. Symbolic of black men's desire to strike a blow for their own freedom was the action of the slave crew of the Confederate gunboat *Planter*.

The *Planter* had a crew of slaves, but her officers were white. At night, in the spring of 1862, while the white officers were asleep in their own homes in Charleston, one of the slave crew—a man named Robert Smalls—smuggled his family and a few relatives aboard. In the dark he fired the ship's boiler, hoisted the Confederate flag and sailed out of Charleston harbor. At sea he pulled down the flag, flew a truce flag in its place and surrendered the *Planter* to a U.S. navy blockade ship. The black crew explained that the *Planter* was their gift from the Confederacy.

Both North and South, the war was seen in a less idealistic way by the common men than by the workers of Europe. In the South it was called a "rich man's war and a poor man's fight"; in the North it was called that too, and "the niggers' war." Many white working men saw it as a fight for black men who would only become competitors for their jobs when freed. By 1863 the Union had to resort to the draft in order to fill the army's ranks, and on March 3 of that year the Enrollment Bill went into effect. The draft was applied by federal registrars and—even though a drafted man could buy an exemption for $300 or pay a substitute to fight for him—it was so bitterly resented that ninety-eight of the registrars were killed in the first four months of the law. Draft riots broke out in various cities. The worst occurred in New York City, where Tammany Hall made much of its role as champion of immigrant minority groups—with the single exception of blacks. For four days anti-draft rioters attacked police, beat black people to death, burned black men's homes and businesses, and attacked draft offices. A black orphanage was burned to the ground; by the end of four days of rioting 1,200 people had been killed.

Still, in spite of Confederate reprisals and Union prejudice, black men continued to enlist. Black men to the number of 186,017 were regularly enlisted as soldiers, in addition to those who served in labor battalions. While 7 per cent of the white population served in the Union Army, 18 per cent of the North's free black population enlisted to fight. Thirty-eight thousand of them gave their lives. As for the Union navy, in whose ships white and black men fought and lived side by side, approximately 25 per cent of the force was composed of black men. An example of black sentiment is expressed in the document below: an appeal to black men by Frederick Douglass.

The Document:

Editorial in *Douglass' Monthly* (formerly the *North Star*), Rochester, New York, March, 1863

WHEN FIRST THE rebel cannon shattered the walls of Sumter and drove away its starving garrison, I predicted that the war then and there inaugurated would not be fought out entirely by white men. Every month's experience during these weary war years has confirmed that opinion. A war undertaken and brazenly carried on for the perpetual enslavement of colored men, calls logically and loudly for colored men to help suppress it. . . .

There are weak and cowardly men in all nations. We have them amongst us. They tell you this is the "white man's war"; that you will be "no better off after than before the war"; that the getting of you into the army is to "sacrifice you on the first opportunity." Believe them not; cowards themselves, they do not wish to have their cowardice shamed by your brave example. Leave them to their timidity, or to whatever motive may hold them back.

I have not thought lightly of the words I am now addressing you. The counsel I give comes of close observation of the great struggle now in progress, and of the deep conviction that this is your hour and mine. In good earnest then, and after the best deliberation, I now for the first time during this war feel at liberty to call and counsel you to arms.

By every consideration which binds you to your enslaved fellow countrymen, and the peace and welfare of your country; by every aspiration which you cherish for the freedom and equality of yourselves and your children; by all the ties of blood and identity which makes us one with the Black men now fighting our battles in Louisiana and in South Carolina, I urge you to fly to arms, and smite with death the power that would bury the government and your liberty in the same hopeless grave. . . .

More than twenty years of unswerving devotion to our common cause may give me some humble claim to be trusted at this momentous crisis. I will not argue. To do so implies hesitation and doubt, and you do not hesitate. You do not doubt. The day dawns; the morning star is bright upon the horizon! The iron gate of our prison stands half open. One gallant rush from the North will fling it wide open, while four millions of our brothers and sisters shall march out to liberty. The chance is now given you to end in a day the bondage of centuries, and to rise in one bound from social degradation to the plane of common equality with all other varieties of men.

Remember Denmark Vesey of Charleston; remember Nathaniel Turner of Southampton; Shields, Green and Copeland, who followed noble John Brown, and fell as glorious martyrs for the cause of the slave. Remember that in a contest with oppression, the Almighty has no attribute which can take sides with the oppressor.

The case is before you. This is our golden opportunity. Let us accept it, and forever wipe out the dark reproaches unsparingly hurled against us by our enemies. Let us win for ourselves the gratitude of our country, and the best blessings of our posterity through all time. The nucleus of this first regiment is now in camp at Readville, a short distance from Boston. I will undertake to forward to Boston all persons adjudged fit to be mustered into the regiment, who shall apply to me at any time within the next two weeks.

"YET ANOTHER NAME": 1865

A plea to continue the
American Anti-Slavery Society

by Frederick Douglass

About The Document:

The black man was no longer a slave, but neither was he free. The very law that emancipated slaves in the District of Columbia—the law that preceded the Emancipation Proclamation—treated black men as outcasts; it included a provision of $100,000 to ship them out of the country and colonize them in a foreign land.

Colonization, as a matter of fact, had always been basic to the "Lincoln Plan"—that and gradual emancipation. Lincoln had originally projected a gradual process of freeing the slaves that would continue at least to the year 1900, to be undertaken by the states with federal assistance for indemnifying the slaveholders. Lincoln always recognized property interests in slaves, and he believed the owners of slaves should be compensated for value surrendered. He also believed that the entire nation, not alone the South, should pay for its complicity in the wrong by sharing in the cost of abolishing it.

As late as a month before his assassination, Lincoln was still considering the idea of voluntary deportation. He had earlier proposed settling freed blacks in the American Isthmus, but the Chiriqui Improvement Company laid claim to that territory, and the plan proved too costly. Lincoln then suggested resettling them in Haiti. (Four hundred Negroes were taken to Haiti at about this time, but most of them died in a smallpox epidemic.) Lincoln had also thought of black colonies in Texas and Florida. In the end, only Haiti and Liberia would agree to accept blacks as American citizens.

An astonishing conversation is recorded between Lincoln

and Benjamin Franklin Butler, a Massachusetts politician and former Union officer, in April 1865. Lincoln had asked Butler to work out the logistics of shipping black men to Haiti or Liberia, and now Butler gave his answer:

> Mr. President, I have gone carefully over my calculations as to the power of the country to export the Negroes of the South and I assure you that, using all your naval vessels and all the merchant marine fleet to cross the seas with safety, it will be impossible for you to transport to the nearest place . . . half as fast as Negro children will be born here.

Clearly the black man was in America to stay. He was not free, though. When Lincoln was assassinated, blacks—who mourned his loss more than most people—were actually to be excluded from the funeral procession by the Washington City Council. Although the Assistant Secretary of War interceded in their behalf, the number of blacks finally permitted in the funeral march was limited—and they walked at the end of the procession. In New York, city officials would not permit any black men to walk in Lincoln's funeral procession.

The Civil War was hardly over when Southern states began enacting "black codes" and "peonage laws" to return the freed slaves to the control of their former masters. Mississippi prohibited black men from owning or even renting land outside of incorporated towns—and left it up to the towns to pass their own laws on the subject. South Carolina and other states forced black men to work as hired farm hands or domestic servants for white employers or to face arrest on charges of vagrancy. By these same laws vagrants were "bound out"; that is, they were rented out as laborers, the employers having the right to pay their fines in lieu of letting them serve jail sentences. Black men were also barred from testifying against white men in court; they could be witnesses in court only if another black man was involved in the case.

Under these conditions, asked Frederick Douglass, what did freedom mean? Their former masters were now their employers. They could not, of course, sell black men. But, said Douglass:

> The employers retained the power to starve them to death, and wherever this power is held, there is the power of slavery.

Far from relaxing, black men felt they must step up their fight for a program that would give them full freedom.

When, at its 32nd Annual Convention in May 1865, William Lloyd Garrison moved to disband the American Anti-

Slavery Society, Douglass led the fight to oppose him. Garrison, president of the Society, felt that the battle had been won and that the Society had served its purpose. Douglass disagreed and, in the address that follows, urged the Society to continue its fight against slavery "under any name."

The Document:

Speech at the 32nd Annual Convention of the
American Anti-Slavery Society, *The Liberator,* May 26, 1865

SEVERAL GENTLEMEN HAVE been so kind as to refer to me in the course of this discussion, and my friend, Mr. May, referred to me as being opposed to the disbandment of this Society at any time during the present year. Having been thus referred to, I wish to put myself properly before the meeting.

I do not wish to appear here in any fault-finding spirit, or as an impugner of the motives of those who believe that the time has come for this Society to disband. I am conscious of no suspicion of the purity and excellence of the motives that animate the President of this Society, and other gentlemen who are in favor of its disbandment. I take this ground; whether this Constitutional Amendment [the Thirteenth] is law or not, whether it has been ratified by a sufficient number of States to make it law or not, I hold that the work of Abolitionists is not done. Even if every State in the Union had ratified that Amendment, while the black man is confronted in the legislation of the South by the word "white," our work as Abolitionists, as I conceive it, is not done. I took the ground, last night, that the South, by unfriendly legislation, could make our liberty, under that provision, a delusion, a mockery, and a snare, and I hold that ground now. What advantage is a provision like this Amendment to the black man, if the Legislature of any State can to-morrow declare that no black man's testimony shall be received in a court of law? Where are we then? Any wretch may enter the house of a black man, and commit any violence he pleases; if he happens to do it only in the presence of black persons, he goes unwhipt of justice. [*Hear, hear.*] And don't tell me that those people down there have become so just and honest all at once that they will not pass laws denying to black men the right to testify against white men in the courts of law. Why, our Northern States have done it. Illinois, Indiana, and Ohio have done it. Here, in the midst of institutions that have gone forth from old Plymouth Rock, the black man has been excluded from testifying in the courts of law; and if the Legislature of every Southern State to-morrow pass a law, declaring that no Negro shall testify in any courts of law, they will not violate that provision of the Constitution. Such laws exist now at the South, and they might exist under this provision of the Constitution, that there shall be neither slavery nor involuntary servitude in any State of the Union. . . .

Slavery is not abolished until the black man has the ballot. While the Legislatures of the South retain the right to pass laws making any discrimination between black and white, slavery still lives there. [*Applause.*] As Edmund Quincy once said,

> While the word "white" is on the statute-book of Massachusetts, Massachusetts is a slave State. While a black man can be turned out of a car in Massachusetts, Massachusetts is a slave State. While a slave can be taken from old Massachusetts, Massachusetts is a slave State.

That is what I heard Edmund Quincy say twenty-three or twenty-four years ago. I never forget such a thing. Now, while the black man can be denied a vote, while the Legislatures of the South can take from him the right to keep and bear arms, as they can—they would not allow a Negro to walk with a cane where I came from, they would not allow five of them to assemble together—the work of the Abolitionists is not finished. Notwithstanding the provision in the Constitution of the United States, that the right to keep and bear arms shall not be abridged, the black man has never had the right either to keep or bear arms; and the Legislatures of the States will still have the power to forbid it, under this Amendment. They can carry on a system of unfriendly legislation, and will they not do it? Have they not got prejudice there to do it with? Think you, that because they are for the moment in the talons and beak of our glorious eagle, instead of the slave being there, as formerly, that they are converted? I hear of the loyalty at Wilmington, the loyalty at South Carolina—what is it worth?

MR. MAY—Not a straw.

MR. DOUGLASS—Not a straw. I thank my friend for admitting it. They are loyal while they see 200,000 sable soldiers, with glistening bayonets, walking in their midst. [*Applause.*] But let the civil power of the South be restored, and the old prejudices and hostility to the Negro will revive. Aye, the very fact that the Negro has been used to defeat this rebellion and strike down the standards of the Confederacy will be a stimulus to all their hatred, to all their malice, and lead them to legislate with greater stringency towards this class than ever before. [*Applause.*] The American people are bound—

bound by their sense of honor (I hope by their sense of honor, at least, by a just sense of honor), to extend the franchise to the Negro; and I was going to say, that the Abolitionists of the American Anti-Slavery Society were bound to "stand still, and see the salvation of God," until that work is done. [*Applause.*] Where shall the black man look for support, my friends, if the American Anti-Slavery Society fails him? [*Hear, hear.*] From whence shall we expect a certain sound from the trumpet of freedom, when the old pioneer, when this Society that has survived mobs, and martyrdom, and the combined efforts of priest-craft and state-craft to suppress it, shall all at once subside, on the mere intimation that the Constitution has been amended, so that neither slavery nor involuntary servitude shall hereafter be allowed in this land? What did the slaveholders of Richmond say to those who objected to arming the Negro, on the ground that it would make him a freeman? Why, they said,

The argument is absurd. We may make these Negroes fight for us; but while we retain the political power of the South, we can keep them in their subordinate positions.

That was the argument; and they were right. They might have employed the Negro to fight for them, and while they retained in their hands power to exclude him from political rights, they could have reduced him to a condition similar to slavery. They would not call it slavery, but some other name. Slavery has been fruitful in giving itself names. It has been called "the peculiar institution," "the social system," and the "impediment," as it was called by the General Conference of the Methodist Episcopal Church. It has been called by a great many names, and it will call itself by yet another name; and you and I and all of us had better wait and see what new form this old monster will assume, in what new skin this old snake will come forth. [*Loud applause.*]

"TO MAINTAIN IN FREEDOM": 1866

In reply to President Andrew Johnson's policies for black people

by Frederick Douglass

About The Document:

The problem of how to deal with the defeated states was left to the new President, Andrew Johnson. President Johnson was from Tennessee, and although he did not like the aristocratic Southern planters who had led the rebellion, he did not like black men either. "Whatever Andrew Johnson may be," Douglass had remarked when Johnson became Vice President, "he certainly is no friend of our race."

A struggle developed between President Johnson and the Northern Republicans who controlled Congress. Johnson favored a lenient attitude toward the Southern states, wanting to readmit them to full participation in the Union quickly and easily. Republicans were intent on treating the South as a conquered territory. Certainly they did not want Southern Democrats ever again to dominate the government and Congress. Partly as a means of retaining control of Congress, the Republicans favored forcing the Southern states to give black men the vote. The votes, they thought, would later help the Republicans and prevent the old ruling class of the South from regaining its power.

Black men, of course, were eager for the franchise. They saw it as their only hope—short of violence—of defending themselves against laws that would keep them in a state not too different from slavery. In 1866 they met in one of many conventions held to examine ways of winning their rights. A committee was appointed to call on President Johnson in the hope that he would recognize the justice of their claims. Frederick Douglass, a member of the committee, reminded the President that Lincoln had given black men guns to help save the Union. Now what they needed was to be given the ballot so that they could save themselves.

President Johnson said that if black men had the vote there would be race war in the South. He was afraid, too, he said, that black men would vote only as their former masters told them to. He proposed that the black man carry out Lincoln's original plan and emigrate to Liberia or Haiti. Johnson would not listen to the arguments of the committee, so Douglass wrote and published a public reply to the President. His reply, which appears below, was widely read and aroused much interest and public discussion.

The Document:

An Open Letter to President Andrew Johnson

MR. PRESIDENT: In consideration of a delicate sense of propriety as well as of your repeated intimations of indisposition to discuss or listen to a reply to the views and opinions you were pleased to express to us in your elaborate speech today, the undersigned would respectfully take this method of replying thereto. Believing as we do that the views and opinions you expressed in that address are entirely unsound and prejudicial to the highest interests of our race as well as to our country as large, we cannot do other than expose the same, and, as far as may be in our power, arrest their dangerous influence. It is not necessary at this time to call attention to more than two or three features of your remarkable address:

1. The first point to which we feel especially bound to take exception is your attempt to found a policy opposed to our enfranchisement, upon the alleged ground of an existing hostility on the part of the former slaves toward the poor white people of the South. We admit the existence of this hostility and hold that it is entirely reciprocal. But you obviously commit an error by drawing an argument from an incident of slavery, and making it a basis for a policy adapted to a state of freedom. The hostility between the whites and blacks of the South is easily explained. It has its root and sap in the relation of slavery, and was incited on both sides by the cunning of the slave masters. Those masters secured their ascendency over both the poor whites and blacks by putting enmity between them.

They divided both to conquer each. There was no earthly reason why the blacks should not hate and dread the poor whites when in a state of slavery, for it was from this class that their masters received their slave catchers, slave drivers, and overseers. They were the men called in upon all occasions by the masters whenever any fiendish outrage was to be committed upon the slave. Now, sir, you cannot but perceive, that the cause of this hatred removed, the effect must be removed also. Slavery is abolished. The cause of this antagonism is removed, and you must see that it is altogether illogical (and "putting new wine into old bottles") to legislate from slaveholding and slave-driving premises for a people whom you have repeatedly declared it your purpose to maintain in freedom.

2. Besides, even if it were true, as you allege, that the hostility of the blacks toward the poor whites must necessarily project itself into a state of freedom, and that this enmity between the two races is even more intense in a state of freedom than in a state of slavery, in the name of heaven, we reverently ask how can you, in view of your professed desire to promote the welfare of the black man, deprive him of all means of defence, and clothe him whom you regard as his enemy in the panoply of political power? Can it be that you recommend a policy which would arm the strong and cast down the defenceless? Can you, by any possibility of reasoning, regard this as just, fair, or wise?

Experience proves that those are most abused who can be abused with the greatest impunity. Men are whipped oftenest who are whipped easiest. Peace between races is not to be secured by degrading one race and exalting another; by giving power to one race and withholding it from another; *but* by maintaining a state of equal justice between all classes. First pure, then peaceable.

3. On the colonization theory you were pleased to broach, very much could be said. It is impossible to suppose, in view of the usefulness of the black man in time of peace as a laborer in the South, and in time of war as a soldier at the North, and the growing respect for his rights among the people and his increasing adaptation to a high state of civilization in his native land, that there can ever come a time when he can be removed from this country without a terrible shock to its prosperity and peace.

Besides, the worst enemy of the nation could not cast upon its fair name a greater infamy than to admit that Negroes could be tolerated among them in a state of the most degrading slavery and oppression, and must be cast away, driven into exile, for no other cause than having been freed from their chains.

FREE TO STARVE: 1865

*A petition protesting
employment conditions*

by the tobacco workers of
Richmond and Manchester, Virginia

About The Document:

The end of slavery left many black people in the South with
no place to go. A Lieutenant Colonel Brinkerhoff wrote in
Mississippi in 1865:

> They are hungry, naked, foot-sore, and homeless and friend-
> less. They are wandering up and down the country, rapidly
> becoming vagabonds and thieves.

Many black men, said Colonel Brinkerhoff, were living on
berries and trying without luck to beg. In most parts of the
South there was little to beg. So completely had the Civil
War exhausted its economy that the outlook for white Southerners was bleak enough. For the black man, conditions were
so serious that white newspapers actually predicted the ex-
tinction of the black race. The Meridian *Clarion* carried an
editorial on August 7, 1865, stating:

> A hundred years is a long time to one man; but to a nation
> or a race, it is but a limited period. Well, in that time the
> negro will be dead. Slavery is abolished now, but in a hun-
> dred years the negro himself will be abolished. Nothing but
> the fiat of the Almighty can stay the hand of his fate . . .

The North freed the slaves; let the North feed them: So
declared the South. In answer, Congress set up the Bureau of
Refugees, Freedmen, and Abandoned Lands, known more
simply as the Freedmen's Bureau. The Bureau was headed by
General Oliver Otis Howard, who announced that its policy
would be to allow black men to choose their own jobs and

employers. They would be paid for their work, and the Bureau would be witness to the contracts they signed with their employers and would see that both parties abided by their terms. The old plantation system of overseers would be abolished. Disputes between white men and black men, or between black men, would be settled by Bureau officers, who would also keep records of marriages where the local courts did not. For those who were without work, the Bureau was authorized to provide food.

The Bureau's most effective accomplishment—it could barely scratch the surface in its short life span of seven years —was in helping to establish 4,000 day, night and industrial schools. Black men responded enthusiastically, enrolling students to the number of a quarter of a million.

One of the Bureau's functions was to settle ex-slaves and poor whites on lands that had been either abandoned during the war or confiscated from Confederate leaders. Many economists agreed with Frederick Douglass' contention that the best hope for the South lay in breaking up the plantations and apportioning them to the freedmen. The slogan "Forty acres and a mule" became the black man's fondest dream— an empty dream, as it turned out. In Mississippi, for example, when the Bureau started operations in the summer of 1865, it held 80,000 acres and 142 town lots—not much land for 400,000 freedmen, but a start. Before the summer was over, however, President Johnson had granted pardons to so many Confederates that less than 35,000 acres remained, and after the general amnesty that followed in the fall, no land at all was left. Some years later Frederick Douglass said that the failure of the Bureau's land reform program had left the black man "on his knees."

On the Sea Islands, off the coasts of Georgia and South Carolina, parcels of land that had been given or sold to the freedmen were suddenly taken away from them and returned to the former owners. The Commander of the U.S. Department of the South, General Saxton, protested to Congress:

> The faith of the government has been pledged these freedmen to maintain them in the possession of their homes, and to break its promise in the hours of its triumph is not becoming to a just government. On some of the islands, the freedmen have established civil governments with constitutions and laws, with all the different departments for schools, churches, building roads, and other improvements.

The attitude of white Southerners toward the Bureau can be judged from the masthead of a Mississippi newspaper:

Breathes there a man with soul so dead,
Who never to himself has said,
G-d d-n the Freedmen's Bureau.

In practice, the Bureau actually worked to black men's disadvantage. The very first regulation it passed said that any
black man who would not take a job and agree to a contract
would be put to work at forced labor and without pay. The
Bureau did suggest a wage scale for black labor, but did not
enforce it.

In Mississippi, during the first nine months of 1866, the
Freedmen's Bureau issued enough food rations to feed 566
persons once a day. Of those 566, about 300 were still in
hospitals or asylums—and after October of that year they
were the only ones to receive aid. Issuing relief rations, the
Bureau felt, would encourage "idleness and independence on
the part of the laborers." Meanwhile, white employers
worked to lower wages. Some said that there would be work
for all if black men would accept one-third of previous
wages; others hoped that, if they held off hiring, the Bureau
would force black men to work for food and clothing only.

One historian has said, "It is difficult to explain the hatred
for the Bureau expressed by so many whites," since the Bureau helped them more than it did the black men.

An example of black working conditions in the South at
this period is shown in the "Complaint of Richmond Tobacco
Workers," presented below. This document is not easy to
read. What the tobacco workers are saying, actually, is that
under slavery they received room, board, and lodging for
doing work their masters got paid for. But in addition, they
were given $9 to $10 per week for the work they did in ex-
cess of the task set.

After emancipation, wages dropped to a point where
blacks could not earn more than $5 per week, and they no
longer received food and lodging. Very clearly, they were
poorer now than they had been as slaves.

The Document:

From J. T. Trowbridge, *A Picture of the Desolated
States; and the Work of Restoration,* 1865–1868,
Hartford, L. Stebbins, 1868

DEAR SIRS WE the Tobacco mechanicks of this city and
Manchester is worked to great disadvantages. In 1858 and

1859 our masters hiered us to the Tobacconist at a prices, ranging from $150 to 180. The Tobacconist furnished us lodging food and clothing. They gave us tasks to performe. all we made over this task they payed us for. We worked faithful and they paid us faithful. They Then gave us $2 to 2.50 cts, and we made double the amount we now make. The Tobacconist held a meeting, and resolved not give more than $1.50 cts per hundred, which is about one days work in a week we may make 600 pounds apece with a stemer. The weeks work then at $1.50 amounts to $9—the stemers wages is from $4 to $4.50 cents which leaves from $5 to 4.50 cents per week about one half what we made when slaves. Now to Rent two small rooms we have to pay from $18 to 20. We see $4.50 cents or $5 will not more then pay Rent say nothing about food clothing medicin Doctor Bills. Tax and Co. They say we will starve through laziness that is not so. But it is true we will starve at our present wages. They say we will steal we can say for ourselves we had rather work for our living. give us a chance. We are Compeled to work for them at low wages and pay high Rents and make $5 per week and sometimes les. And paying $18 or 20 per month Rent. It is impossible to feed ourselves and family—starvation is Cirten unles a change is brought about.

—Tobacco Factory Mechanicks of Richmond and Manchester

"THEY SAID THEY WERE FRIENDS": 1871

*An example of intimidation
against black voters*

by Willis Johnson

About The Document:

Meanwhile, Congress initiated hearings on Reconstruction to find out just what was happening in the South. These hearings, the first large-scale Congressional investigation in our history, made it clear that black men in the South were faring badly. There was, for one thing, widespread terrorism. Two major riots against them, in Memphis and in New Orleans, saw police among the attackers. Of the New Orleans riot, General Philip H. Sheridan—who saw it—said that it was not a riot but "an absolute massacre by the police."

In 1866 the "Radical Republicans" in Congress mustered enough power to seize the initiative from President Johnson and to assume full control over reconstruction policy. The era that followed came to be called "Congressional" or "Radical Reconstruction" (as opposed to Johnson's "Presidential Reconstruction," under which the vanquished South had been permitted to act more or less as it pleased).

Radical Reconstruction launched a new social order. It was virtually a bloodless revolution, so extensive were its reforms; but just as quickly as it came, it disappeared, and most of the reforms with it.

First, Congress passed the Civil Rights Act of 1866, designed to protect freedmen from the black codes. Doubts about its constitutionality led to the Fourteenth Amendment, which incorporated most of the provisions of the new civil rights legislation, guaranteeing equal citizenship rights to the ex-slaves. In addition, the fourteenth Amendment required that all states which had been a part of the Confederacy ratify the Amendment before their seats in Congress would be restored to them.

When Southern states refused to ratify the Amendment, Congress passed the famous Reconstruction Acts. These placed the Southern states under military control until such time as they ratified the Fourteenth Amendment and drew up new state constitutions guaranteeing civil rights to all black men. The Army was to protect every man's right to vote, so that black men would have a voice even in the making of the new constitutions. Later the Fifteenth Amendment gave every citizen the ballot, regardless of race or color.

All this legislation created an interlude of interracial government in the South. With the Union Army protecting their right to vote, many black men entered politics. There were Negro sheriffs, mayors, and judges. Black men sat in state legislatures and in the federal Congress. In South Carolina, they comprised a majority of the state's lower house. Robert Smalls, a former slave who, during the Civil War, had seized the Confederate gunboat *Planter* and delivered it to the Union Navy, served five terms as a Representative from South Carolina. Georgia boasted one black Congressman; Mississippi, two. In all, fourteen black men served in Congress during the Radical Reconstruction period.

For a time, Republicans controlled most of the South. By 1870, free schools were open throughout the South for all children—both black and white. (Practically all the schools were segregated—not more than 1 per cent of the schools in the South were integrated during this period. But there were public schools where before there had been none—for either black or white.) Hospitals, old-age homes, and homes for the deaf and blind were established for the first time. Public buildings, roads, and bridges were built to replace those destroyed during the war. With the support of such Radical Republicans as Representative Thaddeus Stevens and Senator Charles Sumner, it seemed that the fight for full citizenship for black Americans might be won through Congress.

Radical Reconstruction lasted at most ten years, and in some states even less than that. For even as Reconstruction legislation was enacted, white men—all over the South—were working to restore "white supremacy."

The Ku Klux Klan had been founded in 1866 by six former Confederate officers as a social group for war veterans, in Pulaski, Tennessee. The next year, in a move to fight the pro-black legislation of Radical Reconstruction, the group formally reorganized as the "Invisible Empire of the South." Members robed themselves and their horses in white sheets, wore masks and cardboard hats, and in this attire they rode through the countryside at night to terrorize black people exercising their rights as citizens. The Klan's "Dead Books" listed the names of black men and their white allies—primarily, those who supported the Radical Republicans. Black leaders and white schoolteachers figured prominently in these books. Klansmen marched through towns carrying coffins marked with the names of local Republican leaders. A man might wake in the middle of the night to find his house surrounded by robed terrorists, or to find a flaming cross before his house—warning to cease his involvement in behalf of the black man.

The most flagrant means were used to keep black men from voting. White Democrats might simply block the entrance to a polling place and prevent Republicans from entering. Ballot boxes containing Republican votes were stolen. Polling places were opened in secret locations or at unusual times, and only white Democrats were notified; or the polls were manned by hooded riders. A black man who signed a work contract might discover in it a provision nullifying the contract if he should vote Republican. Newspapers in some counties published the names of Republican voters.

The ruthless determination of the whites is illustrated by the campaign plan of the South Carolina Democratic Party before the elections of 1876. Article 12 of the plan stated:

Every Democrat must feel honor-bound to control the vote of at least one Negro, by intimidation, purchase, keeping him away or as each individual may determine, how he may best accomplish it.

Article 16 stated:

Never threaten a man individually. If he deserves to be threatened, the necessities of the times require that he should die. A dead Radical is harmless—a threatened Radical or one driven off by threats from the scene of his operations is often troublesome, sometimes dangerous.

That black men did not take this kind of treatment meekly is illustrated in the story of Willis Johnson, who lived in South Carolina and was an active worker for the Radical Republicans. His story follows, told in his own words before an investigating committee sent by Congress.

The Document:

From *Testimony taken by the Joint Select
Committee to Inquire into the Condition
of Affairs in the Late Insurrectionary
States;* Committee appointed by Congress April 20, 1871.
Hearings held in Columbia, South Carolina, July 3, 1871.

WILLIS JOHNSON (colored) sworn and examined.

Where do you live?

At Leonidas Sim's, in Newberry County.

How long have you lived there?

This year. I lived there one year since I have been free before this year.

What is he?

A planter.

Are you a laborer?

Yes, sir.

Can you read and write?

No, sir.

Were you taught any before you were free?

No, sir.

Have you been taught any since?

No, sir.

Have you been at any time visited by men masked and disguised—Ku-Klux?

Yes, sir.

When?

Last night two weeks ago.

Go on and tell what you saw and what they said and did, telling it in your own way.

When I awoke, as near as I can tell, it was between 12 and 1 o'clock. I heard some one call "Sims." I held still and listened, and heard them walk from his door to my door. I was up-stairs, and I got up and came down-stairs. They walked back to his house again and asked him to put his head out. He did not answer, but his wife asked them who they were. They said they were friends. They walked back to my door again, and just as they got to the door they blew a whistle. Another whistle off a piece answered, and then men seemed to surround the house and all parts of the yard. Then they hallooed, "Open the door." I said nothing. I went to the head of the bed and got my pistol, and leaned forward on the table with the pistol just at the door. They tried with several surges to get the door open, but it did not come open. They went to

1. Diagrams of the lower deck of *Vigilante*, a typical slave ship.

2. Facsimile of unexpurgated Declaration of Independence, in Thomas Jefferson's own handwriting. This is the part deleted from the Declaration by the Founding Fathers.

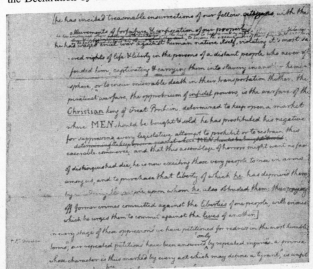

3. Bill of sale for a slave girl. By legal definition, "Negro" meant *slave*; hence the modern trend to avoid the word.

4. Posters like this were common in the days before Emancipation.

RAFFLE

DARK BAY HORSE, "STAR,"

MULATTO GIRL, "SARAH,"

Will be Raffled for

CHANCES AT ONE DOLLAR EACH.

JOSEPH JENNINGS.

5. The "Discovery of Nat Turner," a famous wood engraving. Turner led the first major slave uprising.

6. Daguerreotype of abolitionist leader William Lloyd Garrison. Garrison's *Liberator* never exceeded in circulation 2,700 copies, but the newspaper exerted a powerful influence.

7. Heroine of the Underground Railroad: Harriet Tubman.

8. Sheet music with a message. This cover depicts the escape from slavery of Frederick Douglass when he was twenty.

9. Frederick Douglass as an elder statesman.

10. An unusual photo of John Brown. Five black men participated in Brown's raid at Harpers Ferry.

11. A famous Civil War recruitment poster. The percentage of black men in the Union Army was greater than white, based on population proportion.

MEN OF COLOR, TO ARMS! NOW OR NEVER!

This is our Golden Moment. The Government of the United States calls for every Able-Bodied Colored Man to enter the Army for the **THREE YEARS' SERVICE**, and join in fighting the Battles of Liberty and the Union. A new era is open to us. For generations we have suffered under the horrors of slavery, outrage and wrong; our manhood has been denied, our citizenship blotted out, our souls seared and burned, our spirits cowed and crushed, and the hopes of the future of our race involved in doubts and darkness. But now the whole aspect of our relations to the white race is changed. Now therefore is our most precious moment. Let us Rush to Arms! **Fail Now and Our Race is Doomed** on this the soil of our birth. We must now awake, arise, or be forever fallen. If we value Liberty, if we wish to be free in this land, if we love our country, if we love our families, our children, our homes, we must strike NOW while the Country calls; we must rise up in the dignity of our manhood, and show by our own right arms that we are worthy to be freemen. Our enemies have made the country believe that we are craven cowards, without soul, without manhood, without the spirit of soldiers. Shall we do with this stigma resting on our graves? Shall we leave this inheritance of shame to our children? No! A thousand times No! **We WILL Rise!** The alternative is open to us; let us rather die freemen than live to be slaves. What is life without liberty? We say that we have manhood—now is the time to prove it. A nation or a people that cannot fight may be pitied, but cannot be respected. If we would be regarded Men, if we would forever **SILENCE THE TONGUE OF CALUMNY**, of prejudice and hate, let us rise NOW and fly to arms! We have seen what Valor and Heroism our brothers displayed at **PORT HUDSON** and at **MILLIKEN'S BEND**; though they had just from the galling, poisoning grasp of slavery, they have startled the world by the most exalted heroism. If they have proved themselves heroes, can not we prove ourselves men? **ARE FREEMEN LESS BRAVE THAN SLAVES?** More than a Million White Men have left Comfortable Homes and joined the Armies of the Union to save their Country; annned we brave ours, and swell the hosts of the Union, to save our liberties, vindicate our manhood, and deserve well of our Country?

MEN OF COLOR! All Races of Men—the Englishman, the Irishman, the Frenchman, the German, the American, have been called to assert their claim to freedom and a manly character, by an appeal to the sword. The day that has seen an enslaved race in arms, has, in all history, seen their last trial. We can now see that **OUR LAST OPPORTUNITY HAS COME!** If we are not lower in the scale of humanity than Englishmen, Irishmen, white Americans and other races, we can show it now.

MEN OF COLOR! BROTHERS and FATHERS! WE APPEAL TO YOU! By all your concern for yourselves and your liberties, by all your regard for God and Humanity, by all your desire for Citizenship and Equality before the law, by all your love for the Country, to stop at no subterfuge, listen to nothing that shall deter you from rallying for the Army. Come forward, and at once Enroll your Names for the **Three Years' Service. STRIKE NOW**, and you are henceforth and forever **FREEMEN!**

E. D. Bassett.	John W. Price.	Rev. J. Boulden.	John P. Barr.	Jos. E. Gordon.
Wm. D. Forten.	Augustin Dorsey.	Rev. J. Asher.	Robert Jones.	Samuel Stewart.
Frederick Douglass.	Rev. Stephen Smith.	Rev. J. C. Gibbs.	O. V. Catto.	David B. Bowser.
Wm. Whipper.	N. W. Depee.	Daniel George.	Thos. J. Dorsey, -	Henry Minton.
D. D. Turner.	Dr. J. H. Wilson.	Robert M. Adger.	J. D. Cliff.	Daniel Colley.
Jno. McHummell.	J. W. Cassey.	Henry M. Cropper.	Jacob C. White.	J. C. White, Jr.
A. S. Cassey.	P. J. Armstrong.	Rev. J. B. Reeve.	Morris Hall.	Rev. J. P. Campbell.
A. M. Green.	J. W. Simpson.	Rev. J. A. Williams.	James Needham.	Rev. W. J. Alston.
J. W. Page.	Rev. J. B. Trusty.	Rev. A. L. Stanford.	Rev. Elisha Weaver.	J. P. Johnson.
L. R. Seymour.	J. Morgan Smith.	Thomas J. Bowers.	Elmore Black.	Franklin Turner.
Rev. J. Underdue.	Wm. E. Gipson.	Elijah J. Davis.	Rev. Wm. T. Catto.	Jesse E. Glasgow.

12. A slave pen during Civil War times in Alexandria, Virginia.

13. The New York African Free School, as drawn by a 13-year-old pupil.

14. The Proclamation of Emancipation. The Proclamation freed slaves only in states that were in open rebellion as of January 1, 1863. It did not free slaves in any of the Union states.

15. Ex-slaves wait in front of an office of the Freedmen's Bureau, for job interviews.

16. Ku Klux Klansmen of Reconstruction times. The Klan began as a social club for Civil War veterans.

17. The original leaders of the Niagara Movement, 1905. W. E. B. Du Bois is second from right in second row.

18. Booker T. Washington, the leader who favored compromise.

19. W. E. B. Du Bois, the professor who challenged the leadership of Booker T. Washington.

20. This 1922 march on Washington was organized to protest the lynching of black men. Between 1882 and 1938, the recorded lynchings of black men in the U.S. totaled 3,397.

21. Back-to-Africa leader Marcus Garvey in spectacular Fifth Avenue parade, 1922. His United Negro Improvement Association was the first all-black organization with popular support.

22. Ku Klux Klan parade in Tulsa, Oklahoma, 1923. Note uniformed police marching alongside the klansmen.

23. White men in Detroit started 1942 riot when housing project was opened for blacks. Project was named after Sojourner Truth, noted black abolitionist and women's rights worker of the early 19th century.

24. Attempt to integrate North Little Rock High School in 1957 ended with white students shoving black boys down the school steps.

25. Fifteen-year-old Spottswood Bolling, one of plaintiffs in the 1954 Supreme Court decision that banned segregation in district public schools.

26. Martin Luther King, Jr. celebrates 1956 Montgomery bus boycott victory by riding "up front." One result of boycott was King's rise to national leadership.

27. Historic sit-in at F. W. Woolworth store in Greensboro, North Carolina, 1960. Students, refused service at lunch counter, make use of time to do their homework.

28. To this massive audience at Washington, D. C., in 1963, Martin Luther King, Jr. delivered his famous "I have a dream" speech. Five years later he was assassinated.

29. Mission accomplished, as the 1965 Alabama march which began at Selma ends at Montgomery.

30. Elijah Muhammad, leader of the Black Muslims (the Nation of Islam), addresses annual convention held at Chicago Coliseum.

31. "Summit meeting," 1963. From left to right: John Lewis, then Chairman of SNICK; Whitney Young, Jr. Executive Director, National Urban League; A. Philip Randolph, President of the Brotherhood of Sleeping Car Porters; Martin Luther King, Jr.; James Farmer, then National Director of CORE; Roy Wilkins, Executive Secretary of NAACP.

32. Malcolm X arrives at his home after it was bombed during the night of February 13, 1965.

33. Final leg of James Meredith Freedom March, when Stokely Carmichael's "black power" slogan was first picked up by the nation's press. Left to right: Martin Luther King, Jr., Meredith, Carmichael, and Floyd B. McKissick.

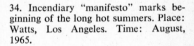

34. Incendiary "manifesto" marks beginning of the long hot summers. Place: Watts, Los Angeles. Time: August, 1965.

35. Members of the Black Panthers of California leave state capitol after protesting laws to restrict the carrying of arms in public.

36. Martin Luther King, Jr. with Floyd B. McKissick, National Director of Congress of Racial Equality (CORE).

37. Militant black power advocate H. Rap Brown, Chairman of Student Non-Violent Coordinating Committee (SNICK).

38. Delegates to the 1967 Newark Black Power Conference. Seated from left to right: Dick Gregory, Ron Karenga, H. Rap Brown, Ralph Featherstone (an officer of SNICK).

GRAND OPENING!

IF YOU DON'T KNOW, LEARN
the
IF YOU KNOW, TEACH
**NEW
REVOLUTIONARY**

**LIBERATION
BOOK STORE**

SAT., sept.9, 11am–7pm

featuring: BOOKS·MAGAZINES
NEWSPAPERS·AND
NEWSLETTERS·ABOUT
THE
**AFRO–AMERICAN LIBERATION
MOVEMENT·LIBERATION
STRUGGLES** in AFRICA, ASIA,
& LATIN AMERICA

421 LENOX·131ST.

LABOR DONATED

39. Poster announces new book store in Harlem. Pamphlets and books on black protest movement can be found here.

POOR PEOPLE'S CAMPAIGN *1968*

SCLC

40. Poor People's Campaign march was officially launched May 2, 1968. It began at the Memphis, Tenn., motel where Martin Luther King, Jr. was assassinated a month before.

41. Demonstrators outside Philadelphia school administration building during ghetto riots of 1967.

10 CENTS

42. Pamphlets depict concerns of ghetto residents. Community control of local schools became a major issue in 1968.

43. The Memphis March—interrupted April 4, 1968, by assassination of **Martin Luther King, Jr.**—is resumed under leadership of Mrs. King. At her right are three of the King children and Harry Belafonte. At her **left** is Ralph Abernathy, who took King's place as head of the Southern **Christian** Leadership Conference.

the wood-pile and got the axe, and struck the front-door some licks, bursted it open, and then went to the back door and burst it open. Nobody had yet come into the house; they had not come in. They said, "Strike a light." Then I dropped down on my knees back of the table, and they struck some matches and threw them in the house, and two of them stepped in the front door, and that brought them within arm's length of me as they stood there. As soon as they did that, I raised my pistol quickly, right up to one's back, and shot, and he fell and hallooed, and the other tried to pull him out. As he pulled him I shot again. As they were pulling, others ran up and pulled him out in the yard, and when the whole party was out in the yard I stepped to the door and shot again, and then jumped to the back door and ran. I got off. I staid away until the next morning; then I came back and tracked them half a mile where they had toted this man and laid him down. I was afraid to go further. Mr. Sims and I were together, and I would not go any further, and he told me to go away; that I ought not to stay there; that he saw the men and saw the wounded man, and was satisfied that he was dead or mortally wounded, and I must leave. Mr. John Calmes, the candidate of the democrats for the legislature, advised me to take a paper and go around the settlement to the white people, stating that I would never vote the radical ticket, and he said he did not think they would interfere with me then. He said that all they had against me was that on election day I took the tickets around among the black people; and he said: "You knocked me out of a good many votes, but you are a good fellow and a good laborer, and we want labor in this country." I told him I would not do that. . . .

"WHOSE LEGISLATURE
IS THIS?": 1868

*A black congressman defends
his right to be seated
in the Georgia House of Representatives*

by Representative Henry M. Turner

About The Document:

In spite of the violence perpetrated against black men by organizations such as the Ku Klux Klan and the White League, black leaders arose who worked hard to educate the freedmen to their political responsibilities and rights as citizens. They went about the country speaking, urging black men to use their rights and to elect men to office who would protect their interests. Such a man was Henry M. Turner.

Turner was educated in the North as a minister and in 1863 was appointed by President Lincoln as chaplain to the First United States black troops. After the war he went to Georgia and worked in the African Methodist Episcopal church. Later, after passage of the Reconstruction Acts, he made thousands of speeches for the Republicans. Of his work, and of its problems, he said in one speech:

> I have been the constant target of Democratic abuse and venom, and white Republican jealousy. The newspapers have teemed with all kinds of slander, accusing me of every crime in the catalogue of villainy; I have even been arrested and tried on some of the wildest charges and most groundless accusations ever distilled from the laboratory of hell.

However, Turner continued, these things had not stopped him:

> I never replied to their slanders nor sought revenge when it hung upon my option; nor did I even bandy words with

the most inveterate and calumnious enemies I have; I invariably let them have their say and do their do.

In 1868 Turner was elected to the Georgia legislature despite white attempts to prevent black voting. The whites had
been effective enough, though, to elect a majority of Democrats—and that majority refused to seat the two Republican
state senators and the twenty-five Republican state representatives on the ground that they were blacks. In the face of
this, after all his efforts and work in the election, Henry M.
Turner could no longer remain silent. On September 3, 1868,
he stood up before the assembled representatives and made a
speech to the men who had refused him his seat. He spoke
from nine o'clock in the morning until three o'clock that afternoon. Parts of the speech follow.

The Document:

Address delivered before the Georgia House
of Representatives, September 3, 1868

MR. SPEAKER: Before proceeding to argue this question upon
its intrinsic merits, I wish the members of this House to understand the position I take. I hold that I am a member of
this body. Therefore, sir, I shall neither fawn or cringe before
any party, nor stoop to beg them for my rights. Some of my
colored fellow members, in the course of their remarks, took
occasion to appeal to the sympathies of Members on the opposite side, and to eulogize their character for magnanimity.
It reminds me very much, sir, of slaves begging under the
lash. I am here to demand my right, and to hurl thunderbolts
at the men who would dare to cross the threshold of my
manhood. There is an old aphorism which says, "Fight the
Devil with fire," and if I should observe the rule in this instance, I wish gentlemen to understand that it is but fighting
them with their own weapon.

The scene presented in this House, today, is one unparal-
leled in the history of the world. From this day, back to the
day when God breathed the breath of life into Adam, no
analogy for it can be found. Never, in the history of the
world, has a man been arraigned before a body clothed with
legislative, judicial or executive functions, charged with the
offence of being of a darker hue than his fellowmen. I know
that questions have been before the Courts of this country,
and of other countries, involving topics not altogether dissim-
ilar to that which is being discussed here today.

But, sir, never in all the history of the great nations of this world—never before—has a man been arraigned, charged with an offence committed by the God of Heaven Himself. Cases may be found where men have been deprived of their rights for crimes and misdemeanors; but it has remained for the State of Georgia, in the very heart of the nineteenth century, to call a man before the bar, and there charge him with an act for which he is no more responsible than for the head which he carries upon his shoulders. The Anglo-Saxon race, sir, is a most surprising one. No man has ever been more deceived in that race than I have been for the last three weeks. I was not aware that there was in the character of that race so much cowardice, or so much pusillanimity. The treachery which has been exhibited in it by gentlemen belonging to that race has shaken my confidence in it more than anything that has come under my observation from the day of my birth. . . .

Whose Legislature is this? . . . They question my right to a seat in this body, to represent the people whose legal votes elected me. This objection, sir, is an unheard of monopoly of power. No analogy can be found for it, except it be the case of a man who should go into my house, take possession of my wife and children, and then tell me to walk out. I stand very much in the position of a criminal before your bar, because I dare to be the exponent of the views of those who sent me here. Or, in other words, we are told that if black men want to speak, they must speak through white trumpets; if black men want their sentiments expressed, they must be adulterated and sent through white messengers, who will quibble, and equivocate, and evade, as rapidly as the pendulum of a clock. If this be not done, then the black men have committed an outrage, and their Representatives must be denied the right to represent their constituents.

The great question, sir, is this: Am I a man? If I am such, I claim the rights of a man. . . .

Postscript To The Document:

Henry M. Turner and the other twenty-four black representatives and two black senators were admitted in the following year's session of the legislature, after massive protests were made to Washington. But in 1869 the Democrats of Georgia were back in complete power. By 1876 Radical Reconstruction in the South was dead. Only in three Southern states—South Carolina, Florida, and Louisiana—did Reconstruction governments remain. Reconstruction died there, too, when in that year's disputed Presidential election those states threw their electoral votes to Rutherford B. Hayes in return for his promise to withdraw federal troops. This was the Hayes-Tilden Compromise, or the Compromise of 1877. When neither Northern nor Southern business interests, needing peace and stability for their markets and cheap labor for their factories, could tolerate the unrest and strife in the South, they made a deal. Translated into political terms, their compromise gave the Presidency to the Republicans and left the Democrats with an unchallenged control of the South that has lasted until today.

Even such a man as Henry M. Turner had to admit defeat, and before his death at the turn of the century he was to declare that black men had no place in the United States. They would be better off, he said, in Africa. He made the statement in 1895:

> I believe that the Negroid race has been free long enough now to begin to think for himself and plan for better conditions than he can lay claim to in this country or ever will. *There is no manhood future in the United States for the Negro.* He may eke out an existence for generations to come, but he can never be a *man*—full, symmetrical and undwarfed.

THE GREAT EXODUS: 1879

The first mass flight
of black men from the South

by a Congressional committee witness

About The Document:

When President Hayes made a good-will tour of the South in the year 1877 and told a group of black men at Atlanta that their rights and interests were safer in the hands of Southern white men than in the hands of the federal government, there could be no doubt about the defeat of Radical Reconstruction. As white men regained control of Southern legislatures, they began to pass "Jim Crow" laws that put an end to the gains achieved during the period when black men had played a part in the political life of the South.

Southern legislatures imposed poll taxes—a special tax that had to be paid in order to vote—and "literacy tests" that required a voter to prove that he could read and *understand* a particular section of the Constitution. Since the test was given by a white man, it is not hard to see that a black man might have difficulty in proving that he "understood" the clause. "Grandfather" clauses stipulated that no one who was entitled to vote before 1867 (when Congress gave the vote to the freedmen), or who was a direct descendant of such a person, need take the test. In effect, this exempted the white man from the literacy test. Through violence and fraud at first, and then through the Jim Crow laws, Louisiana, for example, was able to reduce the number of black men eligible to vote from 130,334 in 1896, to 5,320 in 1900, to 1,342 in 1904.

A system of peonage developed, in which black men were held in virtual slavery working to pay debts that mounted viciously and without end; the debts were even passed from generation to generation. Convicts were leased out to work for private planters on chain gangs. This saved the state the cost of caring for its prisoners; it gave planters the cheapest possible labor; and it gave sheriffs and courts an incentive to arrest and sentence as many black men as possible.

Against this system, black men worked to acquire land, to educate their children, to find a way to live as decent human beings. Many came to the conclusion that there was no hope for them in the South, and very quietly they began to organize to leave.

The first movement of the Great Exodus came in 1879, when more than fifty thousand people left Louisiana. Most of them migrated to Kansas, or to Oklahoma. They were welcomed at first, but as their numbers began to swell, many towns in those states grew alarmed and tried to halt the influx. At some towns along the Mississippi River, boatloads of black men were refused permission to land. Other towns passed ordinances forbidding anyone to enter without money in his pocket. But still, black men did better there than they had at home. They took care of themselves and, as time passed, managed to acquire land and businesses. At Foley, Oklahoma, for example, they established an entirely black community with its own town government, businesses, schools, and churches.

Though the Exodus of 1879 was the largest and most dramatic single outflow of blacks from the South, it established a trend and pattern that still continues. In 1881 there was a major migration out of South Carolina; in 1889 there was one from Alabama. Continually, since that time, black Americans have left the South for the West or for the industrial cities of the North, to find opportunities that have been at least somewhat better than in the South.

The South, of course, was unhappy at the prospect of losing its cheap labor supply. The same tactics used to deprive the black man of his vote now were used to force him to stay. This attempt was less successful, however; increasing numbers of black Americans simply decided that if they could do nothing else, they could leave—and in spite of all obstacles, they did so. The "problem" attracted the attention of Congress, which began investigations to find out who was behind the movement. A sample of what Congress found is contained in the testimony of Henry Adams, one of the men who organized the exodus from Louisiana.

The Document:

From Senate Report 693, 46th Congress,
Second Session, Part 2

QUESTION: Now tell us, Mr. Adams, what, if anything, you know about the exodus of the colored people from the Southern to the Northern and Western States; and be good enough to tell us in the first place what you know about the organization of any committee or society among the colored people themselves for the purpose of bettering their condition, and why it was organized. Just give us the history of that as you understand it.

ANSWER: Well, in 1870, I believe it was, or about that year, after I had left the Army—I went into the Army in 1866 and came out the last of 1869. . . . a parcel of us got together and said that we would organize ourselves into a committee and look into affairs and see the true condition of our race, to see whether it was possible we could stay under a people who had held us under bondage or not. Then we did so and organized a committee.

What did you call your committee? We just called it a committee, that is all we called it, and it remained so; it increased to a large extent, and remained so. Some of the members of the committee was ordered by the committee to go into every State in the South where we had been slaves there, and post one another from time to time about the true condition of our race. . . .

Was the object of that committee at that time to remove your people from the South, or what was it? O, no sir; not then; we just wanted to see whether there was any State in the South where we could get a living and enjoy our rights.

The object, then, was to find the best places in the South where you could live? Yes, sir; where we could live and get along well there and to investigate our affairs—not to go nowhere till we saw whether we could stand it.

How were the expenses of these men paid? Every one paid his own expenses, except the one we sent to Louisiana and Mississippi. We took money out of our pockets and sent him, and said to him you must now go to work. You can't find out anything till you get amongst them. You can talk as much as you please, but you have got to go right into the field and work with them and sleep with them to know all about them.

Have you any idea how many of your people went out in that way?

At one time there was five hundred of us.

Do you mean five hundred belonging to your committee?
Yes, sir.

*I want to know how many traveled in that way to get at
the condition of your people in the Southern States?* I think
about one hundred or one hundred and fifty went from one
place or another.

*And they went from one place to another, working their
way and paying their expenses and reporting to the common
center at Shreveport, do you mean?* Yes, sir.

*What was the character of the information that they gave
you?*
Well, the character of the information they brought to us
was very bad, sir. . . .

*Do you remember any of these reports that you got from
members of the committee?* Yes, sir; they said in several
parts where they was that the land rent was still higher there
in that part of the country than it was where we first organized it, and the people was still being whipped, some of them
by the old owners, the men that had owned them as slaves,
and some of them was being cheated out of their crops just
the same as they was there.

*Was anything said about their personal and political rights
in these reports, as to how they were treated about these?*
Yes, some of them stated that in some parts of the country
where they voted they would be shot. Some of them stated
that if they voted the Democratic ticket they would not be
injured.

*But that they would be shot, or might be shot, if they
voted the Republican ticket?* Yes, sir. . . .

*I am speaking now of the period from 1870 to 1874, and
you have given us the general character of the reports that
you got from the South; what did you do in 1874?* Well,
along in August sometime in 1874, after the white league
sprung up, they organized and said this is a white man's government, and the colored men should not hold any offices;
they were no good but to work in the fields and take what
they would give them and vote the Democratic ticket. That's
what they would make public speeches and say to us, and we
would hear them. We then organized an organization called
the colonization council. . . .

Now, what was the purpose of this colonization council?
Well, it was to better our condition.

In what way did you propose to do it? We first organized
and adopted a plan to appeal to the President of the United
States and to Congress to help us out of our distress, or protect us in our rights and privileges.

Well, what other plan had you? And if that failed our idea
was then to ask them to set apart a territory in the United
States for us, somewhere where we could go and live with
our families. . . .

You preferred to go off somewhere by yourselves? Yes.

Well, what then? If that failed, our other object was to ask
for an appropriation of money to ship us all to Liberia, in
Africa; somewhere where we could live in peace and quiet.

Well, and what after that? When that failed then our idea
was to appeal to other governments outside of the United
States to help us to get away from the United States and go
there and live under their flag. . . .

*Now, let us understand, before we go any further, the kind
of people who composed that association. The committee, as
I understand you, was composed entirely of laboring people?*
Yes, sir.

*Did it include any politicians of either color, white or
black?*

No politicianers didn't belong to it, because we didn't allow
them to know nothing about it . . . we didn't trust any of
them . . .

*Now, when you organized the council what kind of people
were taken into it?* Nobody but laboring men. . . . After the
appeal in 1874, we appealed when the time got so hot down
there they stopped our churches from having meetings after
nine o'clock at night. They stopped them from sitting up and
singing over the dead, and so forth, right in the little town
where we lived, in Shreveport. I know that to be a fact; and
after they did all this, and we saw it was getting so warm—
killing our people all over the whole country—there was several of them killed right down in our parish—we appealed
. . . We had much rather staid there if we could have had
our rights . . . In 1877 we lost all hopes . . . we found ourselves in such condition that we looked around and we seed
that there was no way on earth, it seemed, that we could better our condition there, and we discussed that thoroughly in
our organization along in May. We said that the whole South
—every State in the South—had got into the hands of the
very men that held us slaves—from one thing to another and
we thought that the men that held us slaves was holding the
reins of government over our heads in every respect almost,
even the constable up to the governor. We felt we had almost
as well be slaves under these men. In regard to the whole
matter that was discussed, it came up in every council. Then
we said there was no hope for us and we had better go. . . .

EARLY ANTI-LYNCHING CRUSADES: 1896-1901

An act of self-defense;
debunking a myth;
and a fast of protest

About The Documents:

With the black man deprived of his right to testify in court, he was an open target for a growing wave of violence. In the decade 1890–1899 an average of two black men a week were lynched in the United States. From 1882 (the first year for which records are available) to 1938 the number of black lynchings totaled 3,397. The number lynched outside the former Confederate states was 366, and of these 185 occurred in the border states of Maryland, Kentucky, West Virginia, and Missouri.

Vigilante action, with its inevitable corollary of lynch law, has been throughout history the stamp of the frontier. But in the South it survived and grew steadily even after the frontiers were closed. Writes W. J. Cash in *The Mind of the South:*

> Vigilante action grew so steadily that already long before the Civil War and long before hatred of the black man had begun to play any direct part in the pattern (of more than three hundred persons said to have been hanged by mobs between 1840 and 1860, less than ten per cent were Negroes) the South had become peculiarly the home of lynching.

After the 1880's, the methods of lynching changed. In the early frontier times of the colonies, tarring and feathering and whipping were the usual patterns of lynch law. Later, when it involved outright killing, vigilante groups nevertheless dispatched their victims quickly, by hanging or shooting. It was different when the Ku Klux Klan and the White Leaguers went after the black man. The executions by hanging and shooting were abandoned in favor of burning, often roasting over slow fires. Preliminary torture and mutilation became another feature of lynching. So did the tendency to treat lynchings as festive, frolicsome occasions. A lynching sometimes lasted for days; local white newspapers announced the event, and white families drove hundreds of miles to be on hand at the consummation. Photographs in the Library of Congress record the picnic atmosphere of these lynchings. Men, women, and children are shown waving happily at the photographer; others hold a soda pop in one hand and with the other point at the charred remains of the victim.

As the violence spread, blacks circulated petitions, sent delegations to Washington, and wrote letters to force the nation into an awareness of what was being done to them. An example of this type of action is the *Fast of Protest Appeal* from the National Afro-American Council, reproduced below.

On many occasions they fought back against the violence, and when they did black newspapers reported and encouraged the action. A short article from the Cleveland *Press Gazette* of May 30, 1896, about one black man who refused to submit quietly, is also reprinted below.

White Southerners justified lynching on the ground that it was the only way to cope with a "certain class of crimes." By that, of course, they meant sex crimes committed by black men against white women. In the third document appearing below, Mrs. Ida Wells-Barnett disputes the charge. She points out that only a fraction of black men lynched were ever accused of sex crimes.

The Documents:

An appeal from the National
Afro-American Council to
set aside a day of fasting as
a protest against lynching.
Newspaper article in
New York *Tribune*, May 4, 1899.

THE NATIONAL AFRO-AMERICAN Council of the United States has issued a proclamation calling upon the colored people of this country to set apart Friday, June 2, as a day of fasting and prayer, and has called upon all colored ministers to devote the sunrise hour of that following Sunday, June 4, to special exercises in order that "God, the Father of Mercies, may take our deplorable case in His own hands, and that if vengeance is to be meted out let God himself repay." It sets forth the "indescribable barbarous treatment" of the Negro —refers to role in wars, denounces lynchings "in the most strenuous language." It says, in part:

"We pay out millions of dollars yearly to ride in 'jim-crow' cars, some of them scarcely fit for cattle, yet we are compelled to pay as much as those who have every accommodation and convenience. Indians, Chinamen and every other race can travel as they please. Such unjust laws make the railroad highway robbers. In some sections of the country we may ride for thousands of miles and are denied a cup of tea or coffee because no provision is made, or allowed to be made, to accommodate us with something to eat, while we are ready to pay for it. Waiving hundreds of inconveniences, we are practically outlawed by many States, and also by the general Government in its endorsement of silence and indifference.

"We are dragged before the courts by thousands and sentenced to every form of punishment, and even executed, without the privilege of having a jury composed in whole or in part of members of our own race, while simple justice should guarantee us judges and juries who could adjudicate our cases free from the bias, caste and prejudice incident to the same in this country.

"In many sections we are arrested and lodged in jails on the most frivolous suspicion of being the perpetrators of most hideous and revolting crimes, and, regardless of established guilt, mobs are formed of ignorant, vicious, whiskey-besotted men, at whose approach the keys of these jails and prisons are surrendered and the suspicioned party is ruthlessly forced from the custody of the law and tortured, hanged, shot, butchered, dismembered and burned in the most fiendish manner. Nor is this fate limited to a few unfortunate and monstrous wretches, which we, like other people, doubtless have among our race, but instances have multiplied into hundreds, thousands and tens of thousands. And, horrible to conceive, these mobs no longer conceal themselves in the shadows of the night, but in open day plunder the prisons for the victims of their lawless vengeance and defiantly walk into courts and rob the sheriffs and judges of their prisoners and butcher them without even time to commune in prayer with God, a privilege that no barbaric age has ever denied a soul about to be ushered into the presence of his Maker.

"Owing to these and many other calamitous conditions which time forbids a recital of, unhistoric, unprecedented and dreadfully abnormal, we are impelled by a sense of duty and the instincts of our moral nature to appeal to the Afro-Americans in the United States to put forth some endeavors by ceasing to be longer silent, and to appeal to some judiciary for help and relief. If earth affords none for our helpless and defenceless race, we must appeal to the bar of Infinite Power and Justice, whose Judge holds the destinies of nations in His hands."

Newspaper article in the
Cleveland *Press Gazette,*
May 30, 1896

JACKSONVILLE, FLA.—Jack Trice fought fifteen white men at 3 A.M., on the 12th, killing James Hughes and Edward Sanchez, fatally wounding Henry Daniels and dangerously wounding Albert Bruffum. The battle occurred at Trice's humble home near Palmetto, a town six miles south of here, to prevent his 14-year-old son being "regulated" (brutally whipped and perhaps killed) by the whites. On the afternoon of May 11, Trice's son and the son of Town Marshal Hughes, of Palmetto, fought, the white boy being badly beaten. Marshal Hughes was greatly enraged and he and 14 other white men went to Trice's house to "regulate" his little boy. The whites demanded that the boy be sent out. Trice refused and they began firing. Trice returned the fire, his first bullet killing Marshal Hughes. Edward Sanchez tried to burn the house, but was shot through the brain by Trice. Then the whites tried to batter in the door with a log, which resulted in Henry Daniels getting a bullet in the stomach that will kill him. The "regulators" then ran. A final bullet from Trice's deadly rifle struck Albert Bruffum in the back. The whites secured re-enforcements and returned to Trice's home at sunrise, vowing to burn father and son at the stake; but the intended victims had fled. Only Trice's aged mother was in the house. The old lady was driven out like a dog and the house burned. Posses with bloodhounds are chasing Trice and his boy, and they will be lynched if caught. It is sincerely hoped that both will escape.

Abstract from an article in
the New York *Independent,*
May 16, 1901, titled "Lynching
and the Excuse for It"
by Mrs. Ida Wells-Barnett

. . . . IF THE SOUTHERN citizens lynch Negroes because "that is the only successful method of dealing with a certain class of crimes," then that class of crimes should be shown unmistakably by this record. Now consider the record.

It would be supposed that the record would show that all, or nearly all, lynchings were caused by outrageous assaults upon women; certainly that this particular offense would out-number all other causes for putting human beings to death without a trial by jury and the other safeguards of our Constitution and laws.

But the record makes no such disclosure. Instead, it shows that five women have been lynched, put to death with unspeakable savagery during the past five years. They certainly were not under the ban of the outlawing crime. It shows that men, not a few, but hundreds, have been lynched for misdemeanors, while others have suffered death for no offense known to the law, the causes assigned being "mistaken identity," "insult," "bad reputation," "unpopularity," "violating contract," "running quarantine," "giving evidence," "frightening children by shooting at rabbits," etc. Then, strangest of all, the record shows that the sum total of lynchings for these offenses—not crimes—and for the alleged offenses which are only misdemeanors, greatly exceeds the lynchings for the very crime universally declared to be the cause of lynching. . . . Instead of being the sole cause of lynching, the crime upon which lynchers build their defense furnishes the least victims for the mob. In 1896 less than thirty-nine per cent of the Negroes lynched were charged with this crime; in 1897, less than eighteen per cent; in 1898, less than sixteen per cent; in 1899, less than fourteen per cent; and in 1900, less than fifteen per cent, were so charged.

THE "ATLANTA COMPROMISE": 1895

*Booker T. Washington draws
the parable of the open hand and the
separate but equal fingers*

by Booker T. Washington

About The Document:

Almost everyone has heard or read of Booker T. Washington, the boy who was born a slave and became a man so famous in his own time that the New York *World* called him the "Negro Moses."

The son of a black slave woman and a white slave-owning father, Booker T. Washington went to work in a Virginia salt mine when he was nine years old. Later he managed to attend Hampton Institute in Virginia, where he earned his way as a painter. Still in his twenties, he opened a school in an old church building and shanty in Alabama. There he and his students set about building a school for themselves, with their own labor and with funds raised by their own efforts. In that way, Tuskegee Institute was founded, in 1881.

Washington believed in "thrift, patience and industrial training for the masses," and these principles Tuskegee Institute taught. The Institute became a model. Its spirit of "practical education for community usefulness" spread and attracted considerable support.

Washington taught that it was unwise for black people to press too hard for social, educational, and political equality. He said:

When your head is in the lion's mouth, use your hand to pet him.

This attitude required him to "walk the razor's edge between black pride and white prejudice," and it has been said in defense of Washington's admonitions that to follow them at least made life bearable under the conditions that existed in the South after the failure of Reconstruction.

In 1895, Washington delivered his most famous speech outlining his beliefs, at the Cotton States Exposition at Atlanta, Georgia. It appears below. The Exposition had been organized by Southern businessmen to improve relations with the North and to attract business and trade to the South. Washington's speech, delivered in the Exposition Building, attracted wide attention; to white Americans it made him the spokesman for the entire black race. Booker T. Washington seemed to be telling the black people that they were second-class citizens and might as well learn to make the best of it. That attitude brought him the support of Northern white philanthropists—the millionaire Andrew Carnegie offered to underwrite any project Washington proposed. The nation's leaders in government, education, and industry extolled Washington's virtues. Such support made it possible for Tuskegee Institute to grow and for others like it to be founded in the South, where black men and women supported themselves in schools and learned agricultural and industrial trades. White support of Washington, as well as considerable respect from people of his own race for his accomplishments in education, made him the most powerful black man of his time.

The Document:

Address delivered at the opening of the
Cotton States Exposition, Atlanta, Georgia,
September 18, 1895. From the autobiography
of Booker T. Washington, *Up from Slavery*, 1901

MR. PRESIDENT and Gentlemen of the Board of Directors and Citizens: One-third of the population of the South is of the Negro race. No enterprise seeking the material, civil, or moral welfare of this section can disregard this element of our population and reach the highest success. I but convey to you, Mr. President and Directors, the sentiment of the masses of my race when I say that in no way have the value and manhood of the American Negro been more fittingly and generously recognized than by the managers of this magnificent Exposition at every stage of its progress. It is a recognition that will do more to cement the friendship of the two races than any occurrence since the dawn of our freedom.

Not only this, but the opportunity here afforded will awaken among us a new era of industrial progress. Ignorant and inexperienced, it is not strange that in the first years of our new life we began at the top instead of at the bottom; that a seat in Congress or the state legislature was more sought than real estate or industrial skill; that the political convention of stump speaking had more attractions than starting a dairy farm or truck garden.

A ship lost at sea for many days suddenly sighted a friendly vessel. From the mast of the unfortunate vessel was seen a signal, "Water, water; we die of thirst!" The answer from the friendly vessel at once came back, "Cast down your bucket where you are." A second time the signal, "Water, water; send us water!" ran up from the distressed vessel, and was answered, "Cast down your bucket where you are." And a third and fourth signal for water was answered, "Cast down your bucket where you are." The captain of the distressed vessel, at last heeding the injunction, cast down his bucket, and it came up full of fresh, sparkling water from the mouth of the Amazon River. To those of my race who depend on bettering their condition in a foreign land or who underestimate the importance of cultivating friendly relations with the Southern white man, who is their next-door neighbour, I would say: "Cast down your bucket where you are"—cast it down in making friends in every manly way of the people of all races by whom we are surrounded.

Cast it down in agriculture, mechanics, in commerce, in domestic service, and in the professions. And in this connection it is well to bear in mind that whatever other sins the South may be called to bear, when it comes to business, pure and simple, it is in the South that the Negro is given a man's chance in the commercial world, and in nothing is this Exposition more eloquent than in emphasizing this chance. Our greatest danger is that in the great leap from slavery to freedom we may overlook the fact that the masses of us are to live by the productions of our hands, and fail to keep in mind that we shall prosper in proportion as we learn to dignify and glorify common labour and put brains and skill into the common occupations of life; shall prosper in proportion as we learn to draw the line between the superficial and the substantial, the ornamental gewgaws of life and the useful. No race can prosper till it learns that there is as much dignity in tilling a field as in writing a poem. It is at the bottom of life we must begin, and not at the top. Nor should we permit our grievances to overshadow our opportunities.

To those of the white race who look to the incoming of those of foreign birth and strange tongue and habits for the prosperity of the South, were I permitted I would repeat what I say to my own race, "Cast down your bucket where you are." Cast it down among the eight millions of Negroes whose habits you know, whose fidelity and love you have tested in days when to have proved treacherous meant the ruin of your firesides. Cast down your bucket among these people who have, without strikes and labour wars, tilled your fields, cleared your forests, builded your railroads and cities, and brought forth treasures from the bowels of the earth, and helped make possible this magnificent representation of the progress of the South. Casting down your bucket among my people, helping and encouraging them as you are doing on these grounds, and to education of head, hand, and heart, you will find that they will buy your surplus land, make blossom the waste places in your fields, and run your factories. While doing this, you can be sure in the future, as in the past, that you and your families will be surrounded by the most patient, faithful, law-abiding, and unresentful people that the world has seen. As we have proved our loyalty to you in the past, in nursing your children, watching by the sick-bed of your mothers and fathers, and often following them with tear-dimmed eyes to their graves, so in the future, in our humble way, we shall stand by you with a devotion that no foreigner can approach, ready to lay down our lives, if need be, in defence of yours, interlacing our industrial, commercial, civil, and religious life with yours in a way that shall make the interests of both races one. In all things that are purely social [the speaker flung his hand aloft with the fingers held wide apart] we can be as separate as the fingers, yet [the speaker balled his fingers into a fist] one as the hand in all things essential to mutual progress.

There is no defence or security for any of us except in the highest intelligence and development of all. . . .

The wisest among my race understand that the agitation of questions of social equality is the extremest folly, and that progress in the enjoyment of all privileges that will come to us must be the result of severe and constant struggle rather than of artificial forcing. No race that has anything to contribute to the markets of the world is long in any degree ostracized. It is important and right that all privileges of the law be ours, but it is vastly more important that we be prepared for the exercises of these privileges. The opportunity to earn a dollar in a factory just now is worth infinitely more than the opportunity to spend a dollar in an opera-house.

In conclusion, may I repeat that nothing in thirty years has given us more hope and encouragement, and drawn us so near to you of the white race, as this opportunity offered by the Exposition; and here bending, as it were, over the altar that represents the results of the struggles of your race and

mine, both starting practically empty-handed three decades
ago, I pledge that in your effort to work out the great and
intricate problem which God has laid at the doors of the
South, you shall have at all times the patient, sympathetic
help of my race; only let this be constantly in mind, that,
while from representations in these buildings of the product
of field, of forest, of mine, of factory, letters, and art, much
good will come, yet far above and beyond material benefits
will be that higher good, that, let us pray God, will come, in
a blotting out of sectional differences and racial animosities
and suspicions, in a determination to administer absolute justice, in a willing obedience among all classes to the mandates
of law. This, this, coupled with our material prosperity, will
bring into our beloved South a new heaven and a new earth.

Postscript To The Document:

There were black men who did not agree with Washington:
men who refused to give up their fight for complete equality.
Industrial education was fine, they felt, but it was not the
whole story. W. E. B. Du Bois said: "We shall hardly induce
black men to believe that if their stomachs be full, it matters
little about their brains." Such men felt that Washington
harmed their race by belittling the importance of social and
political equality.

Such men were especially concerned when Washington
began issuing optimistic reports to Europeans about the black
man's situation in the U. S. An example of their concern is
the following reply to those reports signed by twenty-three
black leaders of the National Negro Committee:

To the People of Great Britain and Europe—
    The undersigned Negro-Americans have heard, with great
regret, the recent attempt to assure England and Europe that
their condition in America is satisfactory. They sincerely
wish that such were the case, but it becomes their plain duty
to say that if Mr. Booker T. Washington, or any other person, is giving the impression abroad that the Negro problem
in America is in process of satisfactory solution, he is giving
an impression which is not true.
    We say this without personal bitterness toward Mr. Wash-
ington. He is a distinguished American and has a perfect
right to his opinions. But we are compelled to point out that
Mr. Washington's large financial responsibilities have made
him dependent on the rich charitable public and that, for this
reason, he has for years been compelled to tell, not the whole
truth, but that part of it which certain powerful interests in
America wish to appear as the whole truth.

Our people were emancipated in a whirl of passion, and then left naked to the mercies of their enraged and impoverished ex-master. As our sole means of defence we were given the ballot, and we used it so as to secure the real fruits of the War. Without it we would have returned to slavery; with it we struggled toward freedom. No sooner, however, had we rid ourselves of nearly two-thirds of our illiteracy, and accumulated $600,000,000 worth of property in a generation, than this ballot, which had become increasingly necessary to the defence of our civil and property rights, was taken from us by force and fraud.

Today in eight states where the bulk of the Negroes live, Black men of property and university training can be, and usually are, by law denied the ballot while the most ignorant White man votes. This attempt to put the personal and property rights of the best of the Blacks at the absolute political mercy of the worst of the Whites is spreading each day. . . .

Against this dominant tendency strong and brave Americans, White and Black, are fighting, but they need, and need sadly, the moral support of England and of Europe in this crusade for the recognition of manhood, despite adventitious differences of race, and it is like a blow in the face to have one, who himself suffers daily insult and humiliation in America, give the impression that all is well. It is one thing to be optimistic, self-forgetful and forgiving, but it is quite a different thing, consciously or unconsciously, to misrepresent the truth.

SECTION III

Let No Man Hold Back

"They will be severely criticized and even insulted—but let no man hold back on this account. We shall be fighting a double battle against slavery in the South and prejudice and proscription in the North . . ."

Frederick Douglass

BOOKER T. WASHINGTON CHALLENGED: 1903

W. E. B. Du Bois launches
a new protest movement

by W. E. B. Du Bois

About The Document:

"Jim Crow" was a character in a song of the 1820's, a stereotype of the black man who "turns about and turns about and does jis so." From then on Jim Crow became a common term for the black man, as common as the white prejudices that it connoted, and by the 1880's it had come to refer to any law, ordinance or custom that kept black men apart from white men.

The South's zeal to protect itself from the black men knew no bounds. White mill workers were protected by law from having to look out the same window as black men. Oklahoma's white citizens could feel sure no black voice spoke into their public telephones, as separate phone booths were provided for the black men. Florida kept its white and black textbooks in separate and presumably equal warehouses. Georgia witnesses swore to tell the truth on separate Bibles.

One year after Booker T. Washington's Atlanta Compromise speech, the Supreme Court upheld Jim Crow laws as constitutional. In the famous case of *Plessy v. Ferguson*, the Court decided eight to one that the state of Louisiana was within its rights to arrest Homer Plessy, a black man, for attempting to occupy a railroad car reserved for whites. The decision effectively removed whatever hope the black man had for fighting Jim Crow in the courts.

For a time this decision, coupled with Booker T. Washington's indifference, appeared to stifle the black man's fight for social equality.

It was inevitable, however, that a more militant leadership would emerge. It did—in the North, with the founding by William Monroe Trotter of the Boston *Guardian;* and in the South, in Atlanta, with the publication by W. E. B. Du Bois of *The Souls of Black Folk,* a book that had a greater impact

153

on the black community than any book since *Uncle Tom's Cabin.*

William Monroe Trotter launched the *Guardian* in 1901, with editorial offices in the same building that had housed William Lloyd Garrison's *The Liberator*. The paper's opening editorial attacked Booker T. Washington as a traitor to his race. Du Bois' *The Souls of Black Folk* was a collection of essays and articles, passionately poetical, that he had written as a professor of sociology. The book was published in 1903, when Du Bois was thirty-five. It heralded a new approach of nonviolent activism, and it effectively divided black men in America into two camps: one led by Booker T. Washington and the other by Du Bois and Trotter.

W. E. B. Du Bois was born in Great Barrington, Massachusetts, three years after the close of the Civil War. His ancestors were African, French, and Dutch, but, "thank God," he is said to have exclaimed, "no Anglo-Saxon!"

He entered Fisk University in Nashville as a scholarship student at sixteen. It was his first visit to the South. He began to write articles, then became editor of the *Fisk Herald;* in the summers he taught at a school for sharecroppers in the hills of Tennessee. After completing his studies at Fisk in 1880, he entered the graduate school of Harvard University. Among his teachers there were George Santayana, William James, and Albert Bushnell Hart. There he also came to know Oliver Wendell Holmes and James Russell Lowell. Amid this highly intellectual, protected, ivory-tower environment Du Bois came to believe that ignorance alone caused prejudice, and that prejudice against the black man could be dispelled by "systematic investigation"—by scientific truth and knowledge.

Du Bois studied for two years at the University of Berlin, then returned to Harvard, where, in 1895, he became its first black man to receive a Ph.D. His doctoral dissertation, *The Suppression of the African Slave Trade,* was so well received for its scholarship that it was published as the first volume of the Harvard Historical Studies. For a brief period he taught at Wilberforce University in Ohio, and then he joined the faculty of the University of Pennsylvania. It was here that he made the pioneer sociological study (sociology was then in its infancy) *The Philadelphia Negro: A Social Study,* published in 1899. It is commonly believed that Du Bois was a professor of the University of Pennsylvania. Certainly his Ph.D from Harvard and his scholarly historical studies qualified him for a high university position. The fact is that Du Bois' position at Pennsylvania was never higher than that of assistant instructor. He was at no time introduced to other members of the faculty, and he was never given a teaching assignment. His university work was confined to research.

Du Bois' field investigations were altering his own thinking on prejudice. By the time he accepted an invitation to teach sociology at Atlanta University, he was expressing the conviction that "truth alone is not enough," that it does not "encourage [or] help social reform." There was, Du Bois recalled later, an average of a black man lynched every three and a half days while he was at Atlanta; he could no longer remain "a calm, cool, detached scientist."

Du Bois introduced his most famous essay, politely titled "Of Mr. Booker T. Washington and Others," with a quotation from Byron:

> Hereditary bondsmen! Know ye not
> Who would be free themselves must
> strike the blow?

The essay follows.

The Document:

Essay originally titled "Of Mr. Booker T.
Washington and Others," from *The Souls of
Black Folk*, Atlanta, Georgia, 1903

EASILY THE MOST striking thing in the history of the American Negro since 1876 is the ascendancy of Mr. Booker T. Washington. It began at the time when war memories and ideals were rapidly passing; a day of astonishing commercial development was dawning; a sense of doubt and hesitation overtook the freedmen's sons,—then it was that his leading began. Mr. Washington came, with a single definite programme, at the psychological moment when the nation was a little ashamed of having bestowed so much sentiment on Negroes, and was concentrating its energies on Dollars.

To gain the sympathy and cooperation of the various elements comprising the white South was Mr. Washington's first task; and this, at the time Tuskegee was founded, seemed, for a black man, well-nigh impossible. And yet ten years later it was done in the words spoken at Atlanta:

> In all things purely social we can be as separate as the five
> fingers, and yet one as the hand in all things essential to mutual progress.

This "Atlanta Compromise" is by all odds the most notable thing in Mr. Washington's career. The South interpreted it in different ways: the radicals received it as a complete surren-

der of the demand for civil and political equality; the con-
servatives, as a generously conceived working basis for mutual understanding. So both approved it, and to-day its author
is certainly the most distinguished Southerner since Jefferson
Davis, and the one with the largest personal following.

Next to this achievement comes Mr. Washington's work in
gaining place and consideration in the North. Others less
shrewd and tactful had formerly essayed to sit on these two
stools and had fallen between them; but as Mr. Washington
knew the heart of the South from birth and training, so by
singular insight he intuitively grasped the spirit of the age
which was dominating the North. And so thoroughly did he
learn the speech and thought of triumphant commercialism,
and the ideals of material prosperity, that the picture of a
lone black boy poring over a French grammar amid the
weeds and dirt of a neglected home soon seemed to him the
acme of absurdities. One wonders what Socrates and St.
Francis of Assisi would say to this.

Mr. Washington represents in Negro thought the old attitude
of adjustment and submission; but adjustment at such a peculiar time as to make his programme unique. . . . It has been
claimed that the Negro can survive only through submission.
Mr. Washington distinctly asks that black people give up, at
least for the present, three things,—

First, political power.

Second, insistence on civil rights.

Third, higher education of Negro youth—and concentrate
all their energies on industrial education, and accumulation
of wealth, and the conciliation of the South. This policy has
been courageously and insistently advocated for over fifteen
years, and has been triumphant for perhaps ten years. As a
result of this tender of the palm-branch, what has been the
return? In these years there have occurred:

1. The disfranchisement of the Negro.

2. The legal creation of a distinct status of civil inferiority
for the Negro.

3. The steady withdrawal of aid from institutions for the
higher training of the Negro.

These movements are not, to be sure, direct results of Mr.
Washington's teachings; but his propaganda has, without a
shadow of a doubt, helped their speedier accomplishment.
The question then comes: Is it possible, and probable, that
nine millions of men can make effective progress in economic
lines if they are deprived of political rights, made a servile
caste, and allowed only the most meagre chance for developing their exceptional men? If history and reason give any dis-

tinct answer to these questions, it is an emphatic *No*. And Mr. Washington thus faces the triple paradox of his career:

1. He is striving nobly to make Negro artisans business men and property-owners; but it is utterly impossible, under modern competitive methods, for workingmen and property owners to defend their rights and exist without the right of suffrage.

2. He insists on thrift and self-respect, but at the same time counsels a silent submission to civic inferiority such as is bound to sap the manhood of any race in the long run.

3. He advocates common-school and industrial training, and deprecates institutions of higher learning; but neither the Negro common-schools, nor Tuskegee itself, could remain open a day were it not for teachers trained in Negro colleges, or trained by their graduates.

This triple paradox in Mr. Washington's position is the object of criticism by two classes of colored Americans. One class is spiritually descended from Toussaint the Savior, through Gabriel, Vesey, and Turner, and they represent the attitude of revolt and revenge; they hate the white South blindly and distrust the white race generally, and so far as they agree on definite action, think that the Negro's only hope lies in emigration beyond the borders of the United States. And yet, by the irony of fate, nothing has more effectually made this programme seem hopeless than the recent course of the United States toward weaker and darker peoples in the West Indies, Hawaii, and the Philippines,—for where in the world may we go and be safe from lying and brute force?

The other class of Negroes who cannot agree with Mr. Washington has hitherto said little aloud. They deprecate the sight of scattered counsels, of internal disagreement; and especially they dislike making their just criticism of a useful and earnest man an excuse for a general discharge of venom from small-minded opponents. Nevertheless, the questions involved are so fundamental and serious that it is difficult to see how men like the Grimkes, Kelly Miller, J. W. E. Bowen, and other representatives of this group, can much longer be silent. Such men feel in conscience bound to ask of this nation three things:

1. The right to vote.

2. Civic equality.

3. The education of youth, according to ability. They acknowledge Mr. Washington's invaluable service in counseling patience and courtesy in such demands; they do not ask that ignorant black men vote when ignorant whites are debarred, or that any reasonable restrictions in the suffrage should not

be applied; they know that the low social level of the mass of the race is responsible for much discrimination against it, but they also know, and the nation knows, that relentless color-prejudice is more often a cause than a result of the Negro's degradation; they seek the abatement of this relic of barbarism, and not its systematic encouragement and pampering by all agencies of social power from the Associated Press to the Church of Christ. They advocate, with Mr. Washington, a broad system of Negro common schools supplemented by thorough industrial training; but they are surprised that a man of Mr. Washington's insight cannot see that no such educational system ever has rested or can rest on any other basis than that of the well-equipped college and university, and they insist that there is a demand for a few such institutions throughout the South to train the best of the Negro youth as teachers, professional men, and leaders. . . .

The South ought to be led, by candid and honest criticism, to assert her better self and do her full duty to the race she has cruelly wronged and is still wronging. The North—her co-partner in guilt—cannot salve her conscience by plastering it with gold. We cannot settle this problem by diplomacy and suaveness, by "policy" alone. If worse come to worst, can the moral fibre of this country survive the slow throttling and murder of nine millions of men?

The black men of America have a duty to perform, a duty stern and delicate,—a forward movement to oppose a part of the work of their greatest leader. So far as Mr. Washington preaches Thrift, Patience, and Industrial Training for the masses, we must hold up his hands and strive with him, rejoicing in his honors and glorying in the strength of this Joshua called of God and of man to lead the headless host. But so far as Mr. Washington apologizes for injustice, North or South, does not rightly value the privilege and duty of voting, belittles the emasculating effects of caste distinctions, and opposes the higher training and ambition of our brighter minds, —so far as he, the South, or the Nation, does this,—we must unceasingly and firmly oppose them. By every civilized and peaceful method we must strive for the rights which the world accords to men, clinging unwaveringly to those great words which the sons of the Fathers would fain forget:

We hold these truths to be self-evident: That all men are created equal; that they are endowed by their Creator with certain unalienable rights; that among these are life, liberty, and the pursuit of happiness.

THE NIAGARA MOVEMENT AND THE NAACP: 1905

*Manifesto of the group opposing
the policies of Booker T. Washington*

by W. E. B. Du Bois and others

About The Document:

The issue now was joined, and Booker T. Washington—a master political strategist—sought a rapprochement with Du Bois. In January 1904, Washington called fifty black leaders to meet at Carnegie Hall in New York City. Traveling expenses were to be paid by philanthropist Andrew Carnegie. Washington asked Du Bois to help arrange the meeting, and Du Bois agreed.

As the meeting convened, some of the leaders expressed opposition to Washington, in reply to which Washington proposed the formation of a Committee of Twelve for the Advancement of the Interests of the Negro Race. The proposal was carried. It was left to Washington, Hugh Brown (one of Washington's allies), and Du Bois to appoint the members of the committee. Later, when Du Bois went to New York for the meeting to decide on appointments, he discovered that Washington and Brown had already been in conference for twenty-four hours or more. According to Du Bois, only the persons they had chosen were elected, because they voted two to one against all those he recommended. That summer Du Bois became ill and could not meet with the newly formed Committee of Twelve. He wrote to Washington asking him to postpone the meeting, but it was held despite his absence. Washington was made chairman, and the work of the full committee was delegated to an executive sub-committee, to be named by Washington. The whole organization was now under Washington's command. Du Bois resigned.

In June 1905, Du Bois sent the following letter to selected

black leaders—mostly professionals and intellectuals but including a few businessmen:

> The time seems more than ripe for organized, determined and aggressive action on the part of men who believe in Negro freedom and growth. Movements are on foot threatening individual freedom and our self respect. I write you to propose a Conference during the coming summer. . . .

The conference was planned to be held near Buffalo, New York, in July. Du Bois requested accommodations on the New York side of Niagara Falls, but the hotels refused him. On the Canadian side the hotels were more hospitable, and there, on July 11–13, 1905, twenty-nine black leaders from fourteen states met. To symbolize the power they hoped the movement would generate, and because the meeting was held near the Falls, they called it the Niagara Movement.

An appeal was sent to college students throughout the country to adopt the principles set forth in the objectives of the Niagara Movement, which are reprinted below, and a Junior Niagara Movement for Negro College Students was organized in 1906.

The Niagara Movement held a national meeting at Harpers Ferry and issued a strongly worded address to the nation:

> We will not be satisfied with less than our full manhood rights. . . . We want full manhood suffrage, and we want it now, henceforth and forever.

At dawn the delegates assembled at the locomotive roundhouse where John Brown had made his last stand. Relatives of black men who died with Brown were there, and so was Frederick Douglass' son, Lewis. As the sun rose, the group marched barefoot toward the engine house, singing the *Battle Hymn of the Republic*.

In the summer of 1908, an anti-black riot in Springfield, Illinois, aroused the indignation of a number of white authors, who called upon influential white citizens to aid the black men in their struggle for equality. At the instigation of, among others, Mary White Ovington and Oswald Garrison Villard (grandson of William Lloyd Garrison), a call was issued on February 12, 1909, the centennial of Lincoln's birth, for a meeting to discuss how they could help the black man. The "Call" was written by Villard and signed by fifty-three people, including the educator John Dewey, the social worker Jane Addams, the clergyman John Haynes Holmes, and the editor-novelist William Dean Howells. Du Bois and five other black men also signed. All these persons then attended a national conference in New York City, where a committee was formed, which held several mass meetings in the months that followed. A second conference in May 1910 organized a permanent body, the National Association for the Advancement of Colored People. This organization would play a dominant role in the legal struggle for civil rights during the next half century. (Another important organization, the National Urban League, was founded in 1910 to help rural black families adjust to city life.)

The NAACP included in its leadership most of the blacks involved in the Niagara Movement. Du Bois would have preferred an all-black organization, but funds were lacking; and when the NAACP invited him to help establish the organization, he agreed to come to New York. Offices were set up, with the distinguished Boston attorney Moorfield Storey as president, and Du Bois as director of publicity and research. In November 1910, the first issue of *Crisis,* the official organ of the NAACP, appeared under Du Bois' editorship. He resigned his position at Atlanta University, and continued with the NAACP until 1933.

The original Niagara Movement ceased to exist, but its spirit was continued by William Monroe Trotter, who had helped Du Bois found it. Trotter was a man who refused to compromise on any issue, and in that sense he was a spiritual descendant of the abolitionist William Lloyd Garrison. Editing his militant *Guardian* in Garrison's old office building in Boston, he insisted on complete integration of the black man into the fabric of American life. He had refused to join Du Bois and other black men at the conference that led to the NAACP, saying, "I distrust white folk." He was concerned that white liberals in a black organization would "water down" demands for total integration. Trotter's National Equal Rights League, which he established to take the place of the Niagara Movement, was exclusively a black man's organization.

The Document:

The "Niagara Movement Principles," as drawn up in Buffalo, New York, July 11–13, 1905

Progress: The members of the conference known as the Niagara Movement, assembled in annual meeting at Buffalo, July 11th, 12th, and 13th, 1905, congratulate the Negro-Americans on certain undoubted evidences of progress in the last decade, particularly the increase of intelligence, the buying of property, the checking of crime, the uplift in home life, the advance in literature and art, and the demonstration of constructive and executive ability in the conduct of great religious, economic and educational institutions.

Suffrage: At the same time, we believe that this class of American citizens should protest emphatically and continually against the curtailment of their political rights. We believe in manhood suffrage; we believe that no man is so good, intelligent or wealthy as to be entrusted wholly with the welfare of his neighbor.

Civil Liberty: We believe also in protest against the curtailment of our civil rights. All American citizens have the right to equal treatment in places of public entertainment according to their behavior and deserts.

Economic Opportunity: We especially complain against the denial of equal opportunities to us in economic life; in the rural districts of the South this amounts to peonage and virtual slavery; all over the South it tends to crush labor and small business enterprises; and everywhere American prejudice, helped often by iniquitous laws, is making it more difficult for Negro-Americans to earn a decent living.

Education: Common school education should be free to all American children and compulsory. High school training should be adequately provided for all, and college training should be the monopoly of no class or race in any section of our common country. We believe that, in defense of our own institutions, the United States should aid common school education, particularly in the South, and we especially recommend concerted agitation to this end. We urge an increase in public high school facilities in the South, where the Negro-Americans are almost wholly without such provisions. We favor well-equipped trade and technical schools for the training of artisans, and the need of adequate and liberal endowment for a few institutions of higher education must be patent to sincere well-wishers of the race.

Courts: We demand upright judges in courts, juries selected without discrimination on account of color and the same measure of punishment and the same efforts at reformation for black as for white offenders. We need orphanages and farm schools for dependent children, juvenile reformatories for delinquents, and the abolition of the dehumanizing convict-lease system.

Public Opinion: We note with alarm the evident retrogression in this land of sound public opinion on the subject of manhood rights, republican government and human brotherhood, and we pray God that this nation will not degenerate into a mob of boasters and oppressors, but rather will return to the faith of the fathers, that all men were created free and equal, with certain unalienable rights.

Health: We plead for health—for an opportunity to live in decent houses and localities, for a chance to rear our children in physical and moral cleanliness.

Employers and Labor Unions: We hold up for public execration the conduct of two opposite classes of men: The practice among employers of importing ignorant Negro-American laborers in emergencies, and then affording them neither protection nor permanent employment; and the practice of labor unions in proscribing and boycotting and oppressing thousands of their fellow-toilers, simply because they are black. These methods have accentuated and will accentuate the war of labor and capital, and they are disgraceful to both sides.

Protest: We refuse to allow the impression to remain that the Negro-American assents to inferiority, is submissive under oppression and apologetic before insults. Through helplessness we may submit, but the voice of protest of ten million Americans must never cease to assail the ears of their fellows, so long as America is unjust.

Color-Line: Any discrimination based simply on race or color is barbarous, we care not how hallowed it be by custom, expediency or prejudice. Differences made on account of ignorance, immorality, or disease are legitimate methods of fighting evil, and against them we have no word of protest; but discriminations based simply and solely on physical peculiarities, place of birth, color of skin, are relics of that unreasoning human savagery of which the world is and ought to be thoroughly ashamed.

"Jim Crow" Cars: We protest against the "Jim Crow" car, since its effect is and must be to make us pay first-class fare for third-class accommodations, render us open to insults and discomfort and to crucify wantonly our manhood, womanhood and self-respect.

Soldiers: We regret that this nation has never seen fit adequately to reward the black soldiers who, in its five wars, have defended their country with their blood, and yet have been systematically denied the promotions which their abilities deserve. And we regard as unjust, the exclusion of black boys from the military and naval training schools.

THE BACK-TO-AFRICA MOVEMENT: 1922

A speech outlining the principles of the resettlement movement of the 1920's

by Marcus Garvey

About The Document:

The Back-to-Africa movement never had attracted much support from black people, but in the first part of the 20th century a man named Marcus Garvey stirred the imagination and roused the hopes of thousands with his dream of a black nation ruled by black men.

Garvey was born in Jamaica in 1887, the son of a well-read brick and stone mason. The boy was not formally educated, but he did develop an enormous curiosity about his people through reading in his father's library.

Garvey was apprenticed to a printer at the age of fourteen. A few years later, while working in Kingston, he organized an unsuccessful strike. After a term as publisher of some short-lived radical publications, and an abortive attempt to organize a political party, Garvey emigrated to London, to study the social and economic conditions of blacks throughout the world. He was given a job by an eccentric scholar and publisher, half-black, half-Egyptian, who was impressed with his fiery sincerity. At night he studied at London University. He also read the works of Booker T. Washington and began to correspond with him.

In 1914 Garvey returned to Jamaica and organized the Universal Negro Improvement Association, avowedly to "take Africa, organize it, develop it, arm it and make it the defender of Negroes the world over."

Garvey was impressed with Washington's accomplishments and dreamed of establishing a school like Tuskegee in Jamaica. In 1915 Washington invited Garvey to come to the United States, but by the time he arrived a year later, Washington was dead. His successor, Robert R. Morton, was unenthusiastic about Garvey's African nationalism.

Less than welcome at Tuskegee, Garvey moved to New York, where a large number of West Indians were living in Harlem. There, in 1917, he reorganized the Universal Negro Improvement Association and began to preach his philosophy of black redemption and self-improvement. Garvey was an articulate and passionate speaker, and the UNIA began to prosper. To white people he refused membership; he would not solicit funds from them nor allow them to buy stock in the various business enterprises he set up. But there were white people who supported his movement, just the same. Some were white liberals who, like their counterparts in the American Colonization Society a hundred years before, honestly believed that Garveyism offered the black man his best hope. Some were members of the Ku Klux Klan, who approved of Marcus Garvey and his plan for taking black people out of the United States.

Most black leaders were hostile to Garvey. W. E. B. Du Bois called him a "visionary" but recognized his abilities as a leader. A. Philip Randolph, the trade union leader, accused Garvey of outright exploitation of the black man.

Garvey barnstormed through thirty-eight states, urging the people to learn about the past glories of Africa and arousing pride in being black. Garvey praised everything black. He told his followers that black symbolized strength and beauty, not inferiority. Undesirables, he declared, were to be "white-balled."

By 1919, the UNIA had become a gigantic organization, with branches in every major city of large black population. Within two years black workers had contributed some ten million dollars to the movement.

The 1921 convention of the UNIA in New York was a prime example of Garvey's use of pageantry. Led by Garvey in a uniform of purple, green, and black—with gold-braid trimmings and a helmet crowned with flowing white feathers —50,000 Garveyites and partisans from Harlem marched down Lenox Avenue. With flags and bands they paraded to Madison Square Garden for a mass rally. There they proclaimed Garvey the provisional president-general of Africa. Splendid was the pomp and ceremony of the occasion. There was an invocation by the black archbishop of the African Orthodox Church, which Garvey had created (complete with a black Holy Trinity, a black Christ of Sorrow, and a black Madonna). There were the African Legion, the Black Cross nurses, the African Motor Corps, and the Black Eagle Flying Corps.

Garvey denounced white America (Satan, he said, was white). He told his followers that black men's only hope was to build an independent nation in Africa where they could choose their own leaders. He criticized interracial organizations such as the NAACP for their lack of concern for the ordinary black, and urged black people to do something for themselves.

By the mid-twenties, Garvey had more than a million followers. His most ambitious undertaking was the Black Star Steamship Line, Inc., to transport blacks to their homeland in Africa, and to open up commercial relations with the African continent.

These grandiose schemes collapsed when, in 1923, Garvey was indicted on a charge of using the mails to defraud in connection with the sale of stock in his steamship line. After two years of appeals, Garvey was sentenced to five years in prison. Two years later his sentence was commuted by President Calvin Coolidge, but he was immediately deported to Jamaica.

After that the movement faltered, and although Garvey tried to keep it together from exile, it finally collapsed. Garvey lived the rest of his life in obscurity and died in London in 1940.

Garvey's famous speech outlining the principles of the UNIA appears below.

The Document:

Speech titled "The Principles of the
Universal Negro Improvement Association,"
delivered at Liberty Hall, New York City,
November 25, 1922

OVER FIVE YEARS ago the Universal Negro Improvement Association placed itself before the world as the movement through which the new and rising Negro would give expression of his feelings. This Association adopts an attitude not of hostility to other races and peoples of the world, but an attitude of self-respect. . . .

Wheresoever human rights are denied to any group, wheresoever justice is denied to any group, there the UNIA finds a cause. And at this time among all the peoples of the world, the group that suffers most from injustice, the group that is denied most of those rights that belong to all humanity, is the black group. . . .

We represent a new line of thought among Negroes.

Whether you call it advanced thought or reactionary thought, I do not care. If it is reactionary for people to seek independence in government, then we are reactionary. If it is advanced thought for people to seek liberty and freedom, then we represent the advanced school of thought among the Negroes of this country. We of the UNIA believe that what is good for the other folks is good for us. If government is something that is worth while; if government is something that is appreciable and helpful and protective to others, then we also want to experiment in government. We do not mean a government that will make us citizens without rights or subjects without consideration. We mean a kind of government that will place our race in control, even as other races are in control of their own government. . . .

In view of the fact that the black man of Africa has contributed as much to the world as the white man of Europe, and the brown man and yellow man of Asia, we of the Universal Negro Improvement Association demand that the white, yellow and brown races give to the black man his place in the civilization of the world. We ask for nothing more than the rights of 400,000,000 Negroes.

We of the Universal Negro Improvement Association . . . desire to bring together the 15,000,000 of the United States, the 180,000,000 in Asia, the West Indies and Central and South America, and the 200,000,000 in Africa. We are looking toward political freedom on the continent of Africa, the land of our fathers.

The Universal Negro Improvement Association is not seeking to build up another government within the bounds or borders of the United States of America. The Universal Negro Improvement Association is not seeking to disrupt any organized system of government, but the Association is determined to bring Negroes together for the building up of a nation of their own. And why? Because we have been forced to it throughout the world; not only in America, not only in Europe, not only in the British Empire, but wheresoever the black man happens to find himself, he has been forced to do for himself.

To talk about Government is a little more than some of our people can appreciate. . . . The average . . . seems to say, "Why should there be need for any other government?" We are French, English or American. But we of the UNIA have studied seriously this question of nationality among Negroes—this American nationality, this British nationality, this French, Italian or Spanish nationality, and have discovered that it counts for nought when that nationality comes in conflict with the racial idealism of the group that rules. When our interests clash with those of the ruling faction, then we find that we have absolutely no rights. In times of peace, when everything is all right, Negroes have a hard time, wherever we go, wheresoever we find ourselves, getting those rights that belong to us in common with others whom we claim as fellow citizens; getting that consideration that should be ours by right of the constitution, by right of the law; but in the time of trouble they make us all partners in the cause, as happened in the last war. . . .

The difference between the Universal Negro Improvement Association and the other movements of this country, and probably the world, is that the Universal Negro Improvement Association seeks independence of government, while the other organizations seek to make the Negro a secondary part of existing governments. We differ from the organizations in America because they seek to subordinate the Negro as a secondary consideration in a great civilization, knowing that in America the Negro will never reach his highest ambition, knowing that the Negro in America will never get his constitutional rights. . . . You and I can live in the United States of America for 100 years, and our generations may live for 200 years or for 5,000 more years, and so long as there is a black and white population, when the majority is on the side of the white race, you and I will never get political justice or get political equality in this country. . . .

We are not preaching a propaganda of hate against anybody. We love the white man; we love all humanity. . . . The white man is as necessary to the existence of the Negro as the Negro is necessary to his existence. There is a common relationship that we cannot escape. Africa has certain things that Europe wants, and Europe has certain things that Africa wants . . . it is impossible for us to escape it. Africa has oil, diamonds, copper, gold and rubber and all the minerals that Europe wants, and there must be some kind of relationship between Africa and Europe for a fair exchange, so we cannot afford to hate anybody.

The question often asked is what does it require to redeem a race and free a country? If it takes man power, if it takes scientific intelligence, if it takes education of any kind, or if it takes blood, then the 400,000,000 Negroes of the world have it.

It took the combined power of the Allies to put down the mad determination of the Kaiser to impose German will upon the world and upon humanity. Among those who suppressed his mad ambition were two million Negroes who have not yet forgotten how to drive men across the firing line. . . . When so many white men refused to answer to the call and dodged behind all kinds of excuses, 400,000 black men were ready without a question. It was because we were told it was a war of democracy; it was a war for the liberation of the weaker peoples of the world. We heard the cry of Woodrow Wilson, not because we liked him so, but because the things he said were of such a nature that they appealed to us as men. Wheresoever the cause of humanity stands in need of assistance, there you will find the Negro ever ready to serve.

He has done it from the time of Christ up to now. When the whole world turned its back upon the Christ, the man who was said to be Son of God, when the world spurned Him and spat upon Him, it was a black man, Simon, the Cyrenian, who took up the cross. Why? Because the course of humanity appealed to him. When the black man saw the suffering Jew, struggling under the heavy cross, he was willing to go to His assistance, and he bore that cross up to the heights of Calvary. In the spirit of Simon, the Cyrenian, 1900 years ago, we answered the call of Woodrow Wilson, the call to a larger humanity, and it was for that that we willingly rushed into the war. . . .

We have not forgotten the prowess of war. If we have been liberal minded enough to give our life's blood in France, in Mesopotamia and elsewhere, fighting for the white man, whom we have always assisted, surely we have not forgotten to fight for ourselves, and when the time comes that the world will again give Africa an opportunity for freedom, surely . . . black men will march out on the battle plains of Africa, under the colors of the red, the black and the green.

We shall march out, yes, as black American citizens, as black British subjects, as black French citizens, as black Italians or as black Spaniards, but we shall march out in answer to the cry of our fathers, who cry out to us for the redemption of our own country, our motherland, Africa. . . .

"WE WANT TO LIVE": 1938

Aspirations of black Southern youth

by Edward S. Strong

About The Document:

Already the victim of "last hired, first fired" in the late 1920's, black men suffered massive unemployment during the depression, particularly in the South. By the mid-thirties, almost 70 per cent of the people on relief in Birmingham, Alabama, were black. But the depression brought some positive changes also. The protest movement was intensified, and in 1932 many blacks turned away from their traditional Republicanism to vote for Franklin D. Roosevelt, whose "New Deal" administration appointed more black advisers to government departments than had ever served in high official capacities.

In 1930, a Chicago black newspaper led a boycott against stores that hired only whites. After a five-month struggle, one thousand black people obtained jobs. The most dramatic demand for relief in the early thirties was made by the Bonus Expeditionary Force, a group of twenty thousand unemployed white and black veterans of World War I, who marched on Washington in the spring of 1932 to demand a bonus. This was the famous march that Herbert Hoover routed by the use of tanks and tear gas.

The common desperation born of hunger brought about an unprecedented unity between black and white people. In the South, ten thousand black and white tenant farmers (including Ku Klux Klan members) formed the Southern Tenant Farmers Union with practically "no friction over the race question."

Another outstanding development of the 1930's was the entry of Southern youth into the protest movement. Local organizations of young black people had started to come together in regional assemblies, and by 1937 the first all-South black youth conference was held. A year later, five hundred young blacks met in a second conference held in Chattanooga, Tennessee, to discuss what they wanted and to plan a program to achieve it. Edward S. Strong reported the results of that conference in *Opportunity*.

The Document:

Position paper of the Southern Negro Youth
Conference, as reported in the Urban League magazine
Opportunity, May 1938

IN CHATTANOOGA, TENNESSEE, last month, 500 young colored men and women met in the second all-Southern Negro Youth Conference. They came to express their wants and desires—to plan a new design for living—and in the program that they adopted all their hopes and aspirations for a brighter future were reflected.

What is the aim of young Negroes of the South today? What do they want? How do they propose to move ahead?

The delegates answered these questions simply and unanimously.

We who are young, and who live in the South, want first of all the right to vote. We want the opportunity to serve on juries, to participate in the primary elections of all parties; to be eligible for appointment to all Federal, state, and municipal positions, and to be acceptable as candidates for public office.

To become voters is, of course, a major task. The barriers that we must overcome include abuse of the poll tax, misuse of literacy tests, the continuance of property qualifications and the misinterpretation of state constitutions by the courts. To surmount these obstacles, we realize, we must acquaint ourselves thoroughly with the laws that govern voting in our respective states, so that we first may vote ourselves, and then assist the masses of Negro people to vote. At the same time, we must organize poll-tax-paying clubs and registration centers in every neighborhood to develop the maximum immediate Negro vote possible under existing conditions, and to broaden the base of that vote at each election.

It is as important, we feel, that we win the right to vote in the party primaries as in the general elections because in most sections of the South victory in the Democratic primary is synonymous with election. This right can only be secured when the U. S. Supreme Court reverses its decision which held the primaries to be private affairs. The recent addition of liberal judges to the bench may bring a reversal if somehow a new primary case can be presented.

A second thing we want is work. Three-quarters of a million of us are now out of school and unemployed. The very existence of the NYA [National Youth Administration, founded in 1935 by the Federal government to provide job training for unemployed youths] and the CCC [Civilian Conservation Corps, initiated in 1933 to help unemployed young men find work] is threatened all the time by budget cuts. How to get jobs? How to win economic security? That is one of our major problems.

We feel that the trade-union movement must stand at the heart of any program that we may adopt. That is why we urge further unionization of Negroes and the encouragement of their active participation in bona-fide labor unions, although at the same time we recognize and condemn the openly discriminatory policies of some unions. We want the unions to give us an adequate vocational guidance program and an opportunity for apprenticeship training. We ourselves must work for the further opening up of job opportunities for Negro youth in the Federal, state and local governments, and in private industry.

We want more opportunity for education. We realize that such a program must contain plans to assist Negro youth financially in their efforts to go to school, and so we hope for the passage of the American Youth Act, which would provide Federal assistance to help the states solve their educational problems.

We want to get married. No one will ever know how many thousands of delayed marriages among Negro youth have been caused by the depression. The result in many cases has been a distressing demoralization and an increase in the prevalence of venereal diseases. Our only real hope for a solution lies in bettered economic conditions; but meanwhile we want courses in marriage and homemaking, and in sex education, made available in our schools.

We want an opportunity to develop our talents. We are eager and anxious to contribute to the Negro's cultural heritage as artists, musicians, writers and actors. At present our opportunity for expression is severely limited. We realize that most of us do not possess the ability of a Paul Robeson or a Marian Anderson, but we do feel that if allowed the opportunity, we could make original contributions to science, the arts, drama, literature and music.

We want a religious life. This may seem a bit surprising in view of the prevailing opinion that Negro youth has become increasingly irreligious day by day, but it is none the less true. We cherish the religious heritage of our people and the contribution that has been made through the church to our advancement. The significant feature of our idea of religion is that we insist upon a stricter application of Christian principles to every-day life. We refuse lip-service to the ideal of brotherhood when in practice that ideal is consistently disregarded. We want the church to help us meet concrete life situations.

What must the church do to give us the type of meaningful religious experience we seek? We feel that it must first identify itself with the masses of crucified people of the South. It must become the center of community life, organizing within itself youth and adult groups for Christian social action and promoting fellowship by interdenominational and interracial cooperation.

We want a world of peace. We look with grave concern upon the growth of Fascism and the fascist threat to peace because of the inherent danger of raising the racial myth to a place of major concern in world politics. As a means of obtaining peace we feel that the only workable solution yet proposed is the "quarantine of aggressors" suggested by the President in his speech of last October 5.

These, then, are the aspirations of Southern Negro youth: we want the right to vote, to work, and to complete our education; the opportunity to marry; the chance to express ourselves, the privilege of a satisfactory religious life, and the assurance of a peaceful world.

In short, we want to live!

A. PHILIP RANDOLPH'S MARCH ON WASHINGTON: 1941

*The black man demands
a share in World War II*

by A. Philip Randolph

About The Document:

In the late 1930's, when American involvement in the war already raging in Europe seemed inevitable, black men resented bitterly their exclusion from the nation's defense industries. Of the thirty thousand defense workers in New York City, for example, only 142 were black, and even these few were restricted to such jobs as sweepers, janitors, and elevator operators. Many plants with government contracts refused to hire black labor at all.

In the armed forces, segregation was still the official government policy, a carry-over from the Civil War. Black newspapers reported "race riots at Fort Oswego; discrimination at Fort Devens; Jim Crow conditions at Camps Blanding and Lee; and the edict 'not to shake a nigger's hand' at Camp Upton." The Baltimore *Afro-American* called for thousands of black men to desert rather than serve in army camps in the South.

Increasingly, black men began asking questions like these:

Just how far removed is this brand of democracy that we practice from Fascism, Nazism and barbarism?

and

If you haven't got democracy yourself, how can you carry it to somebody else?

Black leaders pleaded with, and petitioned, the federal

government, the largest employer of civilian and military labor in the country, to meet its responsibilities.

A. Philip Randolph, head of the Brotherhood of Sleeping Car Porters union, said in January 1941 that the government would not act on behalf of blacks until it saw "Ten, twenty, fifty thousand Negroes on the White House lawn." Leaders of all the major black organizations offered to join Randolph, and the March-on-Washington Movement was formed.

In June 1941 it was announced that the March-on-Washington Movement, led by Randolph, with Walter White, Adam Clayton Powell, Jr., and Frank Crosswaith, would rally fifty thousand black men in Washington on July 1, to demand that the federal government take action to stop discrimination in the defense industries and the armed forces.

The idea of a black revolt in a time of crisis threw Washington into a panic. President Roosevelt called the march leaders to Washington and tried to persuade them to call it off. They refused. On June 25, 1941, Roosevelt capitulated and signed the famous Executive Order No. 8802—the Fair Employment Practices Act—banning discrimination in defense plants and government offices and services "because of race, creed, color, or national origin." The march never did take place, since it had achieved its objective.

It was the first time since Lincoln had signed the Emancipation Proclamation that a President had acted to protect the civil rights of black men. The March-on-Washington threat had shown the value, in Randolph's words, of a "non-violent demonstration of Negro mass power" as a tactic of protest.

The Document:

From the article titled "Why Should We March," in the *Survey Graphic*, November 1942

Program of The March On Washington Movement:

1. We demand, in the interest of national unity, the abrogation of every law which makes a distinction in treatment between citizens based on religion, creed, color, or national origin. This means an end to Jim Crow in education, in housing, in transportation and in every other social, economic, and political privilege; and especially, we demand, in the capital of

the nation, an end to all segregation in public places and in public institutions.

2. We demand legislation to enforce the Fifth and Fourteenth Amendments guaranteeing that no person shall be deprived of life, liberty or property without due process of law, so that the full weight of the national government may be used for the protection of life and thereby may end the disgrace of lynching.

3. We demand the enforcement of the Fourteenth and Fifteenth Amendments and the enactment of the Pepper Poll Tax bill so that all barriers in the exercise of the suffrage are eliminated.

4. We demand the abolition of segregation and discrimination in the army, navy, marine corps, air corps, and all other branches of national defense.

5. We demand an end to discrimination in jobs and job training. Further, we demand that the FEPC be made a permanent administrative agency of the U. S. Government and that it be given power to enforce its decisions based on its findings.

6. We demand that federal funds be withheld from any agency which practices discrimination in the use of such funds.

7. We demand colored and minority group representation on all administrative agencies so that these groups may have recognition of their democratic rights to participate in formulating policies.

8. We demand representation for the colored and minority racial groups on all missions, political and technical, which will be sent to the peace conference so that the interests of all people everywhere may be fully recognized and justly provided for in the postwar settlement.

THE MONTGOMERY BUS BOYCOTT: 1955 AND "I HAVE A DREAM": 1963

Martin Luther King
rises to leadership

by Martin Luther King, Jr.

•

About The Document:

Martin Luther King, when leading the famous Montgomery bus boycott, was carrying on a family tradition. His father before him had led a one-man crusade all his life against the buses of Atlanta, Georgia. The father, a sharecropper's son, was the pastor of the Ebenezer Church in Atlanta. He refused to ride the city's public buses after witnessing a brutal attack on black riders by white men. "I don't care how long I have to live with this system," King's father once said, "I will never accept it."

In his *Autobiography,* King wrote that he grew up in "a house of economic security and relative comfort." His mother was the daughter of a successful minister and attended college. During his late teens, King worked in a plant that hired both blacks and whites. There, he wrote, he learned firsthand something his father had taught him: that poor whites are exploited, not just blacks. When he entered Atlanta's Morehouse College as a freshman in 1944, his involvement with racial and economic issues was, as he put it, "substantial."

At Crozer Theological Seminary, he began a quest for what he called "a method to eliminate social evil." He read the works of Thoreau and Walter Rauschenbusch, which impressed him deeply, as well as the social and ethical theories of philosophers from Plato and Aristotle to Rousseau, Hobbes, Mill, and Locke.

During his stay at Crozer, King was exposed to the pacifist attitude in a talk by Dr. A. J. Muste, but King expressed disagreement with pacifism on the ground that though war could never be a positive or absolute good, it could serve to prevent the spread or the growth of destructive forces. It was the nonviolent resistance philosophy of Mohandas Gandhi that appealed to King as "the only morally and practically sound method open to oppressed people in their struggle for freedom."

In 1954, after twenty-one years of school, King had completed the residential requirements for his Ph.D. degree. He was then twenty-seven. While writing his thesis he commuted by plane to Montgomery once a month to preach at the Dexter Avenue Baptist Church, where he had been offered a ministry. On September 1, 1954, King, with his wife and daughter, moved into the Montgomery parsonage as full-time pastor.

He formed a Social and Political Action Committee as an auxiliary of the church. Its job was to keep before the congregation the importance of registering to vote. The committee published a biweekly newsletter on social and political issues. It also established a voting clinic to inform unregistered church members of the pitfalls of discriminatory registration procedures.

After his church program was under way, King joined the local branch of the NAACP and soon was elected to the executive committee. He also joined and became vice president of the Alabama Council of Human Relations, an affiliate of the Southern Regional Council. The ACHR was an interracial organization, whose president was a white minister, and King was criticized by some black men for joining it.

In Montgomery few people challenged the system of segregation. It was grudgingly accepted by black men, and though there were at that time undertones of discontent, the city appeared peaceful on the surface. Even that peace, King wrote, "was achieved at the cost of human servitude." In his book, *Stride Toward Freedom,* he stated:

One place where the peace had long been precarious was on the city-wide buses. . . . There were no Negro drivers, and although some of the white men who drove the buses were courteous, all too many were abusive and vituperative. It was not uncommon to hear them referring to Negro passengers as "niggers," "black cows," and "black apes." Frequently Negroes paid their fares at the front door, and then were forced to get off and reboard the bus at the rear. . . . An even more humiliating practice was the custom of forcing Negroes to stand over empty seats reserved for "whites only." . . . If white passengers were already occupying all of their reserved seats and additional white people boarded the bus, Negroes sitting in the unreserved section immediately behind the whites were asked to stand so that the whites could be seated. If the Negroes refused to stand and move back, they were arrested.

On December 1, 1955, Mrs. Rosa Parks, a Negro seamstress, seated in the black section of a bus in Montgomery, refused to give up her seat to a white male passenger. She was arrested. It was never fully established why Mrs. Parks refused the request. It was established that she was not a "plant" of the NAACP, as has been charged. Perhaps, as Martin Luther King suggested, "the long repressed feelings of resentment on the part of the Negroes had begun to stir." Or perhaps Mrs. Parks was just too tired from her day's work to move.

It is important to know that a year before Mrs. Parks' arrest, a 15-year-old black girl had been pulled off a bus, handcuffed, after refusing to give her seat to a white man. At that time there had been some talk of protesting the arrest by means of a boycott.

Following the arrest of Mrs. Parks, a group of influential black women decided that the time had come for action. They called upon all ministers and civic leaders to stage a bus boycott on December 5 and to hold a city-wide mass meeting that night to determine how long the boycott would be continued.

King was one of the ministers who responded to their call. He described this "Day of Days" in his book *Stride Toward Freedom.*

The Document:

"The Day of Days, December 5" from the
book *Stride Toward Freedom,* Harper & Row,
Publishers, New York, 1958

MY WIFE AND I awoke earlier than usual on Monday morning. We were up and fully dressed by five-thirty. The day for the protest had arrived, and we were determined to see the first act of this unfolding drama. I was still saying that if we could get 60 per cent cooperation the venture would be a success.

Fortunately, a bus stop was just five feet from our house. This meant that we could observe the opening stages from our front window. The first bus was to pass around six o'clock. And so we waited through an interminable half hour.

I was in the kitchen drinking my coffee when I heard Coretta cry, "Martin, Martin, come quickly!" I put down my cup and ran toward the living room. As I approached the front window Coretta pointed joyfully to a slowly moving bus: "Darling, it's empty!" I could hardly believe what I saw. I knew that the South Jackson line, which ran past our house, carried more Negro passengers than any line in Montgomery, and that this first bus was usually filled with domestic workers going to their jobs. Would all of the other buses follow the pattern that had been set by the first? Eagerly we waited for the next bus. In fifteen minutes it rolled down the street, and, like the first, it was empty. A third bus appeared, and it too was empty of all but two white passengers.

I jumped in my car and for almost an hour I cruised down every major street and examined every passing bus. During this hour, at the peak of the morning traffic, I saw no more than eight Negro passengers riding the buses. By this time I was jubilant. Instead of the 60 per cent cooperation we had hoped for, it was becoming apparent that we had reached almost 100 per cent. A miracle had taken place. The once dormant and quiescent Negro community was now fully awake.

All day long it continued. At the afternoon peak the buses were still as empty of Negro passengers as they had been in the morning. Students of Alabama State College, who usually kept the South Jackson bus crowded, were cheerfully walking or thumbing rides. Job holders had either found other means of transportation or made their way on foot. While some rode in cabs or private cars, others used less conventional means. Men were seen riding mules to work, and more than one horse-drawn buggy drove the streets of Montgomery that day. . . .

Around nine-thirty in the morning I tore myself from the action of the city streets and headed for the crowded police court. Here Mrs. Parks was being tried for disobeying the city segregation ordinance. Her attorney, Fred D. Gray—the brilliant young Negro who later became the chief counsel for the protest movement—was on hand to defend her. After the judge heard the arguments, he found Mrs. Parks guilty and fined her ten dollars and court costs (a total of fourteen dollars). She appealed the case. This was one of the first clear-cut instances in which a Negro had been convicted for disobeying the segregation law. In the past, either cases like this had been dismissed or the people involved had been charged with disorderly conduct. So in a real sense the arrest and conviction of Mrs. Parks had a twofold impact: it was a precipitating factor to arouse the Negroes to positive action; and it was a test of the validity of the segregation law itself. I am sure that supporters of such prosecutions would have acted otherwise if they had had the prescience to look beyond the moment.

Leaving Mrs. Parks's trial, Ralph Abernathy, E. D. Nixon, and Rev. E. N. French—then minister of the Hilliard Chapel A.M.E. Zion Church—discussed the need for some organization to guide and direct the protest. Up to this time things had moved forward more or less spontaneously. These men were wise enough to see that the moment had now come for a clearer order and direction.

[Here narrated is the election of officers, which resulted in Dr. King's election as chairman, which "caught me unawares."]

With these organizational matters behind us, we turned to a discussion of the evening meeting. Several people, not wanting the reporters to know our future moves, suggested that we just sing and pray; if there were specific recommendations to be made to the people, these could be mimeographed and passed out secretly during the meeting. This, they felt, would leave the reporters in the dark. Others urged that something should be done to conceal the true identity of the leaders, feeling that if no particular name was revealed it would be safer for all involved. After a rather lengthy discussion, E. C. Nixon rose impatiently:

"We are acting like little boys," he said. "Somebody's name will have to be known, and if we are afraid we might just as well fold up right now. We must also be men enough to discuss our recommendations in the open; this idea of secretly passing something around on paper is a lot of bunk. The white folks are eventually going to find it out anyway. We'd better decide now if we are going to be fearless men or scared boys."

With this forthright statement the air cleared. Nobody would again suggest that we try to conceal our identity or avoid facing the issue head on. Nixon's courageous affirmation had given new heart to those who were about to be crippled by fear.

It was unanimously agreed that the protest should continue until certain demands were met, and that a committee under the chairmanship of Ralph Abernathy would draw up these demands in the form of a resolution and present them to the evening mass meeting for approval. We worked out the remainder of the program quickly. Bennett would preside and I would make the main address. Remarks by a few other speakers, along with Scripture reading, prayer, hymns, and collection, would round out the program.

Immediately the resolution committee set to drafting its

statement. Despite our satisfaction at the success of the protest so far, we were still concerned. Would the evening meeting be well attended? Could we hope that the fortitude and enthusiasm of the Negro community would survive more than one such day of hardship? Someone suggested that perhaps we should reconsider our decision to continue the protest. "Would it not be better," said the speaker, "to call off the protest while it is still a success rather than let it go on a few more days and fizzle out? We have already proved our united strength to the white community. If we stop now we can get anything we want from the bus company, simply because they will have the feeling that we can do it again. But if we continue, and most of the people return to the buses tomorrow or the next day, the white people will laugh at us, and we will end up getting nothing." This argument was so convincing that we almost resolved to end the protest. But we finally agreed to let the mass meeting—which was only about an hour off—be our guide. If the meeting was well attended and the people were enthusiastic, we would continue; otherwise we would call off the protest that night.

I went home for the first time since seven that morning, and found Coretta relaxing from a long day of telephone calls and general excitement. . . .

I went to my study and closed the door. The minutes were passing fast. It was now six-thirty, and I had to leave no later than six-fifty to get to the meeting. This meant that I had only twenty minutes to prepare the most decisive speech of my life. . . . How could I make a speech that would be militant enough to keep my people aroused to positive action and yet moderate enough to keep this fervor within controllable and Christian bounds? I knew that many of the Negro people were victims of bitterness that could easily rise to flood proportions. What could I say to keep them courageous and prepared for positive action and yet devoid of hate and resentment? Could the militant and the moderate be combined in a single speech? . . .

Within five blocks of the church I noticed a traffic jam. Cars were lined up as far as I could see on both sides of the street. It was a moment before it occurred to me that all of these cars were headed for the mass meeting. I had to park at least four blocks from the church, and as I started walking I noticed that hundreds of people were standing outside. In the dark night, police cars circled slowly around the area, surveying the orderly, patient, and good-humored crowd. The three or four thousand people who could not get into the church were to stand cheerfully throughout the evening listening to the proceedings on the loud-speakers that had been set up outside for their benefit. And when, near the end of the meeting, these speakers were silenced at the request of the white people in surrounding neighborhoods, the crowd would still remain quietly, content simply to be present.

It took fully fifteen minutes to push my way through to the pastor's study, where Dr. Wilson told me that the church had been packed since five o'clock. By now my doubts concerning the continued success of our venture were dispelled. The question of calling off the protest was now academic. The enthusiasm of these thousands of people swept everything along like an onrushing tidal wave. . . .

Rev. W. F. Alford, minister of the Beulah Baptist Church, led the congregation in prayer, followed by a reading of the Scripture by Rev. U. J. Fields, minister of the Bell Street Baptist Church. Then the chairman introduced me. As the audience applauded, I rose and stood before the pulpit. Television cameras began to shoot from all sides. The crowd grew quiet.

Without manuscript or notes, I told the story of what had happened to Mrs. Parks. Then I reviewed the long history of abuses and insults that Negro citizens had experienced on the city buses. "But there comes a time," I said, "that people get tired. We are here this evening to say to those who have mistreated us so long that we are tired—tired of being segregated and humiliated; tired of being kicked about by the brutal feet of oppression." The congregation met this statement with fervent applause. "We had no alternative but to protest," I continued. "For many years, we have shown amazing patience. We have sometimes given our white brothers the feeling that we liked the way we were being treated. But we come here tonight to be saved from that patience that makes us patient with anything less than freedom and justice." Again the audience interrupted with applause.

Briefly I justified our actions, both morally and legally. "One of the great glories of democracy is the right to protest for right." Comparing our methods with those of the White Citizens Councils and the Ku Klux Klan, I pointed out that while "these organizations are protesting for the perpetuation of injustice in the community, we are protesting for the birth of justice in the community. Their methods lead to violence and lawlessness. But in our protest there will be no cross burnings. No white person will be taken from his home by a hooded Negro mob and brutally murdered. There will be no threats and intimidation. We will be guided by the highest principles of law and order." . . .

Then came my closing statement. "If you will protest courageously, and yet with dignity and Christian love, when the history books are written in future generations, the historians will have to pause and say, 'There lived a great people—a black people—who injected new meaning and dignity into the veins of civilization.' This is our challenge and our overwhelming responsibility." As I took my seat the people rose to their feet and applauded. I was thankful to God that the message had gotten over and that the task of combining the militant and the moderate had been at least partially accomplished. The people had been as enthusiastic when I urged them to love as they were when I urged them to protest. . . .

When Mrs. Parks was introduced from the rostrum by E. N. French, the audience responded by giving her a standing ovation. She was their heroine. They saw in her courageous person the symbol of their hopes and aspirations.

Now the time had come for the all-important resolution. Ralph Abernathy read the words slowly and forcefully. The main substance of the resolution called upon the Negroes not to resume riding the buses until (1) courteous treatment by the bus operators was guaranteed; (2) passengers were seated on a first-come, first-served basis—Negroes seated from the back of the bus toward the front while whites seated from the front toward the back; (3) Negro bus operators were employed on predominantly Negro routes. At the words "All in favor of the motion stand," every person to a man stood up, and those who were already standing raised their hands. Cheers began to ring out from both inside and outside. The motion was carried unanimously. The people had expressed their determination not to ride the buses until conditions were changed. . . .

Postscript To The Document:

It is interesting to note that until King's election as president of the Montgomery Improvement Association, he had not distinguished himself in any substantial way as a leader; in fact, it was not even he who had organized the original boycott. But in the months to come he was to display the charisma of leadership and to become one of America's most outstanding leaders.

The tactics of the boycott were quickly and efficiently organized. King instituted a system of "dispatch" and "pick-up" for three hundred automobiles. Then the MIA presented its demands to the city for desegregation of the buses.

The demands were refused, negotiations broke down, and the city commissioners announced they were joining the White Citizens Council. The protest movement achieved little in its early stages, but concomitant with its failures came the first indication of King's potential as a leader—and with it, the opportunity to develop his philosophy of nonviolence.

On January 30, 1956, while King was at a mass meeting, his home, with his wife and children in it, was bombed. When King arrived home, he found an angry mob of black men gathered on the lawn. From the porch he spoke to them, and in a matter of minutes he had quieted their anger. The communications media people were there to witness it, and Martin Luther King's national position as a black leader was created that night.

Rebuffed by the City Council, King took the bus desegregation issue into the federal courts, only to be served—along with more than one hundred other blacks—with an indictment by the local grand jury under an anti-boycott statute of 1921. King and the others were jailed, and many more volunteered to go to jail in support of the movement. King's philosophy of nonviolence—his preaching of love within a revolutionary movement—had brought an entirely new dimension to the boycott. On November 13, 1956, the Supreme Court ruled that bus segregation was a violation of the Constitution of the United States.

On December 22, King and other leaders of the Montgomery Improvement Association, along with some white passengers, rode "up front" on a bus through Montgomery. King wrote:

> In a few weeks transportation was back to normal, and people of both races rode together wherever they pleased. The skies did not fall when integrated buses finally traveled the streets of Montgomery.

About The Document:

In the years to follow Dr. King would become undisputed leader of the civil rights movement. The movement reached its climax in the massive March on Washington of August 27, 1963, when a quarter of a million whites and blacks lined either side of the Reflecting Pool in front of the Lincoln Memorial to hear Dr. King's famous "I Have a Dream" speech. Excerpts from that speech follow.

Excerpts from "I Have a Dream"
address delivered at the 1963
March on Washington, D.C.,
by Rev. Martin Luther King

The Document:

I SAY to you today, my friends, though, even though we face the difficulties of today and tomorrow, I still have a dream. It is a dream deeply rooted in the American dream. I have a dream that one day this nation will rise up, live out the true meaning of its creed: "We hold these truths to be self-evident, that all men are created equal."

I have a dream that one day on the red hills of Georgia sons of former slaves and the sons of former slave-owners will be able to sit down together at the table of brotherhood. I have a dream that one day even the state of Mississippi, a state sweltering with the heat of injustice, sweltering with the heat of oppression, will be transformed into an oasis of freedom and justice.

I have a dream that my four little children will one day live in a nation where they will not be judged by the color of their skin but by the context of their character.

I have a dream . . . I have a dream that one day in Alabama, with its vicious racists, with its governor having his lips dripping with the words of interposition and nullification, one day right there in Alabama little black boys and black girls will be able to join hands with little white boys and white girls as sisters and brothers.

I have a Dream Today . . . I have a Dream that one day every valley shall be exalted, every hill and mountain shall be made low. The rough places will be made plain, and the crooked places will be made straight. And the glory of the Lord shall be revealed, and all flesh shall see it together. This is our hope. This is the faith that I go back to the South with.

With this faith we will be able to hew out of the mountain of despair a stone of hope. With this faith we will be able to transform the jangling discords of our nation into a beautiful symphony of brotherhood. With this faith we will be able to work together, to pray together, to struggle together, to go to jail together, to stand up for freedom together, knowing that we will be free one day.

This will be the day when all of God's children will be able to sing with new meaning, "My country, 'tis of thee, sweet land of liberty, of thee I sing, Land where my fathers died, land of the pilgrim's pride, from every mountain side, let freedom ring." And if America is to be a great nation, this must become true.

So let freedom ring from the prodigious hilltops of New Hampshire. Let freedom ring from the heightening Alleghenies of Pennsylvania. Let freedom ring from the snow-capped Rockies of Colorado. Let freedom ring from the curvaceous slopes of California.

But not only that. Let freedom ring from Stone Mountain of Georgia. Let freedom ring from Lookout Mountain of Tennessee. Let freedom ring from every hill and molehill of Mississippi, from every mountain side. Let freedom ring . . .

When we allow freedom to ring—when we let it ring from every city and every hamlet, from every state and every city, we will be able to speed up that day when all of God's children, black and white men, Jews and Gentiles, Protestants and Catholics, will be able to join hands and sing in the words of the old Negro spiritual, "Free at last, Free at last, Great God a-mighty. We are free at last."

THE BLACK MAN AND SELF-DEFENSE: 1962

The case for answering violence with violence

by Robert F. Williams

About The Document:

When Robert F. Williams got out of the Marine Corps in 1955, he returned to his hometown of Monroe, North Carolina, and joined the local chapter of the NAACP. Growing threats of violence from the White Citizens Council and the Ku Klux Klan, which had its southeastern regional headquarters in Monroe, had whittled the membership of the local NAACP chapter down to six, and the well-off middle-class black leadership was proposing to dissolve the chapter altogether. When Williams objected, he was elected president, and the rest of the members, except a Dr. Albert E. Perry, a newcomer, all resigned. Perry became vice-president, and by 1957 he and Williams had rebuilt the local chapter with a membership of working-class people—laborers, farmers, domestics—and a large contingent of returned veterans who, according to Williams, "didn't scare easy."

In 1956 Williams began a drive to integrate Monroe's swimming pool, which had been built with federal funds, and which was closed to blacks. The city officials refused to let black children use the pool; nor would they build a pool in the black community. Williams took legal action. While he was preparing the groundwork for court proceedings, the Ku Klux Klan began a campaign against the NAACP chapter. After holding mass rallies, KKK members would drive through the black neighborhood in motorcades, honking their horns and firing pistols out of the car windows.

A group of pacifist ministers asked the city officials to stop the Klan from driving through the black community, but the request was rejected on the grounds that the Klan was a legal organization having "as much constitutional right to organize as the NAACP."

Appeals to the Governor of North Carolina and President Eisenhower followed, but no aid was forthcoming. It was at this time that the Monroe chapter of the NAACP started to arm itself. It applied for, and received, a charter from the National Rifle Association. Within a year it had sixty members.

In the summer of 1957 an armed motorcade of Klan members opened fire on Dr. Perry's house on the outskirts of the black community. Williams and his followers shot it out with the Klan and turned them back.

Two incidents in the following year brought Williams and the city of Monroe into national prominence. In October, 1958, a seven-year-old white girl kissed a nine-year-old black boy on the cheek. The girl innocently told her mother she had kissed the boy because he was a friend she hadn't seen for a long time and she was so glad to see him again that she kissed him. The mother called the police. The boy, and a friend who was with him at the time, were arrested for rape. Williams reported that he called the national office of the NAACP for help, but they refused to have anything to do with it because they did not like to get involved in a "sex case." The boy and his friend were sentenced to fourteen years in the reformatory. The story first appeared in a London paper, then spread over Europe, where it became a cause for riots and demonstrations. Finally, American papers began to write about the "Kissing Case." The boys were released on February 13, 1959, through the intervention of President Eisenhower.

The national office of the NAACP was thoroughly embarrassed. Roy Wilkins offered Williams a job in Detroit if he would leave Monroe, but Williams refused.

A second court case occurred in 1959. It involved the acquittal of a white man who had raped and beaten a black woman, eight months pregnant. The case incited Williams to reaffirm the right of self-defense. Williams told reporters that black men in Monroe would meet violence with violence if the courts failed to protect them.

Because of his statements to the press concerning the injustice of the Southern courts and the right of black men to defend their homes and families, Williams was suspended by the NAACP. All over the country news broadcasts reported that Williams had received a six-month suspension for advocating violence. Some white pacifist members of Williams' chapter sent a telegram to the national office of the NAACP stating that they were white Southerners, but they protested

Williams' suspension because "they understood the problems of the community and . . . the national office did not."

The NAACP never made the telegram public. Despite national publicity, not a single newspaper reported that the Union County (Monroe) NAACP was an interracial branch nor that its white Southerner members supported Williams' position.

Williams appealed to the NAACP convention but his suspension was upheld, even though the issue created enough delegate sentiment to force the national leadership to insert an endorsement of the concept of self-defense in the NAACP's constitution.

At the end of the six months, instead of going back into office automatically, Williams held an election and was voted back as president. "I didn't want the NAACP national office to think they were doing me any special favor," he said.

In 1960, Williams began to hold sit-ins and to demonstrate for school integration, but he was unable to get any assistance from the national office of the NAACP. In June, 1961, after four years of protest, the Monroe chapter of the NAACP decided to picket the city swimming pool. The picket line closed the pool, and when the pool closed, violence broke out.

Whites fired pistols and rifles over the heads of the picketers, but the local chief of police turned his head and did nothing to stop it. Williams sent a telegram to the U.S. Justice Department, which referred him to the local FBI, which in turn told him it was not a matter for the Justice Department. The FBI men in Monroe told Williams it was a local matter, and they said they had checked with the chief of police, who assured them he would provide ample protection for the pickets.

Two attempts on Williams' life followed, yet the picket line continued. Finally, in a dramatic last-minute rescue from a near-riot confrontation with white citizens, the state police came on the scene. State troopers successfully enforced law and order in Monroe.

The city closed the pool for the rest of the year, and Williams withdrew the picket line. It was at this time that the civil rights Freedom Riders came to Monroe. In their first few hours there, so many Freedom Riders and blacks were arrested that prisoners with legitimate charges against them were set free to make room in the city jail. The shootings and beatings continued, and Monroe's citizens began to arm themselves to defend their lives and their homes.

In his book *Negroes with Guns* Williams describes the ensuing events. He reports that shortly after receiving a call from a police official saying, "In thirty minutes you'll be hanging in the courthouse square," he saw police cars forming a cordon around his block. Gathering together his wife and children, he fled to Canada. Eventually he went to Cuba, where he wrote *Negroes with Guns*. He has since gone on to permanent exile in China, where today he is an active Maoist. The following excerpt from his book is one of the first explicit advocations recorded in the 20th century of the value of violence for the black man in America.

The Document:

Chapter titled "Self-Defense: An American Tradition,"
from *Negroes with Guns*
by Robert F. Williams, Marzani & Munsell, Inc., New York, 1962

THE STRANGLEHOLD of oppression cannot be loosened by a plea to the oppressor's conscience. Social change in something as fundamental as racist oppression involves violence. You cannot have progress here without violence and upheaval, because it's struggle for survival for one and a struggle for liberation for the other. Always the powers in command are ruthless and unmerciful in defending their position and their privileges. This is not an abstract rule to be meditated upon by Americans. This is a truth that was revealed at the birth of America, and has continued to be revealed many times in our history. The principle of self-defense is an American tradition that began at Lexington and Concord.

We have come to comprehend the nature of racism. It is a mass psychosis. When I've described racial conditions in the United States to audiences of foreign newsmen, Cubans and other Latin Americans, they have been shocked to learn of the depths of American race hatred. When I have cited as illustrations such extreme situations as the segregation of telephone party-lines in Union County, or the segregated pet-animal cemetery in Washington, D.C., where an Afro-American cannot bury his dog, they find such things comic as well as pathetic.

Such extreme examples of the racist mentality only appear comic when looked upon as isolated phenomena. In truth they are perfectly logical applications of the premises that make up the racist mentality. Look at the phenomena this way and they are the logical inventions of a thoroughly diseased mind. The racist is a man crazed by hysteria at the idea of coming into equal human contact with Negroes. And this mass mental illness called racism is very much a part of the "American Way of Life."

When Afro-American liberation is finally achieved in the U.S.A., one of the many new developments in such a society will be some sort of institution that will correct those Americans whose minds are thoroughly warped by racism. Somehow a way will be found so that these insane people will be made whole, will be made well again.

This is the time for the Afro-American to act. Our sense of national consciousness and militancy is growing. I speak of the masses of people, the masses of Afro-Americans that I know and have visited; in Jacksonville, Florida; in Atlanta, in Savannah, and in Macon, Georgia; in Columbia, in Charleston, and Greenville, South Carolina. The oppressed and exploited black men that I've met on the streets of Harlem, on the streets of Detroit, and in Chicago. And I speak of the people in Monroe where five years ago, when I started talking about self-defense, I would walk through the streets and many of my black neighbors would walk away to avoid me. Today, despite the FBI manhunt and my exile, despite the frame-up arrests and the shooting since, despite the intimidation campaigns like the one to drive Mrs. Johnson of *The Crusader* staff from Monroe, despite all of this, black Monroe continues its struggle.

As editor of *The Crusader,* I went south in the fall of 1960, deep into Jim Crowland, to observe the freedom struggle. I was confronted with this new wonderful spirit rising throughout Dixie—this determination to break the chains of bondage and the spirit of valor of a people who just a few years ago were submissive peons in civilization's no-man's-land. Daily, I saw the old myth about Afro-Americans being incapable of unity and action exploded.

In Savannah an NAACP leader had contributed $30,000 to the local branch. The branch has a full-time worker and a suite of office space. Pickets and sit-iners have been beaten, and jobs have been lost, but the struggle goes on. The leader is not afraid of violence to himself because the people are with him. In that city an Afro-American union leader said that it had come to pass that the masses of Afro-Americans can see that "We must defend ourselves against violence with violence." That many of them now say that the American white racist needs a good "whipping" to bring him down to earth and to break his white supremacy mania.

I learned in Atlanta that Mr. Elijah Muhammed had made quite an impression and that many Afro-Americans are learning, to the consternation and embarrassment of the black respectable leadership, that he has more to offer than weak prayers of deliverance. A prominent minister in South Carolina said, "Our biggest stumbling block is the Uncle Tom minister—the people must stop paying these traitors." In Atlanta, a university professor, energetic about the new spirit on the part of the Negroes, was very hopeful that new militant leadership would replace the old Uncle Toms, whose days, he was confident, were numbered.

There are exceptions among us. The Uncle Toms, the Judases, and the Quislings of the black "elite" would deny this rising consciousness. They do everything possible to make white Americans think that it is not true, while apologizing to us for the very people who oppress us. Some of these "responsible" Negroes are afraid that militant action damages "amiable race relations." They complain that race relations may deteriorate to a point that many Negroes may lose jobs. What they mean is that they may lose *their* jobs. For the black workers, who are the first to be fired, and last, if ever, to be hired, the situation is so bad it can't deteriorate.

We realize that there must be a struggle within our own ranks to take the leadership away from the black Quislings who betray us. Then the white liberals who are dumping hundreds of thousands of dollars into our struggle in the South to convert us to pacifism will have to accept *our* understanding of the situation or drop their liberal pretensions.

Why do the white liberals ask us to be non-violent? We are not the aggressors; we have been victimized for over 300 years! Yet nobody spends money to go into the South and ask the racists to be martyrs or pacifists. But they always come to the downtrodden Negroes, who are already oppressed and too submissive as a group, and they ask them not to fight back. There seems to be a pattern of some sort of strange coincidence of interest when whites preach a special doctrine to Negroes. Like the choice of theology when the plantation-owners saw to the Christianization of the slaves. Instead of the doctrines which produced the rugged aggressively independent and justice-seeking spirit that we associate with Colonial America as the New England Conscience, the slaves were indoctrinated in the most submissive "trust-your-master" pie-in-the-sky after-you-die form of Christianity.

It is because our militancy is growing that they spend hundreds of thousands of dollars to convert us into pacifists. Because our militancy is growing they come to us out of fear.

Of course, the respectable Negro leadership are the most outspoken exponents of non-violence. But if these people, especially the ministers, are such pure pacifists, why is it that so few, if any, criticize the war preparations of this country? Why is it that so few speak out against the Bomb? Isn't that the sort of preaching one expects and *hears* from sincere pacifists? The responsible Negro leadership is pacifist in so far as its one interest is that we do not fight white racists; that we do not "provoke" or enrage them. They constantly tell us that if we resort to violent self-defense we will be exterminated. They are not stopping violence—they are only stopping defensive violence against white racists out of a fear of extermination.

This fear of extermination is a myth which we've exposed in Monroe. We did this because we came to have an active understanding of the racist system and we grasped the relationship between violence and racism. The existence of violence is at the very heart of a racist system. The Afro-American militant is a "militant" because he defends himself, his family, his home, and his dignity. He does not *introduce* violence into a racist social system—the violence is already there, and has always been there. It is precisely this unchallenged violence that allows a racist social system to perpetuate itself. When people say that they are opposed to Negroes "resorting to violence" what they really mean is that they are opposed to Negroes defending themselves and challenging the exclusive monopoly of violence practiced by white racists. We have shown in Monroe that with violence working *both ways* constituted law will be more inclined to keep the peace.

When Afro-Americans resist and struggle for their rights they also possess a power greater than that generated by their will and their hands. With the world situation as it is today, the most racist and fascist United States government conceivable could not succeed in exterminating 20,000,000 people. We know there is a great power struggle going on in the world today, and the colored peoples control the true balance of power. We also know, from the statistics of the Detroit race riots, that production in this country would fall in forty-eight hours. People everywhere in the world would be ready to support our struggle.

Nor should we forget that these same deceiving pacifist-preaching well-to-do southern blacks profit from the struggle, living lives of luxury while most Afro-Americans continue to suffer. Are they any better than the Negro Quisling in neighboring Charleston, North Carolina—a black man who rode around in a new pink Cadillac with anti-NAACP and anti-integration literature, a huge roll of money, and an expense account, all the blessings of the White Citizens' Council? It is an ironic sign that black Judases are becoming more expensive as the white racist becomes desperate—though it is a small consolation to those of us who suffer from his betrayals.

In Monroe, where we fought the Klan, we were being penalized. There are children there growing up without any education, children without shoes, children without food. Old people without medical attention. For the Monroe Negro, there is no work; there is no welfare. From all the money raised in the North by the official black leadership, no one would send a penny to Monroe, because the white liberals who gave this money considered us to be outlaws and thugs. They preferred to let us suffer rather than to identify themselves with our position. They sent truck convoys into other places in the South, but penalized us because we took a militant stand.

But our children who are growing up without shoes are also growing up with a sense of direction they cannot obtain in the Jim Crow schools. There once was a threat, in Monroe, of Negro teen-age gang war. It abated as the teen-agers resolved their difficulties by coming to understand the problem. It is only natural to expect the black youth to be infected with a desire to do something. Frustrated by less active adults, this desire may be projected in the wrong direction. The vigor of the youth can be channeled into constructive militant actions. It is simply a matter of common sense to have these young Negroes constructively fight racial injustice rather than fight among themselves. Danger is not a respecter of color lines; it is better to bleed for a just cause than to bleed just for the thrill of the sight of blood. Rebellion ferments in modern youth. It is better that it expend itself against its true enemies than against teen-age schoolmates who can't even explain the reasons for their dangerous skirmishes.

The Montgomery bus boycott was perhaps the most successful example of completely pacifist action. But we must remember that in Montgomery, where Negroes are riding in the front of buses, there are also Negroes who are starving. The Montgomery bus boycott was a victory—but it was limited. It did not raise the Negro standard of living; it did not mean better education for Negro children, it did not mean economic advances.

Just what was the issue at hand for the white racists? What sacrifice? Remember that in Montgomery most of the white Americans have automobiles and are not dependent on the buses. It's just like our own experience in Monroe when we integrated the library. I just called the chairman of the board in my county, I told him that I represented the NAACP, that we wanted to integrate the library, and that our own library had burned down. And he said, "Well, I don't see any reason why you can't use the same library that our people use. It won't make any difference. And after all, I don't read anyway." Now, this is the attitude of a lot of white Southerners about the Montgomery bus boycott. The white people who control the city didn't ride the buses anyway; they had their own private cars, so it didn't make any difference to them.

But when Afro-Americans get into the struggle for the right to live as human beings and the right to earn the same amount of money, then they'll meet the greatest amount of resistance, and out of it will come police-condoned or inspired violence. When that happens, the racist must be made to realize that in attacking us he risks his own life. After all, his life is a white life, and he considers the white life to be superior; so why should he risk a superior life to take an inferior one?

Now I believe, and a lot of other Negroes do too, that we must create a black militancy of our own. We must direct our own struggle, achieve our own destiny. We must realize that many Afro-Americans have become skeptical and extremely suspicious of the so-called white liberals who have dominated "Negro" freedom movements. They just feel that no white person can understand what it's like to be a suppressed Negro. The traditional white liberal leadership in civil rights organizations, and even white radicals, generally cannot understand what our struggle is and how we feel about it. They have always made our struggle secondary and after all these years we really never got any place.

They have a patient sense for good public relations. But we're not interested in a good press. We're interested in becoming free. We want to be liberated. To me, oppression is harmful. It is painful. I would wake up in the morning as a Negro who was oppressed. At lunchtime, I would eat as a Negro who was oppressed. At night, I would go to bed as a Negro who was oppressed. And if I could have been free in thirty seconds, it would not have been too soon.

"Too long have others spoken for us," began the first editorial in the first Afro-American newspaper, which began publication in 1827. The truth of these words has not dimmed in the century and a half since they first appeared in *Freedom's Journal*. They are more appropriate than ever.

There are white people who are willing to give us aid without strings attached. They are willing to let us direct our own struggle; they are genuinely interested in the liberation of the Negroes. I wouldn't have been able to remain in the South as long as I did if it had not been for the support that I got from some white people in the North. And I might never have succeeded in escaping the legal-lynching manhunt fomented by the FBI, nor have reached Cuban sanctuary but for the help of whites. They will be willing to continue helping us for the sake of justice, for the sake of human decency. . . .

The tactics of non-violence will continue and should continue. We too believed in non-violent tactics in Monroe. We've used these tactics; we've used all tactics. But we also believe that any struggle for liberation should be a flexible struggle. We shouldn't take the attitude that one method alone is the way to liberation. This is to become dogmatic. This is to fall into the same sort of dogmatism practiced by some of the religious fanatics. We can't afford to develop this type of attitude.

We must use non-violence as a means as long as this is feasible, but the day will come when conditions become so pronounced that non-violence will be suicidal in itself. The day is surely coming when we will see more violence on the same American scene. The day is surely coming when some of the same Negroes who have denounced our using weapons for self-defense will be arming themselves. There are those who pretend to be horrified by the idea that a black veteran who shouldered arms for the United States would willingly take up weapons to defend his wife, his children, his home, and his life. These same people will one day be loud advocates of self-defense. When violent racism and fascism strike at their families and their homes, not in a token way but in an all-out bloody campaign, then they will be among the first to advocate self-defense. They will justify their position as a question of survival. When it is no longer some distant Negro who's no more than a statistic; no more than an article in a newspaper; when it is no longer their neighbors, but it means them and it becomes a matter of personal salvation, then will their attitude change.

As a tactic, we use and approve non-violent resistance. But we also believe that a man cannot have human dignity if he allows himself to be abused; to be kicked and beaten to the ground, to allow his wife and children to be attacked, refusing to defend them and himself on the basis that he's so pious, so self-righteous, that it would demean his personality if he fought back.

We know that the average Afro-American is not a pacifist. He's not a pacifist and he has never been a pacifist and he's not made of the type of material that would make a good pacifist. Those who doubt that the great majority of Negroes are not pacifists, just let them slap one. Pick any Negro on any street corner in the U.S.A. and they'll find out how much he believes in turning the other cheek.

All those who dare to attack are going to learn the hard way that the Afro-American is not a pacifist; that he cannot forever be counted on not to defend himself. Those who attack him brutally and ruthlessly can no longer expect to attack him with impunity.

The Afro-American cannot forget that his enslavement in this country did not pass because of pacifist moral force or noble appeals to the Christian conscience of the slaveholders.

Henry David Thoreau is idealized as an apostle of non-violence, the writer who influenced Gandhi, and through Gandhi, Martin Luther King, Jr. But Thoreau was not dogmatic; his eyes were open and he saw clearly. I keep with me a copy of Thoreau's *Plea For Captain John Brown*. There are truths that are just as evident in 1962 as they were in 1859 when he wrote: [Editor's note: Here Williams gives an excerpt from Thoreau's "Plea for Captain John Brown," which is reprinted on p. 102.]

It is in the nature of the American Negro, the same as all other men, to fight and to try to destroy those things that block his path to a greater happiness in life.

Whenever I speak on the English-language radio station in Havana (which broadcasts for an audience in the United States), I hope in some way to penetrate the mental barriers and introduce new disturbing elements into the consciousness of white America. I hope to make them aware of the monstrous evil that they are party to by oppressing the Negro. Somehow, I must manage to clearly reflect the image of evil that is inherent in a racist society so that white America will be able to honestly and fully see themselves as they really are. To see themselves with the same clarity as foreigners see them and to recognize that they are not champions of democracy. To understand that today they do not really even *believe* in democracy. To understand that the world is changing regardless of whether they *think* they like it or not.

For I know that if they had a glimpse of their own reality the shock would be of great therapeutic value. There would be many decent Americans who would then understand that this society must mend its ways if it is to survive; that there is no place in the world now for a racist nation.

As an individual, I'm not inclined toward "politics." The only thing I care about is justice and liberation. I don't belong to any political party. But I think that as long as the present politics prevails the Negro is not going to be integrated into American society. There will have to be great political changes before that can come about.

Those Americans who most deny the logic of the future are the ones who have driven me into exile. Those people have been cruel. Yet cruel as it may be, this exile was not the end those people had planned for me. But it is not in the hands of today's oppressors to determine my end. Their role in history denies to them an understanding of this, just as their role will not allow them to understand that every true nationalist leader in Africa has been imprisoned or exiled, and that the future leaders of Latin America and Asian national liberation today are experiencing imprisonment, exile, or worse.

The future belongs to to-day's oppressed and I shall be witness to that future in the liberation of the Afro-American.

MALCOLM X AND THE BLACK MUSLIMS: 1964

Two points of view on "black nationalism"

by Elijah Muhammad and Malcolm X

About The Documents:

Around 1930 a dark-skinned peddler of silks and yard goods appeared in Detroit. His name was W. D. Fard. On his door-to-door rounds he said that he was from the Holy City of Mecca and that his mission was to secure "freedom, justice, and equality" for the American black man. Whenever he could, Fard arranged meetings in the homes of those willing to listen to him. He soon had a small, devoted band of followers.

The depression was punching extra holes in the black man's belt. Black men were being laid off while white workers remained on the job, and men who had worked for a long time were being replaced by white newcomers. Fard played on the blacks' growing fear that more and more of them would be forced onto the welfare rolls, and his accusations against the injustice of the white man found an eager audience among black men in Detroit. It is said that eight thousand of them joined Fard's cult in his first four years.

Fard established the first Temple of Islam, which became his permanent headquarters. As the temple grew, Fard organized the "Fruit of Islam," a paramilitary defense corps trained in boxing, karate, and judo. He also organized the Muslim Girls Training Corps, which taught young women domestic skills and the proper behavior for a Muslim wife and mother. Fard's crowning achievement was the University of Islam, where black men were taught how to fight against the "tricknology" of the "blue-eyed devil white man."

By 1933, Fard began to appear less frequently before his followers, which only served to reinforce their belief in his divinity. Fard claimed he was the "Supreme Ruler of the Universe" who had temporarily returned to earth "to redeem and return the Negro to his true religion."

In late 1933, or early 1934, W. D. Fard mysteriously disappeared and was never seen again. His Lost-Found Nation of Islam then fell under the guidance of his heir apparent, Elijah Muhammad, whom Fard had selected to be the "Supreme Minister" over all the other "Ministers of Islam."

Elijah Muhammad was born in Sandersville, Georgia, in 1897, as Robert Poole, one of thirteen children of a Baptist preacher and sharecropper. At the age of sixteen, after completing only four grades of school, Robert Poole ran away from home. He worked at a succession of ill-paid jobs, met and married Clara Evans, and in 1923 moved with her and their two children to Detroit. Poole met Fard in 1931 and became his most dedicated disciple. Later Fard gave him the name Elijah Muhammad, a name he himself had used on occasion.

Following Fard's disappearance there was considerable internal disagreement among members of the Detroit temple. Elijah Muhammad went to Chicago and set up a temple there, and those who believed in Fard's divinity followed him. Without strong leadership, the Detroit temple began to fail, but after a while both temples came under Elijah's authority and both prospered. In 1942, Elijah Muhammad was sentenced to five years in prison for what in those days was referred to as draft-dodging and for influencing young men to evade the draft. After three and a half years he was paroled. He returned to active control of the Muslims in 1946, and set up temples in Milwaukee and Washington, D.C.

In the 1950's a man named Malcolm Little joined the organization. Under the name of Malcolm X this dynamic and articulate spokesman in the next two years became even better known than Muhammad himself. Malcolm X's role in the black protest movement has been the subject of great controversy—and some mystery, but there is no disputing the fact that his rise to power was accompanied by a spectacular expansion of the Muslim organization. By 1961 there were sixty-nine temples and missions in twenty-seven states. Muslim membership was counted somewhere between 100,000 and 200,000.

Malcolm Little was born in Omaha, Nebraska, in 1925. His father was a Baptist minister, who spent as much time preaching Back-to-Africanism as he did religion, and his family suffered the financial consequences. The father was an advocate of Marcus Garvey's Universal Negro Improvement

Association, and he was proud and militant. He was killed, when Malcolm was six, by white men.

Eight children were too many for Malcolm's mother to care for alone. When he was twelve, Malcolm went to Boston to live with a half sister, who tried to encourage him to mingle with the middle-class blacks "on the Hill" in Roxbury. But it was to the "hip" and the "sharp" hangouts in the black ghetto of Boston that Malcolm was lured. In no time he was conking his hair, wearing zoot suits, and escorting white girls about the town.

Malcolm got a job as a sandwich and ice-cream vendor on the Boston–New Haven railroad when he was sixteen. He came to love New York, especially Harlem, where he soon was familiar in the more popular bars. He was hired as a waiter in Small's Paradise, where—listening attentively to the patrons—he became expertly schooled in the hustles.

Because of his red hair, Malcolm became known as "Detroit Red." In a couple of years he was a gun-carrying hood, a drug peddler, a pimp, and a numbers runner—one of the sharpest, toughest of the teen-age Harlem hustlers on the streets. Returning to Boston, he was arrested for armed robbery and sentenced to ten years in jail. He was then twenty-one.

In jail Malcolm took a correspondence course in English and through the efforts of his brother, Reginald, was introduced to "The Nation of Islam." Writers and sociologists who study Elijah Muhammad's movement have commented on the sense of dignity and self-worth that the Muslim organization imparts to its members. This is attested to by the number of ex-cons and ex-junkies who are proud members. Malcolm became a Muslim. He changed his name, in line with organizational policy to reject names imposed by former slave masters. He became Malcolm X.

When he was released from prison he went immediately to Chicago to meet Elijah Muhammad. Elijah took Malcolm under his private tutelage, and Malcolm became totally devoted to the "Messenger of Allah" and his preachings. In the years that followed he became the leading spokesman for the Muslims. He appeared more frequently in public than Muhammad himself, and he began to speak out on topics that went beyond Muslim precepts. The Nation of Islam was unaffiliated with any of the established civil rights groups, but Malcolm believed the organization could play an important role in the struggle for civil rights.

The economic structure of the Muslim society is built along lines very similar to those outlined by Marcus Garvey in his plans for a black nation, the difference being that the

Muslims have been successful where Garvey was not. In many cities the Muslims operate small businesses such as grocery stores, dry-cleaning plants, restaurants, bakeries, and barbershops. The Nation of Islam also has its own newspaper, *Muhammad Speaks,* which began as a biweekly in 1960 and became a weekly in 1965. It is a professionally edited, attractively made-up newspaper, profusely illustrated with photographs and editorial cartoons. In addition to extensive coverage of Muslim activities, the paper reports on legislative and personal acts of discrimination against black men throughout the world. It offers advice on health and stresses the importance of stronger family ties. The paper is edited to follow the Muslim practice of emphasizing the importance of pride in race. The Muslim attitude toward "nationalism"—which early in the black militant movement produced such strong reactions in the white press—is explained in the document by Elijah Muhammad which follows this commentary.

In the early 1960's, the Muslims began to attract the attention of the news media. According to Malcolm X in his autobiography, the press furor over the Muslims began when a television program called "The Hate That Hate Produced" was aired in late 1959. Before long Malcolm X was defending and explaining the Nation of Islam on radio and television discussions and debate programs. The publication of Dr. C. Eric Lincoln's book *The Black Muslims in America* introduced the name "Black Muslims" and brought even more public attention to the cult. It was widely quoted and freely discussed by the news media and fixed in the public mind, despite Malcolm's efforts to prevent the use of the term in reference to the Muslims.

On July 3, 1963, two former secretaries of Elijah Muhammad charged that he had fathered their four children. Malcolm later admitted that as far back as 1955 he had heard such talk about Muhammad but had refused to believe it. Malcolm decided to ask Muhammad himself about the allegations. Muhammad admitted that the stories were true but urged Malcolm not to judge him on moral standards but to analyze his deeds with his own understanding of prophecy and spiritual things. He explained that his adulterous behavior was necessary for him to fulfill in prophecy the lives of Noah, David, and Lot.

That confrontation ended Malcolm's close ties with Elijah Muhammad. But before Malcolm could move on his own, Muhammad moved against him. What happened next is well known. On November 22, 1963, John F. Kennedy was assassinated. During the question-and-answer period of a meeting in New York, Malcolm was asked what he thought about the assassination. He answered that it was a case of "the chickens coming home to roost" and went on to explain that he meant that the same hate in the white man which allowed them to kill innocent black people had spread so far that "it finally had struck down this country's chief of state." The newspapers played up Malcolm's remark but not his interpretation. Muhammad suspended Malcolm for ninety days, and other Muslim leaders mounted an unremitting attack against him.

Malcolm left the Nation of Islam and eventually founded the Muslim Mosque, Inc., in New York City, beginning to formulate the ideology and philosophy of a new movement. At a series of public rallies in Harlem, Malcolm X gave the speech printed in the following pages. The title of the speech was "The Ballot or the Bullet" and its subject was black nationalism.

Shortly after this speech, Malcolm visited Mecca, and Ghana and other African countries. During his travels he spoke with government officials, intellectuals, and diplomats, and he returned to the United States convinced that the problems of black Americans were linked to those of black men everywhere. His attitude toward the white man also underwent a change. Said Malcolm:

> If you attack him because he is white, you give him no out. He can't stop being white. We've got to give the man a chance.

We will never know the final shape of Malcolm X's "new movement," because in 1965 he was assassinated while addressing a group of followers in New York.

The Document:

An editorial from the newspaper
Muhammad Speaks,
reprinted in all editions

What The Muslims Want:

THIS IS THE question asked most frequently by both the whites and the blacks. The answers to this question I shall state as simply as possible.

1. We want freedom. We want a full and complete freedom.

2. We want justice. Equal justice under the law. We want

justice applied equally to all, regardless of creed or class or color.

3. We want equality of opportunity. We want equal membership in society with the best in civilized society.

4. We want our people in America whose parents or grandparents were descendants from slaves, to be allowed to establish a separate state or territory of their own—either on this continent or elsewhere. We believe that our former slave masters are obligated to provide such land and that the area must be fertile and minerally rich. We believe that our former slave masters are obliged to maintain and supply our needs in this separate territory for the next 20 to 25 years—until we are able to produce and supply our own needs.

Since we cannot get along with them in peace and equality, after giving them 400 years of our sweat and blood and receiving in return some of the worst treatment human beings have ever experienced, we believe our contributions to this land and the suffering forced upon us by white America, justifies our demand for complete separation in a state or territory of our own.

5. We want freedom for all Believers of Islam now held in federal prisons. We want freedom for all black men and women now under death sentence in innumerable prisons in the North as well as the South.

We want every black man and woman to have the freedom to accept or reject being separated from the slave master's children and establish a land of their own.

We know that the above plan for the solution of the black and white conflict is the best and only answer to the problem between two people.

6. We want an immediate end to the police brutality and mob attacks against the so-called Negro throughout the United States.

We believe that the Federal government should intercede to see that black men and women tried in white courts receive justice in accordance with the laws of the land—or allow us to build a new nation for ourselves, dedicated to justice, freedom and liberty.

7. As long as we are not allowed to establish a state or territory of our own, we demand not only equal justice under the laws of the United States, but equal employment opportunities—NOW!

We do not believe that after 400 years of free or nearly free labor, sweat and blood, which has helped America become rich and powerful, that so many thousands of black people should have to subsist on relief, charity or live in poor houses.

8. We want the government of the United States to exempt our people from ALL taxation as long as we are deprived of equal justice under the laws of the land.

9. We want equal education—but separate schools up to 16 for boys and 18 for girls on the condition that the girls be sent to women's colleges and universities. We want all black children educated, taught and trained by their own teachers.

Under such schooling system we believe we will make a better nation of people. The United States government should provide, free, all necessary text books and equipment, schools and college buildings. The Muslim teachers shall be left free to teach and train their people in the way of righteousness, decency and self respect.

10. We believe that intermarriage or race mixing should be prohibited. We want the religion of Islam taught without hindrance or suppression.

These are some of the things that we, the Muslims, want for our people in North America.

The Document:

Speech titled "The Ballot or the
Bullet," delivered at the Muslim
Mosque, Inc., New York City,
March 22, 1964

BROTHERS AND SISTERS and friends—and I see some enemies. [*Applause.*] In fact, I think we'd be fooling ourselves if we had an audience this large and didn't realize that there were some enemies present.

This afternoon we want to talk about the ballot or the bullet. The ballot or the bullet explains itself. But before we get into it, I would like to clarify some things. . . . about black nationalism.

The political philosophy of black nationalism only means that the black man should control the politics and the politicians in his own community. [*Applause.*] The time when white people can come in our community and get us to vote for them so that they can be our political leaders and tell us what to do and what not to do is long gone. [*Applause.*] By the same token, the time when that same one white man can send another Negro into the community, to get you and me to support him so he can use him to lead us astray—those days are long gone. [*Applause.*] The political philosophy of black nationalism only means that if you and I are going to live in a black community—and that's where we are going to live, 'cause as soon as you move out of the black community into their community, it's mixed for a period of time, but they're gone and you're right there all by yourself again. [*Applause.*]

The economic philosophy of black nationalism only means that we should own and operate and control the economy of our community. You can't open up a black store in a white community—white men won't even patronize it, and they're not wrong. They've got sense enough to look out for themselves. It's you who don't have sense enough to look out for yourselves. [*Applause.*] The white man is too intelligent to let someone else come and gain control of the economy of his community. But you will let anybody come in and control the economy of your community; control the housing, control the education, control the jobs, control the businesses under the pretext that you are integrated. No, you're out of your mind. [*Applause.*]

We have to become involved in a program of re-education. To educate our people into the importance of knowing that when you spend your dollar out of the community in which you live, the community in which you spend your money becomes richer and richer. The community out of which you take your money becomes poorer and poorer. And then what happens? The community in which you live becomes a slum. It becomes a ghetto. The conditions become run-down, and then you have the audacity to complain about poor housing and a run-down community. Why, you run it down yourselves when you take your dollar out. [*Applause.*] And you and I are in a double trap, because not only do we lose by taking our money someplace else and spending it, when we try and spend it in our own community we're trapped because we haven't had sense enough to set up stores and control the businesses of our community. The man who's controlling the stores in our community is the man who doesn't look like we do. He's the man who doesn't even live in the community. So you and I, even when we try and spend our money in the block where we live or in the area where we live, we're spending it with a man who, when the sun goes down, takes that basketful of money to another part of town. [*Applause.*] So we're trapped, trapped, double trapped, triple trapped. Any way we go we find that we're trapped. . . .

You and I have to make a start, and the definite place to start is right in the community where we live. [*Applause.*] So our people not only have to be re-educated to the importance of supporting black business but the black man himself has to be made aware of the importance of going into business. What we will be doing is developing a situation wherein we will actually be able to create employment for the people in the community. And that will eliminate the necessity of you and me having to act ignorantly and disgracefully boycotting and picketing some cracker someplace else trying to beg him for a job. [*Applause.*] Any time you have to rely upon your enemies for a job you're in bad shape. When you know he is your enemy all the time. Anyhow, you wouldn't be in this country if some enemy hadn't kidnapped you and brought you here. [*Applause.*]. . . .

·We need a self-help program. A do-it-yourself philosophy. A do-it-right-now philosophy. It's-already-too-late philosophy. This is what you and I need to get with. The only time we're going to solve our problem is with a self-help program. Before we can get a self-help program started, we have to have a self-help philosophy. Black nationalism·is a self-help philosophy. This is a philosophy that eliminates the necessity for division and argument, so that if you're black, you should be thinking black. And if you're black, and you're not thinking black at this late date, why, I'm sorry for you. [*Applause.*]

Once you change your philosophy, you change your *thought pattern*. Once you change your thought pattern, you change your attitude. Once you change your attitude, it changes your behavior pattern and then you go on into some action. But as long as you've got a sit-down philosophy, you have a sit-down thought pattern, and as long as you think those sit-down thoughts, you'll be in some kind of sit-down action. They'll have you sittin'-in everywhere. It's not so good to refer to what you're going to do as a sit-in. They right there castrate you. Right there it brings you down. What goes with it? Think of the image of someone sittin'. An old woman can sit. An old man can sit. A chump can sit. A coward can sit. Anything can sit. But you and I been sittin' long enough, and it's time today for us to start doing some standing. And fightin' to back that up. [*Applause.*]

When we look at other parts of this earth upon which we live, we find that black, brown, red and yellow people in Africa and Asia are getting their independence. They're not getting it by singing "We shall overcome." No, they're getting it through nationalism. Every nation in Asia gained its independence through the philosophy of nationalism. Every nation on the African continent that has gotten its independence brought it about through the philosophy of nationalism. And it will take black nationalism to bring about the freedom of 22 million Afro-Americans, here in this country, where we have suffered *colonialism* for the past 400 years. [*Applause.*]

So it's time to wake up. It's got to be ·the ballot or the bullet. The ballot or the bullet. If you're afraid to use an expression like that, you should get on out of the country; you should get back in the cotton patch; you should get back in the alley.

When this country here was first being founded, there were thirteen colonies. The whites were colonized. They were fed up with this taxation without representation. So some of them stood up and said, "Liberty or death." Look, I went to a white school over here in Mason, Michigan. The white man made the mistake of lettin' me read his history books. He made the mistake of teaching me that Patrick Henry was a patriot. And George Washington—wasn't nothin' nonviolent about Old Pat or George Washington. "Liberty or death" was what brought about the freedom of whites in this country from the English. [Applause.] They didn't care about the odds. Why, they faced the wrath of the entire British Empire. And in those days, they used to say that the British Empire was so vast and so powerful, the sun would never set on it. This is how big it was. Yet, these thirteen little scrawny states, tired of being exploited and oppressed and degraded, told that big British Empire, "Liberty or death." And here you have 22 million Afro-Americans, black people today, catchin' more hell than Patrick Henry ever saw. [Applause.] And I'm here to tell you in case you don't know, that you've got a new, a new generation of black people in this country, who don't care anything *whatsoever* about odds. They don't want to hear you old Uncle-Tom-handkerchief-heads talking about the odds. [Applause.]

America today finds herself in a unique situation. Historically, revolutions are bloody. Oh, yes, they are. They haven't ever had a bloodless revolution or a non-violent revolution. That don't happen even in Hollywood. [Applause.] You don't have a revolution in which you love your enemy. And you don't have a revolution in which you are begging the system of exploitation to integrate you into it. Revolutions overturn systems. Revolutions destroy systems. [Applause.] A revolution is bloody. But America is in a unique position. She's the only country in history in a position actually to become involved in a bloodless revolution. The Russian revolution was bloody. The Chinese revolution was bloody. The French revolution was bloody. The Cuban revolution was bloody. And there was nothing more bloody than the American Revolution. But today this country can become involved in a revolution that won't take bloodshed. All she's got to do is give to the black man in this country everything that's due him. Everything. [Applause.]

So it's the ballot or the bullet. Today our people can see that we're faced with a government conspiracy. The Senators who are filibustering concerning your and my rights, that's the government. Don't say it's Southern Senators. This is the government. Any kind of activity that takes place on the floor of the Congress or the Senate, that's the government. Any kind of act that's designed to delay or deprive you and me, right now, of getting full rights, that's the government that's responsible. And any time you find the government involved in a conspiracy to violate the citizenship or the civil rights of a people, then you are wasting your time going to that government expecting redress. Instead, you have to take that government to the world court and accuse it of genocide and all the other crimes that it is guilty of today. [*Applause.*]

So those of us whose political and economic and social philosophy is black nationalism have become involved in the civil rights struggle. We have injected ourselves into the civil rights struggle, and we intend to expand it from the level of civil rights to the level of human rights. As long as you fight it on the level of civil rights, you're under Uncle Sam's jurisdiction. You're going to his court expecting him to correct the problem. He created the problem. He's the criminal. You don't take your case to the criminal. You take your criminal to court. [*Applause.*]

When the government of South Africa began to trample upon the human rights of the people of South Africa, they were taken to the U.N. When the government of Portugal began to trample upon the rights of our brothers and sisters in Angola, it was taken before the U.N. Why, even the white man took the Hungarian question to the U.N. And just this week, Chief Justice Goldberg was crying over three million Jews in Russia, about their human rights, charging Russia with violating the U.N. Charter, because of its mistreatment of the human rights of Jews in Russia. Now, you tell me, how can the plight of everybody on this earth reach the halls of the U.N., and yet you have 22 million Afro-Americans whose churches are being bombed? Whose little girls are being murdered. Whose leaders are being shot down in broad daylight. Now, you tell me, why the leaders of this struggle have never taken it before the United Nations? [*Applause.*] So, our next move is to expand the civil rights struggle to the level of human rights, take it into the United Nations, where our African brothers can throw their weight on our side, where our Asian brothers can throw their weight on our side, where our Latin-American brothers can throw their weight on our side, and where 800 million Chinese are sitting there, waiting to throw their weight on our side. And let the world see that Uncle Sam is guilty of violating the human rights of 22 million Afro-Americans and still has the audacity or the nerve to stand up and represent himself as the leader of the free world. [*Applause.*]

Let the world know how bloody his hands are. Let the world know the hypocrisy that's practiced over here. Let it be the ballot or the bullet. Let him know it must be the ballot or the bullet.

So, I say in my conclusion, the only way we're gonna solve it, we have got to unite, we've got to work together in unity and harmony. And black nationalism is the key. How are we going to overcome the tendency to be at each other's throats that always exists in our neighborhoods? And the reason this tendency exists is that the strategy of the white man has always been divide and conquer. He keeps us divided in order to conquer us. He tells you, I'm for separation and that you're for integration, and he keeps us fightin' with each other. No, I'm not for separation and you're not for integration. What you and I are for is freedom. [*Applause.*] Only you think that integration will get you freedom, I think separation will get me freedom. We both got the same objective. We've just got different ways of getting at it. I studied this man Billy Graham, who preaches white nationalism. That's what he preaches. [*Applause.*] I say, that's what he preaches. The whole church structure in this country is white nationalism. You go inside a white church, that's what they preaching, white nationalism. They got Jesus white, Mary white, God white, everybody white. That's white nationalism. [*Applause.*] So if you walk into a Negro church and you see a white Jesus and a white Mary and some white angels, that Negro church is preaching white nationalism. [*Applause.*] But when you go to a church and you see the pastor of that church with a philosophy and a program that's designed to bring black people together and elevate black people, join that church. [*Applause.*] If you see where the NAACP is preaching and practicing that which is designed to make black nationalism materialize, join NAACP. Join any kind of organization—civic, religious, fraternal, political or otherwise that's based on liftin' the black man up and makin' him master of his own community. [*Applause.*]

It'll be the ballot or it'll be the bullet. It'll be liberty or it'll be death. And if you're not ready to pay that price, don't use the word freedom in your vocabulary.

SNICK AND "BLACK POWER": 1966

A militant leader
explains what he meant when
he introduced the slogan "Black Power"

by Stokely Carmichael

About The Document:

Black protest entered a new phase in the 1960's: the protest of "massive resistance." It began as a sit-in by high-school and college students in Greensboro, North Carolina. In a larger sense it was an extension of the tactic begun when Mrs. Parks had refused to surrender her seat to a white man on a bus in Montgomery, Alabama.

On February 1, 1960, four black students from North Carolina Agricultural and Technical College strode into Greensboro's Woolworth store and sat at the stools of a traditionally all-white lunch counter. They were ignored, but they neither left nor made a disturbance. They sat and waited. After they had sat there for an hour without being served, the lunch counter closed for the day. The students went home. Within two weeks, lunch-counter sit-ins had spread to fifteen cities in five Southern states. Students staged sit-ins at colleges, wade-ins at beaches, kneel-ins at churches.

Late in February, Ella Baker—who was in charge of the Southern Christian Leadership Conference office in Atlanta —called together a number of the student leaders who had participated in the sit-ins. The SCLC—which had grown out of Martin Luther King's successful two-year bus boycott in Birmingham—advanced the students a sum of money to initiate sit-ins on an organized basis. The amount was $800—and with that the Student Nonviolent Coordinating Committee (SNCC or SNICK) was launched.

Shortly after the birth of SNICK the program director of the NAACP—James Farmer—resigned to become National Director of the Congress of Racial Equality (CORE), an organization that for almost two decades had been advocating a

212

program of nonviolent direct action. The transfer of allegiance by an established leader of the moderate NAACP to an organization dedicated to direct action was symbolic of the new mood of impatience even among the older Negro ranks.

Under Farmer's leadership, CORE initiated one of the most dramatic movements of the entire civil rights period— the famous Freedom Rides. An Interstate Commerce Commission ruling had ordered an end to segregated facilities in bus terminals, but throughout the South the order was being assiduously disregarded. The first contingent of seven black and six white Freedom Riders left Washington, D.C., on May 4. At the Rock Hill, South Carolina, bus terminal they were attacked by a white mob; at Anniston, Alabama, one of their buses was attacked and burned; and at Birmingham, they were attacked by young whites armed with metal bars, as the police looked on. Bus drivers refused to take the Freedom Riders farther. The Freedom Riders then flew to New Orleans to stage a mass rally.

They were joined by a group of SNICK students. Throughout that spring and summer, black and white students, sometimes numbering as many as one thousand, took Freedom Rides to face attack, arrest and imprisonment. By autumn they had not accomplished their stated goals, but they had aroused national attention. More important, many young Americans who but a short time earlier were being described by their elders as the "uncommitted generation" had found something to commit themselves to.

In the fall of 1961 SNICK had a hard-core staff of sixteen young people who left school and college to work full time for Negro rights. By 1964 the working staff was 150.

While the Freedom Rides came slowly to an end, one branch of SNICK workers continued to organize sit-in type demonstrations in public parks, public libraries, public swimming pools, etc. Another branch concentrated on voter-registration drives in so-called "dormant" areas of the Deep South, where fear had created such hostility to change that to get one black man to register was a success of consequence.

The first voter registration school was set up in McComb, Mississippi, in August 1961. All that summer hundreds of college students streamed into the state to explain voting requirements to blacks, to help them prepare for their tests, and to stand by them at the places of registration. Volunteers also staffed SNICK's "Freedom Schools" for young children. There were arrests, beatings, and scattered assassinations.

SNICK policy had for some time interpreted the sit-ins and other desegregation demonstrations, not as a means to integration, but as an effort to arouse black people to push for political power. From 1963 to 1966 SNICK workers challenged the very legitimacy of government in the South, first in an effort to organize within the established structure of party politics and, when that failed, outside that structure. The scene of SNICK's baptism in the struggle of power politics was Mississippi.

Not in the 20th century had there been an attempt to organize blacks as a political force. In Mississippi, in 1890, there were 71,000 *more* registered blacks than whites; by 1964, black registration had been reduced to only 6.7 per cent of the 400,000 voting-age black people. (These figures are contained in a report on Negro Voter-Registration in the South by the Voter Education Project of the Southern Regional Council, Atlanta, Georgia, issued April 1, 1964.)

In late 1963 and early 1964, SNICK formed the now famous Mississippi Freedom Democratic Party (MFDP) with a slate of black and white candidates. It represented a black and white coalition, but its goal was to gain seats in the national convention of the Democratic Party to be held in August 1964 at Atlantic City, New Jersey.

Resolutions of support came from the delegations of Michigan, New York, and seven other cities at the convention. Walter Reuther's United Automobile Workers and the ADA (Americans for Democratic Action) also promised to back the new Mississippi party. But the support fell apart in the back rooms of the party regulars.

The convention struggle did give the organization behind it —SNICK—national prominence. SNICK had grown from a small band of student sit-ins to a formidable organization involved in what has been called "protest politics."

SNICK workers were in Selma, Alabama, as early as February 1963, conducting voter-registration drives that by the end of the year, had already led to the arrest of three hundred persons, including SNICK's chairman, John Lewis. It was in January 1965 that Martin Luther King joined the voter-registration drive in Selma. The drive led to more than 3,000 arrests and to the internationally famous Selma-to-Montgomery march of 20,000 persons.

Bordering the county of which Selma is a part is Lowndes County. It was on U.S. Highway 80 in Lowndes County that a young housewife from Detroit was murdered by Ku Klux Klansmen, as she was driving home several civil rights workers from the Selma March. On the same highway, shortly after the murder, stood the sign: "PULL THE LEVER FOR THE BLACK PANTHER." The sign was a call to the residents of Lowndes County to vote for the candidates of a new political party, whose symbol was the black panther.

When SNICK workers moved into Lowndes County in April 1965 to organize a political movement there, not a single black out of 12,500 (80 per cent of the population) was entitled to vote. All the more striking was the proximity of Lowndes County to Montgomery, scene of King's 1955 bus boycott. Close to 18 per cent of the black men in Lowndes actually worked in Montgomery, and at least 60 per cent did their major shopping there.

Leading the new political drive in Lowndes County was twenty-three-year-old Stokely Carmichael, then SNICK's Alabama field secretary. Carmichael, born in Port-of-Spain, Trinidad, had gone to New York's Harlem when he was eleven, then moved to the Bronx and graduated from the Bronx High School of Science. At Howard University (he graduated with a degree in philosophy), he was a leader of the student civil rights organization, the Nonviolent Action Group. As a freshman at college in 1961, he had joined SNICK as a Freedom Rider in Mississippi, and he had served as director of the Second Congressional District's 1964 Mississippi Freedom Democratic Party.

Under Carmichael's leadership, SNICK formed the Lowndes County Freedom Organization (LCFO) as a political party to wrest control of the local sheriff's office and six other offices from the regular Democratic Party. Alabama law requires that political parties use an emblem, and the LCFO chose the black panther to symbolize dignity and strength. Despite a wave of violence that saw two LCFO workers shotgunned to death, over the winter and spring months the party grew in strength. Aided by the 1965 Voting Rights Act, the registration drive recruited 3,900 new voters, and in the May primaries the LCFO voted a slate of candidates to run in the regular November election.

In that election, the Black Panther candidates were to be beaten by the old white tactics of terror, and by truckloads of blacks forced to vote the regular Democratic ticket or lose their jobs. Though the outcome was to discourage many SNICK workers, who would return to the North despondent over their failure, the spring registration drive and the May primary elections were so successful that Stokely Carmichael was elected national chairman of SNICK.

Into the midst of all the turbulent activity in Mississippi, in June 1966, marched James Meredith—(whose enrollment at the University of Mississippi in 1962 had precipitated federal troop intervention to quell the rioting that had followed). Meredith's goal was to prove that the time had at last come when a black man could walk unmolested through his native state in primary election week. On the first day of the march, Meredith was felled by a shotgun blast.

The shooting shocked the nation as few other shootings, lynchings or acts of violence against black men ever had. Meredith had begun his march as an act of individual faith, and as a loner with no organizational support.

An extraordinary meeting took place at Meredith's bedside in a Memphis hospital. There assembled the leaders of all the major black organizations, who had flown to Memphis from headquarters all over the country. There was Martin Luther King of the Southern Christian Leadership Conference; there was Stokely Carmichael of SNICK, with his new ally, Floyd McKissick, a militant who had recently taken command of CORE. Leaders of the traditionally moderate organizations were also on hand: Roy Wilkins of the NAACP and Whitney Young, Jr., of the Urban League.

The leaders had come to convince Meredith that his march must go on—and to lay a strategy that would give it an objective. Meredith agreed—(he left his bed a few days later to rejoin the march). That same night, at a meeting that lasted into the early hours of the morning, the leaders tried to agree on what the objective of the march should be. Some specific, attainable goal was sought by Roy Wilkins and Whitney Young, Jr. Carmichael and McKissick demanded a frontal attack on the whole governmental structure of the South. Martin Luther King fought for a compromise, and what emerged was a "Manifesto," which was signed by King, Carmichael, and McKissick. Wilkins and Young, objecting even to the title, refused to sign it and flew back to New York. The split was to become wider in the days to follow.

The Meredith march, swelled by outraged citizens from every part of the nation, surged on through Mississippi. The leaders maintained an outward show of unanimity, but at the towns where they stopped to address gathering crowds of rank-and-file blacks, they seemed to be talking different languages.

It was in the town of Greenwood that Stokely Carmichael cried out:

> The only way we gonna stop them white men from whuppin' us is to take over. We been saying freedom for six years and we ain't got nothin'. What we gonna start saying now is black power.

From the crowds came the roaring echo: "Black power!" and the newspapers and TV cameras were there to pick it up.

Carmichael had used the slogan many times before in Lowndes County; now overnight black power became the protest cry of the militant wing, especially the young militant wing, of black protest.

One month after the Meredith march, Martin Luther King ran a full-page ad in the *New York Times,* condemning black power as a slogan derived from weakness and desperation, rather than from strength.

King's ad was followed some months later by an even more scathing denunciation of black power issued in the form of a manifesto by the moderate leaders A. Philip Randolph, Bayard Rustin, Roy Wilkins, and Whitney Young, Jr. Their manifesto, titled "Crisis and Commitment," was issued in late 1966. Significantly, Martin Luther King did not sign that manifesto, and through the next two years, through the long hot summers of ghetto violence and the mounting waves of black militancy, there were signs that Dr. King's rhetoric, if not his tactics, was becoming increasingly forceful.

In the article that follows, Carmichael explains what he had in mind when he shouted "black power" to the crowds at Greenwood, Mississippi. It is altogether a different interpretation than the one the white press would give in the years to come. White newspapers, the *New York Times* in particular, would distort the black power concept out of all proportions to its original meaning of political and economic solidarity among black people. The policy of the white press to misconstrue the slogan was unquestionably predicated on the age-old distrust, fear and outright hate of the black man, a fear born in colonial times out of the sense of guilt of white men for the wrongs they inflicted on black men.

Carmichael was, at the time he wrote the article, an advocate of nonviolence, and so was SNICK, the organization he represented. So, too, was another organization then emerging —the Black Panther Party of Oakland, California (an organization formed after the riots in Watts to advise black ghetto residents of their legal rights when apprehended by the police).

White newspapers did not report honestly the modest demands of Stokely Carmichael; the police of Oakland precipitated incident after incident to force the Panthers to take violent action. Carmichael no longer shows moderation. The Black Panthers grow ever more militant, and throughout the land black united fronts are coming into being to gain by any means what white men refuse to grant peacefully.

This is a characteristic of black protest from earliest times. Black leaders start out with moderate demands, but white intransigence prods them into postures increasingly militant. And it is because of this historic fact that the article by Stokely Carmichael has such extraordinary significance.

The Document:

Article titled "What We Want" by Stokely Carmichael,
published in the *New York Review of Books*,
September 22, 1966

ONE OF THE tragedies of the struggle against racism is that up to now there has been no national organization which could speak to the growing militancy of young black people in the urban ghetto. There has been only a civil rights movement whose tone of voice was adapted to an audience of liberal whites. It served as a sort of buffer zone between them and angry young blacks. None of its so-called leaders could go into a rioting community and be listened to. In a sense, I blame ourselves—together with the mass media—for what has happened in Watts, Harlem, Chicago, Cleveland, Omaha. Each time the people in those cities saw Martin Luther King get slapped they became angry; when they saw four little black girls bombed to death, they were angrier; and when nothing happened, they were steaming. We had nothing to offer that they could see, except to go out and be beaten again. We helped to build their frustration.

For too many years, black Americans marched and had their heads broken and got shot. They were saying to the country, "Look, you guys are supposed to be nice guys and we are only going to do what we are supposed to do—why do you beat us up, why don't you give us what we ask, why don't you straighten yourselves out?" After years of this, we are at almost the same point—because we demonstrated from a position of weakness. We cannot be expected any longer to march and have our heads broken in order to say to whites: come on, you're nice guys. For you are not nice guys. We have found you out.

An organization which claims to speak for the needs of a community—as does the Student Nonviolent Coordinating Committee—must speak in the tone of that community, not as somebody else's buffer zone. This is the significance of black power as a slogan. For once, black people are going to use the words they want to use—not just the words whites want to hear. And they will do this no matter how often the press tries to stop the use of the slogan by equating it with racism or separatism.

An organization which claims to be working for the needs of a community—as SNCC does—must work to provide the community with a position of strength from which to make its voice heard. This is the significance of black power beyond the slogan.

Black power can be clearly defined for those who do not attach the fears of white America to their questions about it. We should begin with the basic fact that black Americans have two problems: they are poor and they are black. All other problems arise from this two-sided reality: lack of education, the so-called apathy of black men. Any program to end racism must address itself to that double reality.

Almost from its beginning, SNCC sought to address itself to both conditions with a program aimed at winning political power for impoverished Southern blacks. We had to begin with politics because black Americans are a propertyless people in a country where property is valued above all. We had to work for power, because this country does not function by morality, love, and nonviolence, but by power. Thus we determined to win political power, with the idea of moving on from there into activity that would have economic effects. With power, the masses could make or participate in making the decisions which govern their destinies, and thus create basic changes in their day-to-day lives.

. . . The concept of "black power" is not a recent or isolated phenomenon: It has grown out of the ferment of agitation and activity by different people and organizations in many black communities over the years. Our last year of work in Alabama added a new concrete possibility. In Lowndes County, for example, black power will mean that if a Negro is elected sheriff, he can end police brutality. If a black man is elected tax assessor, he can collect and channel funds for the building of better roads and schools serving black people—thus advancing the move from political power into the economic arena. In such areas as Lowndes, where black men have a majority, they will attempt to use it to exercise control. This is what they seek: control. Where Negroes lack a majority, black power means proper representation and sharing of control. It means the creation of power bases from which black people can work to change state-wide or nation-wide patterns of oppression through pressure from strength—instead of weakness. Politically, black power means what it has always meant to SNCC: the coming-together of black people to elect representatives and to force those representatives to speak to their needs. It does not mean merely putting black faces into office. A man or woman who is black and from the slums cannot be automatically expected to

speak to the needs of black people. Most of the black politicians we see around the country today are not what SNCC
means by black power. The power must be that of a community, and emanate from there. . . .

Ultimately, the economic foundations of this country must
be shaken if black people are to control their lives. The colonies of the U.S.—and this includes the black ghettos within
its borders, north and south—must be liberated. For a century, this nation has been like an octopus of exploitation, its
tentacles stretching from Mississippi and Harlem, to South
America, the Middle East, southern Africa, and Vietnam; the
form of exploitation varies from area to area but the essential
result has been the same—a powerful few have been maintained and enriched at the expense of the poor and voiceless
colored masses. This pattern must be broken. As its grip loos-
ens here and there around the world the hopes of black
Americans become more realistic. For racism to die, a totally
different America must be born.

This is what the white society does not wish to face; this is
why that society prefers to talk about integration. But integration speaks not at all to the problem of poverty, only to
the problem of blackness. Integration today means the man
who "makes it," leaving his black brothers behind in the
ghetto as fast as his new sports car will take him. It has no
relevance to the Harlem wino or to the cotton-picker making
$3 a day. As a lady I know in Alabama once said, "The
food that Ralph Bunche eats doesn't fill my stomach."

Integration, moreover, speaks to the problem of blackness
in a despicable way. As a goal, it has been based on complete
acceptance of the fact that in order to have a decent house or
education, blacks must move into a white neighborhood or
send their children to a white school. This reinforces, among
both black and white, the idea that "white" is automatically
better and "black" is by definition inferior. This is why integration is a subterfuge for the maintenance of white supremacy. It allows the nation to focus on a handful of Southern
children who get into white schools, at great price, and to ig-
nore the 94% who are left behind in unimproved all-black
schools. Such situations will not change until black people
have power—to control their own school boards, in this case.
Then Negroes become equal in a way that means something,
and integration ceases to be a one-way street. Then integration
doesn't mean draining skills and energies from the ghetto into
white neighborhoods; then it can mean white people moving
from Beverly Hills into Watts, white people joining the
Lowndes County Freedom Organization. Then integration becomes relevant.

To most whites, black power seems to mean that the Mau Mau are coming to the suburbs at night. The Mau Mau are coming, and whites must stop them. Articles appear about plots to "get whitey," creating an atmosphere in which "law and order must be maintained." Once again, responsibility is shifted from the oppressor to the oppressed. Other whites chide, "Don't forget—you're only 10% of the population; if you get too smart, we'll wipe you out." If they are liberals, they complain, "What about me?—don't you want my help any more?" These are people supposedly concerned about black Americans, but today they think first of themselves, of their feelings of rejection. Or they admonish, "You can't get anywhere without coalitions," when there is in fact no group at present with whom to form a coalition in which blacks will not be absorbed and betrayed. Or they accuse us of "polarizing the races" by our calls for black unity, when the true responsibility for polarization lies with whites who will not accept their responsibility as the majority power for making the democratic process work.

White America will not face the problem of color, the reality of it.

From birth, black people are told a set of lies about themselves. We are told that we are lazy—yet I drive through the Delta area in Mississippi and watch black people picking cotton in the hot sun for 14 hours. We are told, "If you work hard, you'll succeed"—but if that were true, black people would own this country. We are oppressed because we are black—not because we are ignorant, not because we are lazy, not because we're stupid (and got good rhythm); but because we're black.

I remember that when I was a boy, I used to go to see Tarzan movies on Saturday. White Tarzan used to beat up the black natives. I would sit there yelling, "Kill the beasts, kill the savages, kill 'em!" I was saying: Kill me. It was as if a Jewish boy watched Nazis taking Jews off to concentration camps and cheered them on. Today, I want the chief to beat hell out of Tarzan and send him back to Europe. But it takes time to become free of the lies and their shaming effect on black minds. It takes time to reject the most important lie: that black people inherently can't do the same things white people can do, unless white people help them.

The need for psychological equality is the reason why SNCC today believes that blacks must organize in the black community. Only black people can convey the revolutionary idea that black people are able to do things themselves. Only they can help create in the community an aroused and continuing black consciousness that will provide the basis for political strength. In the past, white allies have furthered white supremacy without the whites involved realizing it—or wanting it, I think. Black people must do things for themselves: they must get poverty money they will control and spend themselves, they must conduct tutorial programs themselves so that black children can identify with black people. This is one reason Africa has such importance: The reality of black men ruling their own nations gives blacks elsewhere a sense of possibility, of power which they do not now have. . . .

I have said that most liberal whites react to "black power" with the question, What about me? rather than saying: Tell me what you want me to do and I'll see if I can do it. There are answers to the right question. One of the most disturbing things about almost all white supporters of the movement has been that they are afraid to go into their own communities—which is where the racism exists—and work to get rid of it. They want to run from Berkeley to tell us what to do in Mississippi; let then look instead at Berkeley. They admonish blacks to be nonviolent; let them preach nonviolence in the white community. They come to teach me Negro history; let them go to the suburbs and open up freedom schools for whites. Let them work to stop America's racist foreign policy; let them press this government to cease supporting the economy of South Africa.

There is a vital job to be done among poor whites. We hope to see, eventually, a coalition between poor blacks and poor whites. That is the only coalition which seems acceptable to us, and we see such a coalition as the major internal instrument of change in American society. SNCC has tried several times to organize poor whites; we are trying again now, with an initial training program in Tennessee. It is purely academic today to talk about bringing poor blacks and whites together, but the job of creating a poor-white power bloc must be attempted. The main responsibility for it falls upon whites. Black and white can work together in the white community where possible; it is not possible, however, to go into a poor Southern town and talk about integration. Poor whites everywhere are becoming more hostile—not less—partly because they see the nation's attention focused on black poverty and nobody coming to them. Too many young middle-class Americans, like some sort of Pepsi generation, have wanted to come alive through the black community; they've wanted to be where the action is—and the action has been in the black community.

Black people do not want to "take over" this country. They don't want to "get whitey"; they just want to get him off their backs, as the saying goes. It was for example the exploitation by Jewish landlords and merchants which first created black resentment toward Jews—not Judaism. The white man is irrelevant to blacks, except as an oppressive force. Blacks want to be in his place, yes, but not in order to terrorize and lynch and starve him. They want to be in his place because that is where a decent life can be had.

But our vision is not merely of a society in which all black men have enough to buy the good things of life. When we urge that black money go into black pockets, we mean the communal pocket. We want to see money go back into the community and used to benefit it. We want to see the cooperative concept applied in business and banking. We want to see black ghetto residents demand that an exploiting landlord or storekeeper sell them, at minimal cost, a building or a shop that they will own and improve cooperatively; they can back their demand with a rent strike, or a boycott, and a community so united behind them that no one else will move into the building or buy at the store. The society we seek to build among black people, then, is not a capitalist one. It is a society in which the spirit of community and humanistic love prevail. The word love is suspect; black expectations of what it might produce have been betrayed too often. But those were expectations of a response from the white community which failed us. The love we seek to encourage is within the black community, the only American community where men call each other "brother" when they meet. We can build a community of love only where we have the ability and power to do so: among blacks.

As for white America, perhaps it can stop crying out against "black supremacy," "black nationalism," "racism in reverse," and begin facing reality. The reality is that this nation, from top to bottom, is racist: that racism is not primarily a problem of "human relations" but of an exploitation maintained—either actively or through silence—by the society as a whole. Camus and Sartre have asked, can a man condemn himself? Can whites, particularly liberal whites, condemn themselves? Can they stop blaming us, and blame their own system? Are they capable of the shame which might become a revolutionary emotion?

We have found that they usually cannot condemn themselves, and so we have done it. But the rebuilding of this society, if at all possible, is basically the responsibility of whites —not blacks. We won't fight to save the present society, in Vietnam or anywhere else. We are just going to work, in the way we see fit, and on goals we define, not for civil rights but for all our human rights.

THE CASE FOR
BLACK SEPARATISM: 1967

The Conference on Black Power
adopts a momentous resolution

by Robert S. Browne

About The Document:

Newark is the hub of the industrial complex of northeastern New Jersey. More than 50 per cent of the city's approximately half million people are black, representing one of the highest black population percentages in the United States. Politically and economically, however, the city is dominated by whites. Even its black ghetto, the Central Ward, is represented by white men.

Of the 150 ghetto riots that occurred in various parts of the United States during 1967, Newark, with twenty-three killings—twenty-one of them black—was second only to Detroit, with forty-three killings, thirty-three of them black.

In the late summer of 1967, about seven hundred black delegates from various parts of the country assembled in Newark's Central Ward, at a meeting place called the Spirit House, to participate in the Conference on Black Power.

Ron Karenga, leader of the extremist black nationalist organization US was present, and so was H. Rap Brown, as president of SNICK. Nonviolent political activists were also present; for example, Horace Sheffield, of the United Automobile Workers, and Owen Brooks, director of the Delta Ministry (the civil rights division of the National Council of Churches).

Also attending the Conference were Floyd B. McKissick, national chairman of CORE, and Jesse Jackson, of the Southern Christian Leadership Conference, who had marched throughout Chicago the previous summer trying to move black people into white neighborhoods.

The seven hundred delegates to the Black Power Confer-

ence met in closed sessions, and journalists and others who
tried to get into the Spirit House were asked to leave. The one
thing the newsmen obtained was the text of a resolution calling for "a national dialogue on the desirability of partitioning
the United States into two separate and independent nations,
one to be a homeland for white and the other to be a homeland for black Americans." Considering the diversity of outlook of the delegates, the adoption of the resolution was of
extreme significance, particularly because its wording had
been amended from the floor, implying a consensus arrived at
through debate and compromise. The text of the resolution
follows:

*Whereas the black people in America have been systemati-
cally oppressed by their white fellow countrymen*

*Whereas there is little prospect that this oppression can be
terminated, peacefully or otherwise, within the foreseeable
future*

*Whereas the black people do not wish to be absorbed into
the larger white community*

*Whereas the black people in America find that their inter-
ests are in contradiction with those of white America*

*Whereas the black people in America are psychologically
handicapped by virtue of their having no national homeland*

*Whereas the physical, moral, ethical, and esthetic standards
of white American society are not those of black society and
indeed do violence to the self-image of the black man*

*Whereas black people were among the earliest immigrants
to America, having been ruthlessly separated from their fa-
therland, and have made a major contribution to America's
development, most of this contribution having been uncom-
pensated, and*

*Recognizing that efforts are already well advanced for the
convening of a Constitutional Convention for the purpose of
revising the Constitution of the U. S. for the first time since
America's inception, then*

*Be it resolved that the Black Power Conference initiate a
national dialogue on the desirability of partitioning the U. S.
into two separate and independent nations, one to be a homeland for white and the other to be a homeland for black
Americans.*

The man who read the resolution to the Conference for
adoption was a black man, Professor Robert S. Browne. Assistant Professor of Economics at Fairleigh Dickinson University, he lived in Cambodia and Vietnam from 1955-61,
and returned to the U.S. to become one of the first critics of
this country's involvement in the Vietnam war, and one of the
first to equate the black freedom movement with the anti-war

effort. In the article that appears below, Professor Browne relates the events that led the Black Power Conference to adopt the resolution. The insights he displays make a remarkable summation of what the black protest movement is all about.

The Document:

Article published in *Ramparts*, December 1967

. . . CLEARLY, this is not a radical resolution. Like the Declaration of Independence, it enumerates some of the felt grievances of the people. But it is more moderate in tone than Jefferson's Declaration and its action clause stops considerably short of that of the 1776 document. Significantly, it asks not for separation but merely for dialogue. In this sense, it is possibly the mildest resolution which the Conference adopted.

Nevertheless, as the press reported, this resolution received perhaps the most thunderous ovation of the entire Conference. Obviously, this enthusiasm was not due to the resolution's moderation but to the fact that reference to an all-black state touched deep sensitivity in the emotions of the audience. All of those who applauded and approved the resolution can by no stretch of the imagination be considered active partisans of the idea of a separate state. But just as surely, as black people have become progressively more disillusioned at the prospect of ever finding a dignified niche for themselves in American society, so have they become more eager to explore any avenue which may offer greater promise. What the support for the resolution unmistakably revealed was the depth of the despair about white America which is now prevalent in the black community; and therein lies its significance.

Taken at face value, the resolution is far from an expression of racism or hate. Rather, it is a straightforward effort to explore an obvious means of minimizing racial friction by suggesting some fair basis for the physical separation of the contending parties. Partitioning of the U.S. into separate black and white nations will conceivably appeal to both the Southern white racist and the Northern black nationalist, and it can with equal inaccuracy be characterized as painfully conservative or wildly radical. The intent of the resolution, however, is to free the partition concept from the deadly embrace of extremists and to afford it consideration by moderates of both races. The social climate in America is being transformed at a dizzying pace, and those who summarily dismiss the partition concept as being too radical to merit serious consideration risk committing the classic error of ignoring the pleas of the moderate center and thereby sentencing the country to the terror of the irresponsibles on the two extremes.

A certain amount of hostility toward any modification of the American political structure is only natural. Indeed, the nation's bloodiest war was fought under the banner of "preserving the Union." so that on sentimental grounds alone the resistance to partitioning can be expected to be massive. But primitive emotion is scarcely a sound guide for policy. Besides, sensitive persons must with increasing frequency ask themselves if there really remains much of a Union to preserve.

One of the few lessons which history teaches us is that nothing created by man is immutable, least of all his political architecture. Only those who are completely lacking in historical perspective are likely to believe that the U.S. has settled its political form and its geographical boundaries for all time. The political realist is not only aware that man-made institutions are never eternal; he realizes that it is not even desirable that they should be. Rather, they must be amenable to constant reshaping to meet changing conditions. The hope which underlies the partition resolution is that the anticipated initial hostile reaction to the proposal can be gradually stripped away and replaced by non-hysterical discussion and analysis as to whether or not partitioning of the national territory offers a promising solution to our racial quandary.

As this dialogue progresses, serious exploration and research will be required probing the legal, political, economic and sociological implications of partitioning and of population relocation. Assumptions will have to be made regarding just what portions of the present territorial U.S. will be included in each of the two nations and how assets will be apportioned. The mechanisms for negotiating such a partitioning will have to be examined intensively, as well as the basis for recognition of official negotiators for the black community. The answers to such questions obviously cannot be found in one month or in one year. Ultimately, the proposal may well prove unworkable because some of these questions may prove unanswerable. But the mere fact that the modalities of implementation are difficult to formulate is certainly no reason to prejudge the merits of the proposal and to dismiss it from consideration as a viable alternative if it seems to speak to the needs of a large segment of the population.

There is ample historic precedent for national partitioning, the most appropriate contemporary model probably being the division of the former British India into today's India and Pakistan. This schism, which was made along religious rather than racial lines, was accompanied by personal hardships of such magnitude that one hesitates to refer to it as a model. A substantial portion of these human tragedies, however, appear to have stemmed from the precipitous manner in which the entire matter of partitioning was agreed to and effectuated. Only during a brief period was partition given really serious consideration and then, suddenly, because of political pressures, it was abruptly approved and implementation begun—an implementation which involved the relocation of tens of millions of people. An atmosphere of extreme bitterness and hostility prevailed throughout the area and in such circumstances atrocities were easily predictable. The grossly inadequate administrative preparations for so gigantic an undertaking also contributed to the widespread hardships which occurred. By encouraging a national dialogue, the Black Power resolution hopes to diffuse the intense emotionalism which the proposal is certain to arouse, and to stimulate serious planning as to how such a project could best be carried out, thus avoiding many of the pitfalls which befell India and Pakistan.

It should not be overlooked that such racially white and culturally Western countries as Canada, Belgium and Spain all harbor strong separatist movements. The separatists in these countries are not considered a lunatic fringe but constitute a significant political force. In these countries the dialogue proceeds at a leisurely pace and continuous efforts are made to accommodate the nation to the demands of the ethnic or linguistic minority. It is also noteworthy that in the examples of classical decolonization, violence has tended to occur principally when dialogue and national planning were absent (e.g., Ireland, Indonesia, Algeria) and to have been largely avoided where honest dialogue was permitted (Ghana, Zambia, French Africa).

I frankly do not know how many blacks would favor a separatist solution of the type proposed. Many of us suffer from a serious inferiority-complex about our race and may doubt our ability to operate a successful nation, despite the inspiring example of several of the African countries which came into independence with handicaps of illiteracy and lack of capital far more serious than those we would face. My experience suggests that the number of blacks who would support the idea of partitioning is nevertheless sufficient to warrant serious national consideration of its feasibility. I have listened to the voices of my people and I know that they are desperate. Talk of violence and of revolution hangs heavy in the atmosphere of both black and white America. Not surprisingly, black leadership is in the vanguard of those who recognize and articulate the need for drastic changes in American society. However, the black community's role in effecting these changes remains unresolved. Partition has the significant advantage of offering a path which, with proper goodwill, can be trod nonviolently. It has the disadvantage of speaking primarily to the basic problem facing black America and not to the problems of the total society. Clearly, *some* new path will have to be taken to relieve the desperation of black Americans. Partition is being offered as one way out. Does white America have an equally reasonable counter-proposal?

The sources of this desperation of the Negro should have been fairly well known by now. In case they were not, the resolution's drafters took the Jeffersonian view that "a decent respect of the opinions of mankind requires that they should declare the causes which impel them to the separation." Yet, in their formalized brevity, the "whereas" clauses of the resolution hardly convey the full panoply of frustrations which have driven some blacks to an endorsement of separatism.

Unquestionably, the gloomy statistics on black unemployment, income, housing and disease create the general framework for this despair—statistics which the Negro must read against the background of a decade of both unprecedented national civil rights activity and unprecedented national prosperity. The black community clearly sees itself getting a progressively smaller share of the pie as the pie itself grows ever larger. Coupled with these economic statistics are the sociological ones: schools are more segregated than ever before; cities are more ghettoized in 1967 than in 1937.

For the upper-middle-class Negro, as for most whites, these figures on the deterioration of the Negro's position since World War II are sometimes difficult to grasp, for on the surface much progress is in evidence. Well-scrubbed, nattily dressed Negroes are to be seen working in myriad sorts of establishments from which they were formerly barred; they are increasingly seen at private social functions of upper-class whites; they are even to be glimpsed occasionally in advertisements for well-known products, and in non-stereotype roles in TV and film entertainment. A Negro sits on the Supreme Court, another sits on the Federal Reserve Board, and one has been elected to the Senate from a primarily white constituency.

Indeed, it is these very strides which have been, at least in part, responsible for the current crisis in Negro leadership. The traditional leaders point with pride to their accomplishments and conclude that they are pushing matters at as fast a pace as the white society will permit. Meanwhile, the great bulk of the black community sinks ever lower, increasingly resentful of its worsening position vis-a-vis the black elite as well as vis-a-vis the whites. As a result, the black masses are becoming politicized, are developing a class consciousness, and are rejecting the existing Negro leadership. An unexpected, although possibly temporary, interruption in this process of polarization of the black community occurred last winter as fallout from the Adam Powell incident. The manner in which virtually all segments of the white community openly supported the attack on Congressman Powell, the supreme symbol of black achievement of power in America, served as an eyeopener to all blacks, whatever their level of sophistication and economic achievement. If Powell, the epitome of power, was not safe, then clearly no black man was safe and it was obviously naive to think otherwise. The Powell incident, by the very grossness of its racism, built a precarious bridge between the increasingly bitter, increasingly segregated black masses, and the increasingly affluent, increasingly integrated black middle class. Their interests were once again shown to be identical, even if involuntarily so.

Clearly, it is as a measure of self-defense that the black community has begun to draw together and even to discuss separatism. Let every liberal white American ponder this.

The bridge between the two segments of the black community is by no means a stable one, largely because of the schizophrenia of the black middle class. Whereas the black masses, both those in the rural South and those who have flooded into Northern cities in the past quarter century, aspire primarily for a higher standard of living and for freedom from the indignities and oppressions which their blackness has attracted to them, the middle-class Negroes have developed more subtle tastes. To varying degrees, these Negroes have become "assimilated" into white society and lead lives which are spiritually dependent upon the white community in a way that the mass of Negroes could never comprehend. For them, an integrated America is fast becoming a reality and the thrust of their effort is to extend the integration concept to every corner of the country. Their schizophrenia arises from the inescapable reminders of their vulnerability. Even with a Ph.D., a Nobel prize, a Congressional Medal of Honor or a vast fortune, a Negro is still a "nigger" to many (most?) white Americans and the society does not let him forget it for very long. Nor does the sensitive Negro really want to forget it; he wants to change it.

But perhaps the most unsettling of all the factors affecting the mental health of the black man in this white society is the matter of identification. It can be exemplified by the poignant, untold agony of raising black, kinky-haired children in a society where the standard of beauty is a milk-white skin and long, straight hair. To convince a black child that she is beautiful when every channel of value formation in the society is telling her the opposite is a heartrending and well-nigh impossible task. It is a challenge which confronts all Negroes, irrespective of their social and economic class, but the difficulty of dealing with it is likely to vary directly with the degree to which the Negro family leads an integrated existence. A black child in a predominantly black school may realize that she doesn't look like the pictures in the books, magazines and TV advertisements, but at least she looks like her schoolmates and neighbors. The black child in a predominantly white school and neighborhood lacks even this basis for identification.

This identity problem is, of course, not peculiar to the Negro. Minorities of all sorts encounter it in one form or another—the immigrant who speaks with an accent; the Jewish child who doesn't celebrate Christmas; the Oriental whose eyes are slanted. But for the Negro the problem has a special dimension, for in the American ethos a black man is not only "different," he is classed as ugly and inferior. This is not an easy situation to deal with, and the manner in which a Negro chooses to handle it will both be determined by and a determinant of his larger political outlook. He can deal with it as an integrationist, accepting his child as being ugly by prevailing standards and urging him to excel in other ways to prove his worth; or he can deal with it as a black nationalist, telling the child that he is not a freak but rather part of a larger international community of black-skinned, kinky-haired people who have a beauty of their own, a glorious history and a great future. In short he can replace shame with pride, inferiority with dignity, by imbuing the child with what is coming to be known as black nationalism. The growing popularity of this viewpoint is evidenced by the appearance of "natural" hair styles among Negro youth and the surge of interest in African and Negro culture and history.

Black Power may not be the ideal slogan to describe this new self-image which the black American is developing, for to guilt-ridden whites the slogan conjures up violence, anarchy and revenge. To frustrated blacks, however, it symbolizes unity and a newly found pride in the blackness with which the Creator endowed us and which we realize must always be our mark of identification. Heretofore this blackness has been a stigma, a curse with which we were born. Black Power means that this curse will henceforth be a badge of pride rather than of scorn. It marks the end of an era in which black men devoted themselves to pathetic attempts to be white men and inaugurated an era in which black people will set their own standards of beauty, conduct and accomplishment.

Is this new black consciousness in irreconcilable conflict with the larger American society? In a sense, the heart of the American cultural problem has always been the need to harmonize the inherent contradiction between racial (or national) identity with integration into the melting pot which was America. In the century since the Civil War, the society has made little effort to find a means to afford the black minority a sense of racial pride and independence while at the same time accepting it as a full participant in the larger society. Now that the implications of this failure are becoming apparent, the black community seems to be saying, "Forget it! We'll solve our own problems." Integration, which never had a high priority among the black masses, is now being written off by them as being not only unattainable but actually harmful—driving a wedge between the black masses and the so-called Negro elite. To these developments has been added the momentous realization by many "integrated" Negroes that, in the U.S., full integration can only mean full assimilation—a loss of racial identity. This sobering prospect has caused many a black integrationist to pause and reflect, even as have his similarly challenged Jewish counterparts. Thus, within the black community there are two separate challenges to the traditional integration policy which has long constituted the major objective of established Negro leadership. There is the general skepticism that the Negro, even after having transformed himself into a white blackman, will enjoy full acceptance into American society; and there is the longer-range doubt that even should complete integration somehow be achieved, it would prove to be really desirable, for its price may be the total absorption and disappearance of the race—a sort of painless genocide.

Understandably, it is the black masses who have most vociferously articulated these dangers of assimilation, for they have watched with alarm as the more fortunate among their ranks have gradually risen to the top only to be promptly "integrated" off into the white community—absorbed into another culture, often with undisguised contempt for all that had previously constituted their heritage. Also, it was the black masses who first perceived that integration actually increases the white community's control over the black one by destroying black institutions, and by absorbing black leadership and coinciding its interests with those of the white community. The international "brain drain" has its counterpart in the black community, which is constantly being denuded of its best trained people and many of its natural leaders. Black institutions of all sorts—colleges, newspapers, banks, even community organizations—are all experiencing the loss of their better people to the newly available openings in white establishments, thereby lowering the quality of the Negro organizations and in some cases causing their demise or increasing their dependence on whites for survival. Such injurious, if unintended, side effects of integration have been felt in almost every layer of the black community.

If the foregoing analysis of the integration vs. separatism conflict exhausted the case for partition then we might conclude that the problems have all been dealt with before, by other immigrant groups in America. (It would be an erroneous conclusion, for while other groups may have encountered similar problems, their solutions do not work for us, alas.) But there remains yet another factor which is cooling the Negro's enthusiasm for the integrationist path: he is becoming distrustful of his fellow Americans.

The American culture is one of the youngest in the world. Furthermore, as has been pointed out repeatedly in recent years, it is essentially a culture which approves of violence, indeed enjoys it. Military expenditures absorb roughly half of the national budget. Violence predominates on the TV screen and the toys of violence are best selling items during the annual rites for the much praised but little imitated Prince of Peace. In Vietnam, the zeal with which America has pursued its effort to destroy a poor and illiterate peasantry has astonished civilized people around the globe. In such an atmosphere the Negro is understandably restive about the fate his white compatriots might have in store for him. The veiled threat by President Johnson at the time of the 1966 riots—suggesting that riots might beget pogroms and pointing out that Negroes are only ten per cent of the population—was not lost on most blacks. It enraged them, but it was a sobering thought. The manner in which Germany herded the Jews into concentration camps and ultimately into ovens was a solemn warning to minority peoples everywhere. The casualness with which America exterminated the Indians and later interned the Japanese suggests that there is no cause for the Negro to feel complacent about his security in the U.S. He finds little consolation in the assurance that if it does become necessary to place him in concentration camps it will only be as a means of protecting him from uncontrollable whites: "protective incarceration," to use governmental jargonese.

The very fact that such alternatives are becoming serious topics of discussion has exposed the Negro's already raw and sensitive psyche to yet another heretofore unfelt vulnerability —the insecurity which he suffers as a result of having no homeland which he can honestly feel his own. Among the major ethno-cultural groups in the world he is unique in this respect. As the Jewish drama during and following World War II painfully demonstrated, a national homeland is a primordial and urgent need for a people, even though its benefits do not always lend themselves to ready measurement. For some, the homeland constitutes a vital place of refuge from the strains of a life led too long within a foreign environment. For others, the need to reside in the homeland is considerably less intense than the need for merely knowing that such a homeland exists. The benefit to the expatriate is psychological, a sense of security in knowing that he belongs to a culturally and politically identifiable community. No doubt this phenomenon largely accounts for the fact that both the West Indian Negro and the Puerto Rican exhibit considerably more self-assurance than does the American Negro, for both of the former groups have ties to an identifiable homeland which honors and preserves their cultural heritage.

It has been marveled that we American Negroes, almost alone among the cultural groups of the world, exhibit no sense of nationhood. Perhaps it is true that we do lack this sense, but there seems to be little doubt that the absence of a homeland exacts a severe if unconscious price from our psyche. Theoretically, our homeland is the U.S.A. We pledge allegiance to the stars and stripes and sing the national anthem. But from the age when we first begin to sense that we are somehow "different," that we are victimized, these rituals begin to mean less to us than to our white compatriots. For many of us they become form without substance; for others they become a cruel and bitter mockery of our dignity and good sense; for relatively few of us do they retain a significance in any way comparable to their hold on our white brethren.

The recent coming into independence of many African states stimulated some interest among Negroes that independent Africa might become the homeland which they so desperately needed. A few made the journey and experienced a newly-found sense of community and racial dignity. For many who went, however, the gratifying racial fraternity which they experienced was insufficient to compensate for the cultural estrangement which accompanied it. They had been away from Africa for too long and the differences in language, food and custom barred them from experiencing the "at home" sensation which they were eagerly seeking. Symbolically, independent Africa could serve them as a homeland: practically, it could not. Their search continues—a search for a place where they can experience the security which comes from being a part of the majority culture, free at last from the inhibiting effects of cultural repression and induced cultural timidity and shame.

If we have been separated from Africa for so long that we are no longer quite at ease there, then we are left with only one place to make our home, and that is this land to which we were brought in chains. Justice would indicate such a solution in any case, for it is North America, not Africa, into which our toil and effort have been poured. This land is our rightful home and we are well within our rights in demanding an opportunity to enjoy it on the same terms as the other immigrants who have helped to develop it. . . .

Certainly partition would entail enormous initial hardships. But these hardships should be weighed against the prospects of prolonged and intensified racial strife stretching into the indefinite future. Indeed, the social fabric of America is far more likely to be able to withstand the strains of a partitioning of the country than those of an extended race war. Indeed, if it happened that the principle of partition were harmoniously accepted by most Americans as the preferable solution, it is possible that only voluntary transfers of population would be necessary. Conceivably, no one would be forced to move against his will. Those Negroes who wanted to migrate to the new nation ("New Africa"?) could do so, and their counterparts could move to the United States. The France-Algeria arrangements could be used as a model. (To put the question of mass transference of populations into its proper perspective, it is well to remember that the U.S. is currently witnessing one of history's great demographic movements, although most Americans are totally unaware of it. In the past 25 years, some four million Negroes, roughly 20 per cent of the total Negro population, have migrated from the rural South to the cities of the North and West. History records few such massive population transfers.)

There is an excellent chance that, following partition, neither nation would be overtly racist. The basis for the present racial animosity would be largely removed by the very act of separation. Reciprocal tourism might very well become a leading industry for both nations, for the relations between the races would finally be on a healthy, equalitarian basis. A confederation of the two states, perhaps joined by Canada, Mexico and other nations, could conceivably emerge at some future time.

Divorce is an inherent aspect of the American tradition. It terminates the misery of an enforced but unhappy union, relieves the tension and avoids the risk of more serious consequences. It is increasingly apparent to blacks and whites alike that their national marriage has been a disastrous failure. Consequently, in the search for ways to remedy this tragic situation, divorce should obviously not be ruled out as a possible solution. The Black Power Conference resolution asks America to do no more than to give it serious consideration.

Even in the black ghettos it may require considerable time before the idea of partitioning can be evaluated dispassionately, for the Negro has never rejected the indoctrination which he receives in "Americana"; rather, his problem is that he has accepted it too readily, only to discover that it was not meant to apply to him.

But the mood of the ghetto is in a state of unprecedented change and in this new climate a sense of nationhood is groping for expression. It may hold within it the key to mental health for black America, and its ultimate outcome cannot now be foreseen. It may lead to two separate nations or it may lead us toward some as yet untried type of human community vastly superior to the present system of competing nationalisms. The new world community which mankind so desperately needs may rise phoenix-like from the collapsing, unworkable old order. Intelligent, imaginative men must not shrink from exploring fearlessly any avenue which might lead mankind to this new world community. Men may sometimes hate other men. Fortunately, they do not hate mankind. This is the solid foundation upon which we must try to build.

"THE RIOT COMMISSION" REPORT: 1968

*A black psychologist
finds a "fatal flaw"*

by Dr. James A. Tillman, Jr.

About The Document:

The explosion of burning and looting that wracked seventy-two cities in twenty-two states during the summer of 1967 subsided with the coming of fall, and the nation counted its casualties: eighty-three persons killed, most of them black. Fall and winter seemed to bring a period of calm. By February the *New York Times* could quote this comment on civil rights legislation by a U.S. Congressman: "The trouble is no one seems to care any more."

The season was nearing an end when, on February 8 in Orangeburg, South Carolina, police fired into a crowd during a student sit-in to desegregate a bowling alley. Three black youths were killed. The winter months passed without a major riot, however.

Below the surface calm, Americans—black and white—were reacting to the previous long hot summer and wondering what the next summer would bring.

During the winter 1967–68, black men struggled for self-determination through economic self-help programs, such as Operation Breadbasket, headed by the Rev. Jesse Jackson, to upgrade black employees and to market black manufactures. CORE encouraged black farmer cooperatives, black credit unions, and black entrepreneurs in rural districts, while in New York, Dr. Thomas Matthew sponsored "green power" (meaning "money power") programs for blacks in the ghettos of Harlem and the Bronx.

Meanwhile, white police forces across the nation were stockpiling what they euphemistically called "anti-riot hardware"—riot guns, crowd control chemicals such as MACE, and armored cars and armored tanks. And while the police stockpiled weapons for all-out war, the National Advisory Commission on Civil Disorders—the "Riot Commission" created by the President to investigate the causes of the summer riots—held hearings and gathered and sifted the evidence.

At winter's end, the facts uncovered by the Commission proved so alarming, and so contrary to the comfortable prejudices of those who dismissed the riots as the work of Communists or of a minority of well-organized black revolutionists, that the Commission members ended their deliberations early and released their report four months in advance of the date in July that the President had requested. The Commission found "no evidence that all or any of the disorders or the incidents that led to them were planned or directed by any organization or group, international, national or local." Moreover, the Commission reported that almost half of the 1967 riots had been precipitated by police violence against black people. The Report stated:

> This is our basic conclusion. Our nation is moving toward two societies, one white, one black—separate and unequal. . . . The most fundamental [cause of the riots] is the racial attitude and behavior of white Americans toward black Americans. . . . Race prejudice has shaped our history decisively; it now threatens to affect our future. . . . White racism is essentially responsible for the explosive mixture which has been accumulating in our cities since the end of World War II.

National response to the Report, both from blacks and whites, seemed to express relief that the problem had been openly traced—for the first time in history by an official government agency—to the fact that ours is a racist society. So profound was the relief, in fact, that few seemed to notice that while the Report placed the blame for the race crisis on attitudes that exist within the white community, it failed to propose any significant ways of dealing with those very attitudes and prejudices. The Commission recommendations were all aimed at easing the physical hardships of the black ghetto communities, without aiming to correct the causes of white racism. Clearly the Commission had fallen victim itself to the trap it spelled out for whites in general when it further stated:

> What white Americans have never fully understood—but what the Negro can never forget—is that white society is deeply implicated in the ghetto. White institutions created

it, white institutions maintain it and white society condones it.

Yet if white institutions created, maintain and condone the black ghettos, how can the ghettos be improved if the white institutions remain unchanged? Paraphrasing the philosophers Camus and Sartre, Stokely Carmichael has asked:

Can whites, particularly white liberals, condemn themselves?

The question is a vital one. The Commission did the job it was appointed to do (to ascertain the causes of the riots), and it laid the blame squarely at the door of the white community. And yet, a very few months later, the House Un-American Activities Committee proposed concentration camps for future rioters, defining them as "mixed Communist and black nationalist elements." The recommendations, issued early in May 1968, urged identification cards for ghetto dwellers for "the control and organization of the inhabitants."

In the document that follows, James A. Tillman, Jr., a black psychologist in Syracuse, New York, and a former executive director of the Crusade for Opportunity, discusses the flaw in the Riot Commission Report.

The Document:

Statement prepared for inclusion
in this book by Dr. James A. Tillman, Jr.

WHILE THE Riot Commission found white racism to be the cause of riots, it significantly failed to make a single recommendation designed to point the way to programs intended to get at white racism within the white community. In fact, the so-called black leaders who have rushed out to praise the report, in uncritical terms, have failed to ask this relevant question: If white racism is the cause of race riots, how can we reasonably expect America to develop the will and commitment to even implement the programs recommended by the report, unless and until we have begun to deal realistically with white racism in the white, not black, community?

The Commission, then, again left the sin and illness of white racism untouched with respect to future programs. If white racism is the cause, then shouldn't something be done about it in the white community? To all but the completely venal and stupid, the obvious answer is YES! Why, therefore, did the Commission completely fail to recommend programs designed to consciously and deliberately rid the whites of their white racist attitudes? The answer, given American history and contemporary dynamics, is obvious; such recommendations would have required the Commission to further admit, as I have been saying for many years, that whites are mentally ill with respect to race and that white racism is a collective mental illness, which needs and requires systematic treatment.

The report is calculated to bamboozle unthinking and uncritical whites and blacks by recommending only programs designed to improve the physical lot of blacks. These are necessary but not sufficient. The whites badly need improvement too! They need improvement psychologically which will enable them to begin to live in a state of mental health. The Commission, given its agreement that white racism is the central cause of race riots, should have made action recommendations concerning the massive mental health programs which are now needed in the white community. If the Commission had made such recommendations, its report might show America new paths.

Because the Commission failed to make such recommendation with respect to the white community, its report simply makes a bad situation worse. Confession and contrition are not enough on the part of whites. If the Commission had recommended both—1) programs to improve the physical lot of blacks and 2) programs designed to improve the mental and emotional health of whites, its report might have greater merit.

The tragic fact is that such programs as are recommended by the Commission can not be mounted, so long as the power to initiate and implement such programs rests with the white community, until whites have begun to come to grips with their own insecurities which cause them to need, and to live by, white racism. . . .

Postscript To The Document:

The question remains, Can white people change their racist attitudes? In a society that does more to encourage people to exploit and to make a profit out of one another, than to help one another, the possibility of eradicating white racism depends upon our ability and our will to affect profound economic changes. Racism infects all our institutions, and economic reform alone will not cure it, however. The philosophies of our churches certainly need to be re-examined. Our school texts will have to be rewritten to feature the role of blacks and other minorities (not just revised with supplements tacked on the end). The books we publish will have to challenge cherished beliefs and "tell it like it is."

There is wonderful hope in the student activism taking place on college campuses and in high schools today. Young people's attitudes have yet to be totally warped by false notions of racial superiority, and we would do well to include in school curricula courses that question the value systems and preconceptions of our elders. School authorities on their own will do little more than add a course here and a course there on Black History or Black Literature. That is hardly enough. In the end it will devolve upon young people to prod their elders into doing more. Through organizing workshops on race relations, through freely giving and taking in study and discussion groups, young people can materially hasten a future free of race hate.

Toward this end, Dr. Tillman—the writer of the document presented above—has prepared a guide to assist young people in forming workshops and study and discussion groups on how they may root out racist attitudes. Details on the availability of the guide appear on page 248 of this book.

A paramount question white people must grapple with is the role they are to play in the movement for black equality. Few people realize why SNICK decided against white participation in the mid-1960's. So many white students came to Lowndes county during the famous registration drives that SNICK workers found they were devoting inordinate time to answering questions and to briefing the white volunteers. The resentment of whites when SNICK decided to conserve its energies and to go it alone as an all-black organization is an indication of how superficial the liberal white commitment to the black cause really is. One would be hard put to name a white leader who in modern times answers to the commitment of a Tom Paine, a William Lloyd Garrison, or a John Brown. In addition, many white liberals are hurt at being denied what is basically an unconscious desire to play the great-white-father within the movement. They do not see that until the black man speaks for himself, leads himself, decides for himself, and even makes mistakes for himself, there will be no true equality.

EPILOGUE

The misunderstood legacy
of Martin Luther King, Jr.

DESPITE THE FINDINGS of the Riot Commission, police stock-piling of anti-riot weapons and the preparation for forcible repression of civil protest continued ominously.

Ominous, too, was the silence of President Johnson who had ordered the creation of the Commission. Persons close to Lyndon Johnson said that he was angry at the Commission's failure to praise his own efforts in the cause of civil rights. When, a week after the report was made public, reporters pressed Johnson for comment, all he would say was that he regarded the report as "recommended reading." We are all aware of President Nixon's cavalier dismissal of the Report.

Martin Luther King, Jr., appealing for contributions to the imminent Poor People's Campaign, stated in a letter dated "April 1968":

> The national government is playing Russian roulette with riots; it gambles with another summer of disaster. Not a single basic social cause of riots has been corrected. Though ample resources are available they are squandered substantially on war. . . . The nation has been warned by the President's Commission that our society faces catastrophic division in an approaching doomsday if the country does not act.

Martin Luther King's words seem almost an echo of the two-hundred-year-old prophecy of Thomas Jefferson: "I tremble for my country when I reflect that God is just; that his justice cannot sleep forever."

Just as the proposals of the House Un-American Activities Committee echoed the sentiment expressed so long ago in the laws of Virginia, 1723:

> Laws for the better governing of Negroes, Mulattoes and Indians. Inasmuch as the present laws are found insufficient to restrain their tumultuous and unlawful meetings, or to punish the secret plots and conspiracies carried on amongst

them, and known only to such . . . that some further provision be made, for detecting and punishing all such dangerous combinations in the future. . . .

To generate the people's "relentless pressure," which he saw as necessary to force the government to take action, Dr. King and the Southern Christian Leadership Conference organized for a massive march of poor people, both white and black, on Washington, D.C. King warned of massive civil disobedience in the nation's capital, of tying up traffic, of boycotting schools, of sit-ins at government offices—in a "last desperate demand to avoid the worst chaos, hatred and violence any nation ever encountered."

Early in April 1968, Martin Luther King, Jr., was in Memphis, Tennessee, to lead demonstrations in support of that city's black sanitation workers who were on strike for better wages and conditions. On the evening of April 4, while he stood chatting with his co-workers on the second floor balcony of a Memphis motel, Martin Luther King, Jr., was shot from ambush. He died within the hour, without regaining consciousness.

Reaction to Dr. King's death was immediate and monumental. Government "leaders" urged black people to remember Dr. King's message of love and nonviolence. The white institutions that had refused to listen to Dr. King's demands for justice now seemed terribly concerned lest black men fail to listen to his call for "restraint." And indeed, their fears of what black reaction to King's assassination might be seemed to be justified as violence broke out in 125 cities, expressing the explosive rage of people whose principal spokesman for the hope of justice without bloodshed, of peace without slavery had been killed.

In the aftermath of Dr. King's death, confusion arose as to the true meaning of his message. Many leaders seemed bent on twisting Dr. King's commitment to nonviolence into a message of passive acceptance. Repeatedly, continually, Dr. King insisted that the strength of the black man's cause lay in his superior moral position: the position of a people demanding what is theirs by right and making those who would deny them responsible for the violence of their own repression. This, Dr. King said, required black people to refrain from *committing* violence, but certainly not to refrain from demanding their rights in the most militant ways possible. Nor did he ask black people to refrain from disobedience to laws passed contrary to their human dignity.

Dr. King's courage and willingness to face the violence of his people's oppressors cannot for a moment be questioned; it was clearly evident in his life as well as in his death.

Perhaps in reading over many times the speech made by Henry David Thoreau to a Concord audience on the night that John Brown was hanged, the true legacy of King's life and death can be sensed.

The implication of the speech by Senator Harry F. Byrd of Virginia, the day after Dr. King's death, seemed to be that King was responsible for his own death. Those who organize mass demonstrations, Byrd said, "become themselves the victims of the forces they set in motion." Noting that Dr. King often spoke of nonviolence, Senator Byrd stated, "Violence all too often attended his action and, at the last, he himself met a violent end." The attempt to make Dr. King's death an act of his own responsibility is assuredly an expression of the same white inability to condemn itself pronounced by Camus and Sartre and by Stokely Carmichael, Julius Lester and Eldridge Cleaver.

For hundreds of years the white race has wronged the black race. Perhaps in a conscious recognition of the debt owed by whites to blacks, and in an honest effort to repay that debt, white Americans can find a means of reorienting their consciousness toward a people whose persons they stole, whose labor, and whose contributions to the nation they flagrantly denied. White Americans may be unable to condemn themselves, to accept the guilt of their ancestors. But they can acknowledge a debt; and in their acceptance of indebtedness, white men can provide compensations for black men similar to the compensatory benefits given to G.I.'s to make up the losses they sustain.

Time is running out on Thomas Jefferson's prophecy. We have been spared its full vengeance by the release of pent-up emotions during the long hot summers. Yet the repressive tactics of the police—along with the false charges of Communist subversion increasingly being levelled against black men's organizations—are leading black men to ever-increasing militancy and give foreboding imminence to Jefferson's awful vision.

AVAILABLE SOURCES
OF THE DOCUMENTS

The seven major collections of black history are contained in the libraries that follow, listed in alphabetical order, with addresses and names of the chief librarian or curator. With each listing appears an abbreviation to designate the collection.

Following the collections is the list of documents in the same sequence as they appear in this book, together with the designated abbreviations for the collections.

By specifying the *full* title as it appears in the text preceding each document (in most cases first lines only are given below), the reader may request from the named library the original document, or if it is brief, a photostatic copy at a small service charge.

Henry P. Slaughter Collection and the Countee Cullen Memorial Collection, Trevor Arnett Library, ATLANTA UNIVERSITY, Atlanta, Georgia 30314 (Miss Lillian Miles, Curator) A

Special Collections FISK UNIVERSITY LIBRARY, Nashville, Tenn. 37203 (Miss Bernice M. Armstead, Curator) F

George Foster Peabody Collection of Negro History HAMPTON INSTITUTE, Hampton, Virginia (Dr. Hillis D. Davis, Director) HAMP

Negro Collection HOWARD UNIVERSITY LIBRARY, Washington, D.C. 20001 (Mrs. Dorothy Porter, Curator) HOW

New York Public Library SCHOMBURG COLLECTION, 103 West 135th St., N. Y., N. Y. 10030 (Mrs. Jean B. Hutson, Curator) S

Tuskegee Institute Collection TUSKEGEE INSTITUTE, Tuskegee, Alabama (Mrs. Annie King, Chief Librarian) T

James Walden Johnson Collection YALE UNIVERSITY LIBRARY, New Haven, Conn. 06520 (Donald Gallup, Curator) Y

SECTION I

A FAMOUS CURSE
Old Testament, King James version. Available almost anywhere.

THE "RICHES" OF THE NEW WORLD: 1494
Letter published in Barcelona, etc. None of the collections listed have this document. It is available at the New York Public Library, 42nd Street, Reference Room.
Memorial brought by Antonio de Torres, etc. Y

THE AFRICAN SLAVE TRADE: 1746
The National and Private Advantages of the African Trade Considered, etc. Y

COLONIAL SLAVE STATUTES: 1630–1740
The Statutes at Large of Virginia, etc. A Y
The Statutes at Large of South Carolina, etc. A Y
Records of the Colony of Rhode Island, etc. Y
Archives of Maryland, etc. Y

"AN HEIGHT OF OUTRAGE AGAINST HUMANITY": 1775
Pennsylvania Journal, etc. S Y

THE DELETED CLAUSE: 1776
Facsimile print of Thomas Jefferson's original draft of the Declaration of Independence, in his own handwriting, available from the Photoduplication Service, Library of Congress, Washington, D.C. 20540, for $2.70.

COLONIZATION SCHEMES: 1817
Thoughts on African Colonization or an Impartial, etc. A F
HAMP HOW S T Y

DAVID WALKER'S APPEAL: 1828
David Walker's Appeal in Four Articles, etc. H S

WALKER'S APPEAL CONDEMNED: 1830–31
The Genius of Universal Emancipation, etc. S
The Liberator, etc. S

THE CONFESSIONS OF NAT TURNER: 1831
The Confessions of Nat Turner, etc. The original tract is too worn for photostating. However, the tract was reprinted in 1905 by the Negro Monograph Co., Washington, D.C. (Comparisons with the original show that it is an accurate reprint.)
F HAMP HOW S T Y

"LET SOUTHERN OPPRESSORS TREMBLE!": 1831
The Liberator, etc. S Y

THE UNDERGROUND RAILROAD: 1836
Reminiscences, etc. F HAMP HOW S T Y

"YOU ARE EMPANELLED AS A JUROR": 1839
American Slavery As It Is, etc. (Although this was written by Theodore D. Weld it was originally published without his name on the title page.) A F HAMP HOW S Y

A CALL TO REBELLION: 1843
Memorial Discourse, etc. A F HAMP HOW S Y

"THE NORTH STAR SHALL LIVE": 1847
The North Star, etc. S

"PLEA FOR CAPTAIN JOHN BROWN": 1860
  Echoes of Harpers Ferry, etc. A F HAMP HOW S

SECTION II

"MEN OF COLOR, TO ARMS!": 1863
  Douglass' Monthly, etc. S

"YET ANOTHER NAME": 1865
  The Liberator, etc. HOW Y

"TO MAINTAIN IN FREEDOM": 1866
  The Life and Writings of Frederick Douglass International Publishers, New York (1950–1955) A F HAMP HOW S
  T Y

FREE TO STARVE: 1865
  Trowbridge, J. T., *A Picture of the Desolated States*, etc. HOW
  S Y

"THEY SAID THEY WERE FRIENDS": 1871
  Testimony taken by the Joint Select Committee, etc. Available from Library of Congress, Washington, D.C., 20540.

"WHOSE LEGISLATURE IS THIS?": 1868
  Address delivered, etc. A

THE GREAT EXODUS: 1879
  Senate report 693, etc. Available from Library of Congress, Washington, D.C., 20540. Request "Congressional Serial Set" No. 1899.

EARLY ANTI-LYNCHING CRUSADES: 1896–1901
  New York *Tribune*, etc. Y
  Cleveland *Press Gazette*, etc. F
  New York *Independent*, etc. S

THE "ATLANTA COMPROMISE": 1895
  Up From Slavery, etc. A F HAMP HOW S T Y

SECTION III

BOOKER T. WASHINGTON CHALLENGED: 1903
  The Souls of Black Folk, etc. A F HAMP HOW S T
  Y

THE NIAGARA MOVEMENT AND THE NAACP: 1905
  "Niagara Movement Principles," etc. S

THE BACK-TO-AFRICA MOVEMENT: 1922
  Speech contained in "Aims and Objects," a pamphlet published

by the U.N.I.A., 1924, reprinted by University Place Book
Store, 69 University Place, New York, N.Y. 10003.

"WE WANT TO LIVE": 1938
   Opportunity, etc. F HAMP HOW S T Y

A. PHILIP RANDOLPH'S MARCH ON WASHINGTON: 1941
   Survey Graphic, etc. A F HOW S T Y

THE MONTGOMERY BUS BOYCOTT: 1955 and "I HAVE A DREAM": 1963
   Stride Toward Freedom, etc.
   "I Have a Dream," etc. A F HAMP HOW S T

THE BLACK MAN AND SELF-DEFENSE
   Negroes with Guns, etc. F HAMP HOW S T

MALCOLM X AND THE BLACK MUSLIMS: 1964
   Muhammad Speaks, etc. F HAMP HOW S T
   "The Ballot or the Bullet" speech by Malcolm X was delivered
before various audiences in 1964. It is available on record and
tape; also in the book *Malcolm Speaks*, Merit Publishers, N.Y.,
1965. A F HAMP S Y

SNICK AND "BLACK POWER": 1966
   New York Review of Books, etc. HAMP S T

THE CASE FOR BLACK SEPARATISM: 1967
   Ramparts, etc. A S T

THE "RIOT COMMISSION" REPORT: 1968
   "The Fatal Flaw in the Riot Report." Copy of the full state-
ment available gratis from Dr. James A. Tillman, Jr., 1123
Euclid Ave., Syracuse, N.Y. 13210. The discussion guide men-
tioned on page 241 is titled *What Is Your Racism Quotient? A
Layman's Guide for Detecting and Treating Racism* by James
A. Tillman, Jr., and Mary Norman Tillman, $1 per copy, less
in bulk quantities.

INDEX

SIGNET Specials of Interest

☐ **CONCERNING DISSENT AND CIVIL DISOBEDIENCE by Abe Fortas.** An Associate Justice of the United States Supreme Court offers a valid alternative to violence as he defines the limits and scope of civil disobedience.
(#D3646—50¢)

☐ **MIAMI AND THE SIEGE OF CHICAGO: An Informal History of the Republican and Democratic Convention of 1968 by Norman Mailer.** From the pen of "the best writer in America" (Book Week), comes a unique and deeply moving report of the shame of Miami and the shambles of Chicago during the 1968 presidential conventions.
(#Q3785—95¢)

☐ **HOW TO GET OUT OF VIETNAM: A Workable Solution to the Worst Problem of Our Time by John Kenneth Galbraith.** The distinguished economist, political theorist, and bestselling author offers a practical plan for U.S. withdrawal from "a war we cannot win, should not wish to win, are not winning, and which our people do not support."
(#S3414—35¢)

☐ **I PROTEST! By David Douglas Duncan.** A powerful condemnation of the war in Vietnam in photographs and text by the world-famous photographer who was assigned by Life Magazine and ABC News to cover the action in Khe Sanh.
(#N3546—$1.00)

☐ **VIOLENCE: AMERICA IN THE SIXTIES by Arthur Schlesinger, Jr.** One of the most eminent historians of our time speaks out on the emerging pattern of violence in America and suggests ways in which we might uncover the roots of hatred and move towards self-control.
(#D3747—50¢)

THE NEW AMERICAN LIBRARY, INC., P.O. Box 2310, Grand Central Station, New York, New York 10017

Please send me the SIGNET BOOKS I have checked above. I am enclosing $_____(check or money order—no currency or C.O.D.'s). Please include the list price plus 10¢ a copy to cover mailing costs. (New York City residents add 5% Sales Tax. Other New York State residents add 2% plus any local sales or use taxes.)

Name_____

Address_____

City_____State_____Zip Code_____
Allow at least 3 weeks for delivery